CROOKED,
BUT NEVER COMMON

CROOKED, BUT NEVER COMMON

THE FILMS OF PRESTON STURGES

STUART KLAWANS

Columbia University Press *New York*

Columbia University Press
Publishers Since 1893
New York   Chichester, West Sussex
cup.columbia.edu
Copyright © 2023 Columbia University Press
All rights reserved

Library of Congress Cataloging-in-Publication Data
Names: Klawans, Stuart, author.
Title: Crooked, but never common : the films of Preston Sturges / Stuart Klawans.
Description: New York : Columbia University Press, 2023. | Includes bibliographical references and index.
Identifiers: LCCN 2022013872 (print) | LCCN 2022013873 (ebook) | ISBN 9780231207287 (hardback) | ISBN 9780231207294 (trade paperback) | ISBN 9780231556903 (ebook)
Subjects: LCSH: Sturges, Preston—Criticism and interpretation. | Comedy films—United States—History and criticism. | Motion pictures—United States—History—20th century. | Motion picture producers and directors—United States—Biography. | Screenwriters—United States—Biography.
Classification: LCC PN1998.3.S78 K55 2023 (print) | LCC PN1998.3.S78 (ebook) | DDC 791.4302/33092—dc23/eng/20220604
LC record available at https://lccn.loc.gov/2022013872
LC ebook record available at https://lccn.loc.gov/2022013873

Columbia University Press books are printed on permanent and durable acid-free paper.

Cover image: *The Lady Eve* (1941), Paramount Pictures/Photofest.
© Paramount Pictures
Cover design: Chang Jae Lee

For Bali, Jake, and Ruby

CONTENTS

Instead of an Introduction: A Rhetoric of Preston Sturges   1

1 Ya Can't Get Away from Arithmetic: *The Great McGinty*   11

2 He Thinks He Has Ideas: *Christmas in July*   33

3 I'm Not a Poet, I'm an Ophiologist: *The Lady Eve*   65

4 As You Are, So Shall You Remain: *Sullivan's Travels*   95

5 Topic A: *The Palm Beach Story*   133

6 Homo Sapiens, the Wise Guy: *Triumph Over Pain*   165

7 Psycholology: *The Miracle of Morgan's Creek*   193

8 That's All You Know How to Hurt: *Hail the Conquering Hero*   231

9 You Arouse the Artist in Me: *The Sin of Harold Diddlebock*   261

10 Every Emotion Was Exaggerated: *Unfaithfully Yours*   285

Instead of a Conclusion: A Genealogy of Preston Sturges   317

Acknowledgments   337
Notes   341
Bibliography   349
Index   353

CROOKED, BUT NEVER COMMON

Sturges on set with Claudette Colbert and Joel McCrea for *The Palm Beach Story*. Courtesy The Museum of Modern Art

INSTEAD OF AN INTRODUCTION

A Rhetoric of Preston Sturges

I'm here to talk about someone who changed film history, as the first person in Hollywood's sound era to direct movies, great ones, from scripts he'd written himself.

A child of divorce, he grew up divided in his loyalties between a slightly unreliable, arts-besotted mother and a practical, much-loved father figure. After spending some formative years in Chicago, where he breathed the peculiar atmosphere of the world's biggest boomtown—its air of proud raffishness and cultural ambition—he carried his formidable energy to New York and achieved fame in the theater. Movie studios took notice. He flirted with them while playing hard to get and negotiated terms so favorable that many of the workers already indentured in the bungalows looked forward to his getting his comeuppance.

The dawn of the 1940s found him winning acclaim in Los Angeles as a dazzling figure who promised to bring the movies into a new era of sophistication. By 1948, his Hollywood career was essentially over.

Adjusting for a few distortions and omissions, this little profile fits not one mold-breaking Golden Age filmmaker but two, Preston Sturges and Orson Welles (whose *Heart of Darkness* was initiated at the same time as *The Great McGinty* and, if not abandoned, might have beaten it to the writer-director finish line). So much for the first duty of authors introducing books: convincing readers that my hero is singularly important.[1]

As much as I enjoy and admire Sturges's work—as much as I recognize that the man responsible for it was not just distinctive but remarkably odd—I acknowledge that the confluence of forces that delivered him into Hollywood's front rank and then swept him out of it again did much the same for Welles. To help this book's fortunes, I ought to assure you that Sturges has a unique claim on your attention for having surfed the period's breakers of social, cultural, economic, and institutional change; but really, you can pick among many.

And if you're among the people who find Sturges's films especially appealing, you've got writers other than me to guide you. Among them are Sturges's biographers Diane Jacobs and James Curtis; the indispensable editor of nine of the published screenplays, Brian Henderson; a tradition of distinguished commentators including James Agee, Manny Farber and W. S. Poster, André Bazin, Andrew Sarris, Richard Corliss, Penelope Houston, Veronica Geng, and James Harvey; and Sturges himself, whose unfinished memoir (adapted and edited by his widow Sandy Sturges as *Preston Sturges by Preston Sturges*) is a rich source of provocative insights and not-quite-dependable yarns.

Out of respect for my predecessors, I will not offer yet another overview of Sturges's life. As my opening gambit with Welles ought to suggest, I also will veer from the "biographical-psychological interpretation" of the films (as Henderson calls it).[2] Sturges himself set the terms for such a reading through his self-publicizing in the early 1940s. The sharp divisions he portrayed in his early life between female and male parenting, European and American settings, the ridiculous pretensions of artists and the plain dealing of men of affairs established a framework for discussing his movies (and also finding fault with them) that has been useful to writers since Agee. I don't intend to dismantle that framework or ignore the anecdotes that deck it with vivid colors. I just want to make it wobble a bit, as reality does.

If you have come with me even this far, it must be because you have watched Sturges's films and want to add to your enjoyment by reading about them. I assume that now and then you will appreciate being reminded of details that may have slipped your memory; but even though I will run through the major films chronologically, from *The Great McGinty* (released in 1940) through *Unfaithfully Yours* (1948), I will provide neither the freestanding plot summaries nor the grand thematic wrap-ups that might fill *Sturges for Dummies* (an audience that wouldn't like him, anyway).

So what kind of guidebook am I introducing?

The answer begins with the philosopher and sometime film theorist Stanley Cavell. I wrote my first essay about Sturges for a conference in Cavell's honor organized by Henry Abelove at the Wesleyan Center for the Humanities. Invited to think about any aspect I chose of Cavell's writings on film, I asked if it was significant that *The Palm Beach Story* is missing from his magisterial *Pursuits of Happiness: The Hollywood Comedy of Remarriage*. My brief answer was, yes and no.[3] I concluded that an analysis of *The Palm Beach Story* would bring into Cavell's study a mass of detail that neither corroborates nor contradicts his thesis but might enrich an understanding of Sturges's way of thinking. My longer answer is this book.

I follow Cavell in believing that Sturges's movies—like many other films produced in the studio era—can be understood to unfold like reasoned arguments about subjects of real concern. That is to say, they can be read. It's an unsurprising proposition, or ought to be, if only because high-end movies took months to develop from idea to finished product, required a considerable investment of capital, and drew on the expertise of multiple collaborators, many of whom (including the producers) were manifestly intelligent. The people who made movies often had the time, ability, and incentive to think them through. And yet longstanding prejudice holds that it's outlandish to think of these movies as meaningful, let alone intellectually coherent.

The U.S. Supreme Court codified this prejudice in 1915 in the case of *Mutual Film Corporation v. Industrial Commission of Ohio*, ruling that movies were not artistic statements but commercial products (like tinned meat) and therefore enjoyed no First Amendment protection. Writers who found work in Hollywood while feeling they had lowered themselves—they should have been busy instead with novels and plays—openly adopted this dismissive attitude and liked to reinforce the image of Los Angeles as Tinseltown. (The locus classicus is Herman Mankiewicz's often-quoted, perhaps apocryphal telegram sent in 1925 to Ben Hecht, urging him to relocate from New York: "Millions are to be grabbed out here and your only competition is idiots.") When his turn came, Sturges joined in the chorus, dedicating what would become his best-known film, *Sullivan's Travels*, to the notion that movies are a form of popular entertainment and should not pretend to be anything else.

With flagrant disregard for history, I will violate the avowed preference of my author by attempting to trace ideas through his movies, much as I will ignore how the era's distribution system reinforced his position, making it hard for audiences to think about analyzing films. Almost nobody at the studios in 1940 expected a movie to be watched after it had traveled its course from first-run city theaters to the last rural outposts. Film archives were few, revival houses and film societies scarce, and there was as yet no omnipresent, insatiable televisual industry. People who suspected that it might be possible to read a film could test their hypothesis only on current releases, and then only by returning to a theater over and over with the rank-and-file movie-mad.

Today, by contrast, the materials and tools of film history are widely accessible, and a fair number of people have used them frequently enough to have taken something like Cavell's position. If you are among them and suspect that a studio movie written from scratch and directed by a single person might be particularly interesting to read, then this book is for you.

Its goal is to increase your pleasure in Sturges by following the trains of thought, ambiguities, and semicovert artistic impulses that emerge in his films on a second viewing, or a fifth. Sometimes an apparent formal discontinuity—surprising in a work by such a meticulous craftsman, and therefore easily overlooked—will lead to the discovery. At other times the clue will lie in Sturges's cultural milieu—from the lingering words of old vaudeville songs to the overpowering influence of George Bernard Shaw—traces of which can be detected in the films, if you look. A modest exercise; but I hope it will show that Sturges's movies are hilarious, audacious, and touching in proportion to their being meaningful.

Cynicism about social and political arrangements, yearning for and disillusionment with romantic love, defiance of prudery, enthusiasm for self-invention (especially by women who have little other choice), and horror at the thought of living out a perpetual, unvarying cycle—these are among the themes that run consistently through the films. Serious enough; but because Sturges expressed them at a frantic pace, using antic plot reversals, bursts of slapstick, and a gallery of character actors who make you wonder if life is just an endless round of the same strangely familiar mugs, many critics and film historians have begrudged him his status as a great filmmaker. They own up to his achievement while adding a quibble or two: *jokey, stagy, compromised, self-defeating*. Having traced the course of his thought, I would like to remove those qualifiers.

As it happens, one of the chief distractions from thinking your way through the films is their most universally admired trait: the dialogue. Few screenwriters have been as witty as Sturges. None has rained down words on every situation in such a mist of eccentricity and delight.

Nobody denies that Sturges had an unsurpassed ability to "spritz dialogue," as he put it; but until you consider his favorite ways to make words funny and the implications of those methods, it's difficult to get past the introductory stage and move on to real business. The challenge is all the greater because Sturges's fans are never happy until all their favorites have been quoted. (The good news when you write about Sturges: your book is full of marvelous lines. The bad news: they're all his.) In the coming pages, I will do my best to cite the greatest hits—but for now, as an entry point to his worldview, here is an abbreviated rhetoric of Preston Sturges.

He plays with the dangers, pleasures, and plasticities of language by deploying parody, doubletalk, double entendre, personification, metaphor, metonymy, parallel construction, self-contradiction, sudden candor, dialect, diatribe, cant, argot, and enough elegant variation to fill a thesaurus. Examples will abound throughout this book. For now, I will focus on the three devices that, taken together, reveal the most about him.

The first might be called hypoarticulation. Sturges's characters sometimes talk a lot while saying nothing at all. Here is the Boss's chauffeur in *The Great McGinty*:[4]

And then she says, "You and who else?" and I says, "Oh, yeah," and she says, "Yeah is right," and I says, "So what?" and she says, "So when?" and I says, "You and me both," and she says, "And that goes double for me," and I says, "Oh, yeah!" And then the operator says, "Deposit another twenty-five cents for three minutes," so I hang up on her.

In extreme cases, a character's words may get pulled so far out of shape that they cease to belong to any known language at all, while remaining weirdly comprehensible. This is what happens with Toto, the little gigolo in *The Palm Beach Story*, whose principal, hypoarticulated utterance is "Grittinks!"

The contrasting device is hyperarticulation, in which characters speak with an eloquence unexpected from their type and unnecessary to the situation. This is what happens in *Christmas in July* when a department store salesman listens with mounting excitement to his colleague's enumeration of the advanced features of the latest convertible sofa, and then bursts out in peroration: "There is no limit to man's ingenuity!"

The point to observe is that hypoarticulation occurs infrequently in Sturges's films, whereas hyperarticulation is everywhere. Even when wringing laughter out of stereotypes of Black speech, as did so many other Hollywood writers, Sturges brings out the wittiness in the dialect, atypically building up rather than tearing down the character's worldliness and intelligence. Here is the Pullman porter in *The Palm Beach Story*, replying to the question of whether the film's heroine got off his train alone: "You might practically say she was alone. Gentleman she get off with gimme ten cents from New York to Jacksonville. She's alone, but she don't know it."

Directly related to this preference for hyperarticulation is Sturges's aversion to malapropism, or the substitution of a wrong word for the right one based on a similarity of sound: a device used frequently by other comic writers to get a laugh out of a character's ignorance or low status.[5] It's true that Muggsy in *The Lady Eve* asks "a hypodermical question" when he's in a sharply probing mood. But when the blundering radio announcer in *Christmas in July* fears having run into a "fox pass," he commits a mispronunciation, not a malapropism, and calls up the strangely appropriate image of a strait that only the sly can escape. Perhaps Wormy in *The Sin of Harold Diddlebock* is guilty of malapropism when he hears someone mention "posterity" and babbles, into his booze, "Posterity is just around the corner," but then again, he's right.

That almost no one in a Sturges film ever grabs at the completely wrong word testifies to the cheerful disdain in which the author holds realism, as well as a pleasure in language that he imparts generously to his characters, the shady and street-educated no less than the rich and polished. You rightly expect that his admiration for successful cheats and con artists will extend to their efflorescent patter; but he also holds out a fellow writer's understanding toward Mr. Noble, the speechifying mayor and furniture manufacturer in *Hail the Conquering Hero*, whose painful stabs at creativity arouse condescension but also an amused sympathy.

To Sturges, almost everyone (however inept) may participate in the gaiety of invention that language affords. He does not merely flaunt his revelry with words. He shares it with his characters, with a democratic impulse that at times may seem counter to his travesties of political and commercial sham, his mockery of romantic sappiness and the simpleminded conventions of popular narrative. With the boulevardier sophistication and bohemian élan that he acquired when very young, he feels himself above all that. And yet he reserves his harshest judgment for the aristocrat and artist who matches his own overwhelming rhetorical power: Sir Alfred de Carter in *Unfaithfully Yours*. Almost everyone else, whether clever at using words or laughably clumsy with them, may be excused for trying to get by in a world that on average is absurd and at worst feels like a trap.

Of course, Sturges's dialogue is not the sole factor in summoning up that world, while suggesting a forgiving attitude toward its inhabitants. He is also formidable at developing characters, inventing plots, and building narrative structures. I will often have occasion to remark, with awe, on these authorial skills, but my purpose is to go beyond them by thinking about how they come to life: in the expressions, tones of voice, and gestures of the actors, in the surroundings realized by a studio's departments of wardrobe, makeup, production design, and music, in the images concocted under the soundstage lights.

What's on the screen is always richer, trickier, and more charged with meaning than what's in the script, however flabbergasting that may be. So I end this nonintroduction, and my rhetorical analysis as well. From here on, I'm looking at the films.

1

YA CAN'T GET AWAY FROM ARITHMETIC

The Great McGinty

The occasion is a cold election night; the setting, a city that shares many street names with Sturges's native Chicago and many traditional practices too, such as filling homeless men with free soup and then paying them two dollars a head to vote for the mayoral incumbent. In a Park District tool shed behind the breadline, where an excitable ward-heeler has set up shop, a hulking vagrant newly recruited to cast a vote demands to know the reward for doing it twice.

"Two votes will get you four fish," the ward-heeler tells him.
"And three is six?"
"And four is eight. Ya can't get away from arithmetic."

Such is the inescapable logic of *The Great McGinty*, which upon its release in 1940 marked the beginning of Sturges's career as a Hollywood writer-director. As well tooled and slippery as a ball bearing, as conclusive as a physics experiment, *The Great McGinty* is the product of an imagination so diagrammatic that each wisecrack seems to be connected by a straight line to its balancing retort.

12 ⁂ YA CAN'T GET AWAY FROM ARITHMETIC

The links are sometimes scarcely longer than a breath. When the bum returns to the tool shed after a brisk montage sequence, with paper chits tucked into every fold of his clothing to prove he's voted thirty-seven times, the arithmetical ward-heeler cries, "Sixty-four bucks!" and can't get away from the rebuke, "*Seventy*-four."

Other connections run across almost the full length of the film. Early on, the bum rides in the back seat of an armored limousine with the city's gangster Boss, who in his expansive Slavic manner allows this rising hustler to keep all the protection money he's collected. The loot, the Boss says, had been written off anyway. "Then what's the idea of sending me out?" the bum shouts, and is calmly told, "I'm glad you didn't disappoint me.

McGinty succeeds, the first time, in not saying thank-you to the Boss.
Courtesy Photofest

For a minute I was afraid you were going to say thank you." Those words of gratitude do finally come, near the end, after the bum has been broken out of jail and is once more riding in the limousine, which now serves as a getaway car. Turning to the Boss, he at last says, "Thank you," very quietly, and is slapped down with a curt, "Why don't you shut up for a change?"

The back-and-forth bounces of dialogue, the rise and fall of the action, the parallel movements of the camera (tracking right to left across the meager fare served to the men on the breadline, then right to left across the Boss's lavish election-night buffet): all these might tempt you to think you could commit the movie's form to graph paper, as easily as you could sum up its genre as satire and its subject matter as the ways of big-city politics.

And yet this story about misbehavior on the grand scale also contains a lot that evades measurement, placement, and definition. The bum's name, for example—what is it?

Except for having been called "Dan" in a remote-seeming prologue, during a scuffle that almost drowns out the monosyllable, this hobo Anyman begins the movie with no name at all. Or, rather, he has many—Rufus J. Widdicombe, Emanuel Goldberg, Dr. Heindrich L. Schutzendorf, all read out in polling places from dubious voter rolls. After that, a mere Funny Guy, Tough Guy, Lug, or Slug seems good enough. At the level of social observation, this harping on anonymity attests to the interchangeability of men reduced to urban poverty. At the level of theme, it sharpens Sturges's parody of the democratic myth that any American, however nondescript, may rise like Lincoln to high office.

But there seems to be something more to the protagonist's namelessness, which continues even after he has been through a round of bathing and barbering and has acquired a glaring new suit. He isn't called anything in particular until well into the movie, after he's been made an alderman. It's almost as if the moniker "Dan McGinty" had been slapped on him for purposes of electioneering, at orders from the Boss—a man who also happens to lack a proper name.

This strange surplus of anonymity was integral to the film from its inception, in 1933. The original version of the screenplay, titled *The Vagrant*, called the protagonist O'Hara—almost as forgettable a name as a character can have. The titles of subsequent drafts—*The Story of a Man*, *The Biography of a Bum*—preserved this preference for generality. Sturges did not give his character an identity that could stick until he sold the script to Paramount in 1939; and even then he perhaps hinted at something provisional by plucking the name from an old song.

"Down Went McGinty" was a music-hall number from 1889 by Joseph Flynn, about an Irishman who goes out one Sunday in his best suit, only to fall into gambling, drinking, fighting, and the river. By choosing to name his character after Flynn's comic reprobate, Sturges may have been slyly suggesting that his own "Dan McGinty" was born of artifice, having descended from a stage Irishman. But Sturges went further, as if insisting on the precedent. He proposed *Down Went McGinty* as a title for the film—as if this movie, on which he was pinning all his hopes, would somehow get a commercial boost from a song that was fifty years old and half-forgotten.

Paramount's marketing department covered up some of these traces of Sturges's thought process by retitling the project *The Great McGinty*. But hints of "Down Went McGinty" linger. Sturges had Paramount's excellent composer Frederick Hollander base the movie's theme music on Flynn's tune, which generations have now heard without a clue as to its identity. And the movie's period, which is ostensibly the twenties, often feels more like Flynn's era of gaslight and vaudeville. The mists of an outdated song hover for unknown reasons around this otherwise arithmetical movie. And the protagonist who materializes out of them is a shape-shifter, whatever name his long-lost parents might have given him.

The man known as McGinty goes through the film with few consistent traits other than a short temper and a talent for fisticuffs. A creature of the streets, he knows how to guard his pockets from a prostitute, believes a Jew is bent forward by the weight of his nose, and when unimpressed with someone's manliness is apt to let fly with a fag joke—all of which is more realistically crude as portraiture than Hollywood usually permitted itself, in gangster pictures let alone in comedies. But these characteristics, despite their novelty, come down to sociological observation. What defines McGinty as a *person* is that almost nothing defines him. Depending on the circumstances, he can be disheveled or slicked-back, clean-shaven or raffishly mustached, terse, voluble, patient, abrupt, jocular, threatening, wised-up, ingenuous, curious, gloating, or remorseful. Although solid enough in body for a physics experiment, thanks to being played by thick, square-faced Brian Donlevy, he seems to change physically with each turn of the plot: His cheeks thin or fill out, his long-browed eyes narrow or open wide. The transformations go beyond what you'd normally expect from the Paramount wardrobe and makeup departments and an actor's bag of tricks. It's as if McGinty's human essence were little more than a fluid easily poured from one container to another.

In later films, Sturges would often thrust his characters into situations slippery with fraud or misunderstanding, to which they would comically struggle to adapt. But the first of his protagonists, McGinty, is an exception, as the only one of his characters who remakes himself perpetually and likes it. The distinction is all the more striking when you consider how frequently Sturges relies in his other films on fixed dramatic types, and how often his people discover they can't escape their place in the world. (We'll see that with the movie director in *Sullivan's Travels* who keeps trying to go on the road as a hobo and keeps finding himself back in Hollywood; or with Charles, also known as Hopsie, the hapless romantic hero of *The Lady Eve*, of whom his future father-in-law truly says, "A mug's a mug in everything.") With Dan McGinty, though, Sturges lets loose an imp of the amorphous, whom the film's mathematical rigor must strain to reimprison—even though the narrative's flashback structure guarantees that everything will eventually return to where it started.

"Never heard of him?" a delighted Boss asks a political crony after floating McGinty's name as a possible mayoral candidate. "That's just what I'm talking about!" The Boss wants a beefy, all-American nonentity as a front man, and he's got one, to his own satisfaction and the requirements of the plot. But the audience might be a little more demanding, wanting to understand what might be involved in *The Great McGinty*'s contest between inexorable logic and uncertain identity.

With earlier American sound movies, whose scripts were composed by relay teams of writers, it would be a mug's game to tease out traces of a filmmaker's memories and feelings. A director's broad themes, characteristic motifs, and elements of personal style, yes. Anything more specific and individual, no. It was only with *The Great McGinty* that a Hollywood studio produced a movie dreamed up from scratch and committed to celluloid by a single person, with the attendant possibility of the artist's feelings being expressed, disguised, or concealed.

A disclaimer: Yes, something new came into the world with *The Great McGinty*, which means that the story of its origin matters, especially in accounting for the film's unexpected, almost unnecessary depth of emotion. But I don't believe the accounting can be done on a strictly biographical-psychological basis. That method tends to work backward from the more explicit features of a body of work, finding their imaginative source in the best-known (that is, most vigorously publicized) parts of the artist's life. The obscure and covert generally get less consideration, as do aspects of the work that might have resulted not only from psychic motivations but also from negotiations with economic and structural circumstance. So it is with Sturges, who preferred to be reticent about some parts of his life—because of professional norms, I believe, rather than personal discomfort—and did not represent them outright in his films. Those parts, though tacit, are important to *The Great McGinty*—as important as the protagonist's missing name.

As evidence, notice how odd it is—suspect, even—that the surface of *The Great McGinty* shows no sign of the film's genesis. This is the most brashly urban of Sturges's movies, rivaled only by *Christmas in July* in its grit and bustle and comparable only to *Sullivan's Travels* in depicting breadlines and drifters—and yet its roots lie neither in city life nor in the Depression. The picture began its slow germination amid a mid-1920s pastoral idyll, before Sturges had even tried to be a writer.

He and the first of his heiress wives, Estelle de Wolfe Mudge, were then living on her income on a rural estate they'd bought in Westchester County, New York. Sturges later recalled these rich, lazy days on a millpond as his "country gentleman" period. Hard times followed. In January 1927, Estelle abruptly told Sturges she was through with him and would be leaving for Paris, alone. Despite being a twenty-nine-year-old man of the world,

Sturges was so surprised and devastated that he fled to Chicago (the closest thing he had to a home) and the care of his adoptive father, Solomon, a businessman who had been young in the gaslight era. There Sturges brooded upon suicide, until by chance he witnessed the unappetizing spectacle of a construction worker's death, upon which he decided he might as well return to New York City and find a way to make a living. It took about a year for him to settle on playwriting as his métier, and another to achieve a hit on Broadway with *Strictly Dishonorable*. At last he was the man he felt he was meant to be: famous for his wit and rich in his own right. By that time he was married to a second beautiful heiress, Eleanor Hutton, who was even wealthier than the first.

While caught up in this sudden rise, Sturges apparently didn't waste time thinking back to Andrew J. McCreery—an old neighbor from the lost Westchester estate—or the anecdotes this retired New York City magistrate had spun for him. As Sturges was to recall decades later in his memoirs, "It was he who told me about politics and how Tammany got the vote out in bad weather; how repeat voters vote under the names of many people, some of whom are deceased and some only sick in bed. . . . Over time I learned from him many other things about politics which would have been of the utmost value to me had I been a writer, for instance, or a motion picture director who wanted to make a film on the subject."[1] But Sturges did not become that man until after he'd blundered himself out of his first success. In less than four years, his miscalculations and headstrong behavior ended his Broadway career, his first Hollywood contract, and his second marriage.

By summer 1933, all he had left was the impending release of a new movie, *The Power and the Glory*—and he could make an exceptional claim of authorship for it. This was one of the rare films of the era to have originated from a screenplay written on speculation and left unaltered by other hands. The producer and distributor, Fox, was promoting Sturges's script as an historic work of art and would go so far as to display a copy under glass in the lobby of the Gaiety Theatre on Broadway. The picture was set for a premiere in August. In the excitement of the months before the opening, Sturges wrote *The Vagrant*, based in part on McCreery's tales of machine politics.

I can only speculate about why, at this moment, Sturges chose to revisit these stories about turn-of-the-century Tammany Hall. Brian Henderson, the excellent editor of Sturges's published screenplays, aptly remarks that *The Vagrant* "is a sort of comic version of *The Power and the Glory*" and proposes that Sturges might have seen it as the next film in a projected cycle about success in America.[2] In *The Power and the Glory*, an honest man from a small town rises from poverty to wealth and renown and then loses everything; in *The Vagrant*, the same course is taken by a scheming big-city bum. It also might be relevant that in the years that had passed since Sturges's own rise with *Strictly Dishonorable*, bums had proliferated in the cities, and so had the public works meant to rescue them—projects favored by the new Roosevelt administration but disliked by men such as Solomon Sturges, who saw them as instances of fiscal imprudence, if not engines of corruption. There's also another layer. Sturges mingled the tales he'd heard about Tammany with his recollections of the vivid old-time politicians, such as Bathhouse John Coughlin and Michael "Hinky Dink" Kenna, who had ruled the Chicago of his childhood, and so deepened the personal associations of *The Vagrant* (even if nobody else would know the associations were there).

But whatever might have prompted him to turn just then to a comic story about politics and graft, his immediate hopes were dashed. By the time he put the finishing touches on the screenplay, in September 1933, *The Power and the Glory* had been declared a disappointment at the box office. Sturges now desperately needed to sell a script; he'd been pouring borrowed money into the hull of a fifty-two-foot schooner he'd grandly bought, and he was behind on the rent on his apartment on Fifth Avenue, the one he wasn't living in, just down the block from St. Patrick's Cathedral. But Fox, Universal, and Warner Bros. all rejected *The Vagrant*. According to Sturges's memoirs, the studios found its setting "too sordid" and its story "too much concerned with politics. Politics would not interest women at all, and women made up the majority of the audiences."[3]

This rejection was a double blow, since Sturges had imagined that he would not only sell *The Vagrant* but also negotiate to direct it, in effect lifting himself close to the level of Chaplin. Virtually no one else in Hollywood both wrote and directed anymore; Chaplin could do so only because he was still the world's greatest star and operated as a one-man studio. But with the perceived failure of *The Power and the Glory*, Sturges had to abandon his aspirations and degrade himself to the status of a screenwriter on contract, soothed only by the balm of a liberally applied salary. For the next six years, though, as he worked his way up at Universal and Paramount, he kept pressing for the opportunity to direct—and the script he drew from the trunk, again and again, was *The Vagrant*.

In August 1939, he famously offered the rights to Paramount for one dollar—according to the best of his biographers, Diane Jacobs, the studio's lawyers insisted that he raise the price to ten—with the stipulation that he would direct.[4] Then, from September through November, he thoroughly rewrote the screenplay in preparation for a December start of production. Back in 1933, he'd abased himself by going on contract; but this flurry of revision showed he'd learned a lot about screenwriting from his years in the bungalows.

One of those lessons was how to organize screen time effectively. The working script published in Henderson's edition is already a marvel of balance and parallelism; and as Henderson argues, Sturges was even more rigorous when he took over the script as its director, subjecting it to a slashing revision in rehearsals and on the set. The three-act structure that emerged is at once effortless to follow and deliberately misleading and comes packaged within an elaborate frame story that seems blatantly irrelevant.

Draw up a chart with approximate running times and you can see both the symmetry of the scheme and its cunning disproportions:

Frame Story (6 minutes): Trouble in a cheap South American bar. A U.S. expatriate (Louis Jean Heydt) attempts suicide in the men's room and is restrained by the gruff Yankee bartender. The bartender seats the man and his rumba-dancer girlfriend (Steffi Duna) on a pair of stools and begins to tell them about his former wealth and glory.

Act One (20 minutes): Rise of the bum from breadline to alderman's office under the aegis of the Boss.

Interlude (2 minutes): Reflections in the South American bar.

Act Two (33 minutes): Rise of McGinty to mayor and governor, while his sham marriage (invented for the sake of his campaigns) turns into a true one.

Interlude (2 minutes): Further reflections in the South American bar.

Act Three (17 minutes): Fall of McGinty—a victim of his desire to live up to his wife's ideals—and his flight from jail with the Boss.

Frame Story (2 minutes): Concluding trouble in South America, and suggestion that the bartender's yarn about himself might have been true.

The brief resumptions of the South American story neatly separate the acts, while also providing occasions to tell the audience, through dialogue, to expect an upswing or downturn in McGinty's fortunes when the main narrative resumes. Even an inattentive first-time viewer can intuit the plan of the film and estimate how far the action has progressed. An alert viewer will guess more, noticing in particular that a new character appears at the beginning of act 2, framed in the kind of lingering head-and-torso shot that movies reserve for consequential figures.

This is Catherine (Muriel Angelus), the secretary with whom McGinty will form a supposedly chaste union of political convenience. Sturges plays fair with the audience by introducing her as someone who will most likely be important. But in the way he then proceeds to shift the narrative tone, distort the viewer's sense of time, and prepare the dramatic coup at the start of act 3, he is as devious as a card sharp, or Alfred Hitchcock.

The trick is to lull the viewer into forgetting about the Boss while the disproportionately long second act plays out. The Boss appears only once after McGinty wins election as mayor, and that's in a crowd scene, to which he contributes a single line of dialogue. During the gubernatorial campaign, the Boss doesn't show up at all. Throughout this period of McGinty's headiest triumph, his one constant companion is Catherine. It's true that she domesticates this political beast who has stalked in from the wilds of Skid Row. But she also abets him in his malfeasance and serves as the audience's affectionate surrogate in observing his shenanigans. She does so from the moment she looks up at an aldermanic campaign poster for McGinty and says to his photograph, with an indulgent smile, "Aren't you ashamed of yourself?"

Indeed, he ought to be—but the distinguishing splendor of *The Great McGinty* is the good cheer that it grants to crookedness. Satirical inversions of accepted values had been a part of English-language drama since *The Beggar's Opera*, but they were rare in American movies and had never yet been carried through with Sturges's roughhouse glee. McGinty has fun when he lies to people and gouges money from them, and Catherine (despite her disapproval) enjoys watching him do it. She's just crooked enough to be his soul mate. If she eventually makes an honest man of McGinty—with disastrous consequences—she also prefigures Sturges's adventure-seeking heroines, who are (to paraphrase Jean from *The Lady Eve*) not as good as a naïve man would imagine a good woman to be.

When McGinty, pacing in his Prohibition-era office early in act 2, decides he wants a drink, Catherine knows the bootleg bourbon is filed under E, and she doesn't hesitate to accept one for herself. And when McGinty complains to her that the Boss wants him to find a wife, she pauses only briefly before volunteering: "*I'd* do it for you, Mr. McGinty." With her blond locks wreathed about her head in fashionable milkmaid style, Catherine looks pure enough as she makes this offer. But given Muriel Angelus's habit of keeping her lips breathlessly parted at all times and emitting a gasp at the end of each line, Catherine comes across from the first as being aroused by McGinty. Little wonder that when the couple at last consummates their marriage, after months of supposedly sexless cohabitation, they give the impression of tumbling into a union expressly forbidden by the Production Code. Their wedding, though lawful, had been fake; the lust looks real.

Not that Catherine is wholly at odds with her sweet hairstyle. She has her good-girl side, which comes out, for example, when she leads her children in prayer. Then again, she deceives McGinty by keeping the children secret until after the wedding. And what about bland-faced George (Allyn Joslyn), the "old friend" who takes her to dinner every night while she's living with McGinty and repeatedly proposes "marriage"? Maybe Catherine is chaste with George, too—but in that case, is she really virtuous to keep the poor fish on the line? By the end of act 2, Catherine is ready to expose her hard edge: she tells governor-elect McGinty that he's become "strong enough" to clean up the tenements and put an end to child labor. It sounds less like an encouragement than an order; its sternness hints that Catherine now feels *she's* strong enough and is ready to displace the Boss in her husband's public life.

If female ticket-buyers disliked thinking about politics and would have found his movie "sordid," as Sturges claimed he'd been told, this Catherine-dominated act 2 would not have done enough to improve his script's fortunes. But perhaps his explanation of why the studios in 1933 had declined to produce *The Vagrant* shouldn't be taken entirely at face value. It's hard to imagine the story that would have been too sordid for Warner Bros. back then. And even though movies about politics were indeed rare at that time, studios were willing to bet that ticket-buyers, female or otherwise, would watch Wallace Beery in *The Secret Six*, Warren William and Bette Davis in *The Dark Horse*, or Tully Marshall in *Afraid to Talk*. Whatever the actual reason for the studios' demurral—a reluctance, perhaps, to buy a spec script from a writer who had just flopped and now insisted on directing—Sturges's explanation for why the studios rejected *The Vagrant* seems at best incomplete.

McGinty and Catherine just before their fall. Courtesy Photofest

His memoirs make *The Vagrant* sound like nothing but a grand tour of municipal corruption—which is, admittedly, how people like to remember the film. The exuberant fraudulence of *The Great McGinty* is intoxicating: not only the ripe names of the phantom voters and the garbled hokum of the campaign

("Don't forget the mayor who didn't forget to remember the less fortunate") but also the empty menace of the Boss's bodyguard (without his gun, a mere "violet"), the sham pugnacity of William Demarest as the ward-heeler (quick to bark, quick to back off), and the imposture of the businesses that McGinty is sent to shake down—the genteel fortune-telling parlor that you can assume fronts for a brothel, the interior decorator's showroom furnished with little more than the fumes of a speakeasy, the office where the bail bondsman is probably booking wagers over the phone. All this is unsurpassed as cynical comedy.

But something other than political chicanery is at the structural and emotional core of the movie: the marriage with

McGinty, an anonymous racketeer, shaking down a business that can't speak its name. Courtesy Photofest

Catherine. This is the part that Sturges passes over in his memoirs when he recounts the initial failure of *The Vagrant*. His omission can't be attributed to shyness about affairs of the heart; his memoirs offer an almost self-lacerating narrative of his romantic disasters. Why then, when recounting his initial failure to sell *The Vagrant*, didn't he at least mention the fictional romance he'd built into his movie?

I think Sturges's puzzling reticence on this subject may be related to the surplus anonymity that is the other mystery of *The Great McGinty*. Both seem to spring from the defeats Sturges had suffered in his career and his marriages, and from the way he recovered from them by remaking himself as a hired man in the bungalows. He could discuss such matters openly, but not as influences on his movies.

For those of us living after the rise of auteurism, it's easy to imagine that the purpose of attaining writer-director status was to enable self-expression; but at the height of the studio system, the price for the opportunity to direct a film, as Sturges knew, was the obligation not only to efface but to deny the presence of anything personal, including an artistic impulse. The dictum that film directing was just "a job of work," as John Ford liked to say—Ford, one of Hollywood's most prestigious and profoundly artistic filmmakers—expressed and also helped enforce this reluctance to put on airs. Behind the ethic of self-abnegation stood a method of organization that made films seem like any assembly-line product, and a legal framework that established movies as having the First Amendment status of tinned meat. And behind those conditions, which were particular to filmmaking, loomed the vast American tradition of anti-intellectualism. The nation's greatest satirist, Mark Twain, had preemptively guarded himself against accusations of deep thinking in the notice he posted at the start of *Adventures of Huckleberry Finn*:

"Persons attempting to find a motive in this narrative will be prosecuted; persons attempting to find a moral in it will be banished; persons attempting to find a plot in it will be shot." He shucked off suspicions of having anything meaningful to say; and so did his heir, Preston Sturges, while working in an art form much more self-consciously commercial than literature.

If a painful experience, known only to himself and his circle, were to filter into a script, or perhaps even prompt its composition, Sturges was obligated to deny that it had anything to do with him as a writer and director. The workplace ethic decreed that the failed husband and scuffling debtor buried inside him could be nothing more in *The Great McGinty* than a shapeless shadow, as nameless and obscure as a bum on a breadline. The interests of the mass audience were everything to the studios, and to Sturges as a proud entertainer; the subjective interests of an author, not even worth mentioning.

And yet if Sturges's personal history had not informed the movie, the final part of *The Great McGinty* could not begin on a note of such dread.

Act 3 starts with McGinty, newly sworn in as governor, walking slowly and solemnly into his office, alone, approaching the camera head-on from a distance. When he at last halts, the reverse shot shows that the chair behind the governor's desk is already occupied. Sitting there is the man Sturges has enticed you to forget throughout act 2, the man Catherine will fail to maneuver to the side—the Boss. At this point, you can feel something in the movie snap shut.

Why does the reappearance of this man feel more like a shock than a surprise? Why is the cut to him so disturbing? Maybe it's because you can't evade the Boss, any more than you can get away from arithmetic.

Despite all the blini-savoring, English-mangling joie de vivre that Akim Tamiroff brings to the role, the Boss in act 3 at last takes on his true form as the relentless force that will always claim the seat of power. In a past life, as he tells McGinty, he would have been a robber baron on a hill. In his present life, he is inevitably the sole proprietor of all political parties. Translate him into screenwriting terms, and he might be the diagrammatic principle. The amorphous McGinty strutted through act 2 as if he could determine his own shape; Catherine, who can be almost as hard to pin down as her husband, danced rather than marched beside him in his campaign parade, as if reveling in her freedom; but stern necessity, the boss of screenplays (and all of us), now reasserts itself. You can almost hear Sturges's iron logic closing across McGinty and Catherine with a clang. Before act 3 goes much further, McGinty will literally be behind bars.

In films to come, Sturges would frequently play Houdini with his characters, springing them magically from the constraints in which he'd trapped them. (These liberations, delayed until just a minute or two before the movie's end, are generally achieved in a slapstick prestissimo.) But here, in the movie he'd wanted to make as his directorial debut, he insists that McGinty and Catherine live out the consequences of the narrative: ruin for him, heartbreak and loneliness for her.

It seems to me that when Sturges poured the Tammany Hall anecdotes he'd heard at the Westchester millpond into *The Great McGinty*, he could not easily separate them from the memory of his first marriage and divorce, an episode that perhaps lurks behind the doomed act 2 idyll of Catherine and McGinty. I also suspect that recurring marital collapses (and repeated career failures) established a pattern that Sturges regarded almost as a law of nature, which he imposed upon his lovers as the only legislation that is *not* defied in *The Great McGinty*.

It may even be that a hint of the suicidal brooding of the younger Sturges made its way into the movie, in the obtrusively long frame story.

Any moviegoer can see that the prologue, so different in tone from the romp that follows, far exceeds the requirements of a plot setup, and many viewers will feel that the maudlin Yankee who sets off the action outlasts his welcome. But documentary evidence suggests that this weak, desperate man was as important to Sturges as his cocky bartender. Here is the final puzzle of *The Great McGinty*.

As Diane Jacobs notes in her account of the film's inception, Sturges wrote a one-paragraph summary of *The Vagrant* in 1933, when he was in the midst of composition: "There are two men exiled in Mexico. One of them was a banker [*sic*] cashier, honest all his life except for one crazy minute. He had to get out of the country. The other was a crooked politician, dishonest all his life except for one crazy minute. . . . He also lands in Mexico."[5] Almost seven years later, when Sturges directed the film, he began it with a title card: "This is the story of two men who met in a banana republic. One of them was honest all his life except one crazy minute. The other was dishonest all his life except one crazy minute. They both had to get out of the country."

So a Newtonian law of screenwriting persisted, from first to last. Every character has an equal and opposite counterpart, and the sides must balance, algebraically if not arithmetically. Six or seven minutes of drama about the suicidal embezzler must somehow weigh as much as the seventy-five minutes of the bartender's comedy.

Maybe they did for Sturges, who seems to have loaded the drunken, self-pitying cashier with the remembered burden of his breakdown in 1927, along with contempt for the fool he'd once been. That ought to have been enough to balance the equation—but only for the author. If moviegoers sense that an equivalence has been struck between the frame story and the main narrative, they will probably do so only during the final two minutes.

A single question accomplishes the trick. Back at the bar, after McGinty has recalled how the Boss rescued him despite having been betrayed, the bank cashier, confused or perhaps incredulous, asks, "Why didn't he kill you?"

"I never could figure that out," McGinty says.

To the Yankee's girlfriend, this reply proves that McGinty's yarn is as false as the campaign promises of a Chicago alderman. But to an audience that has experienced the dreadful return of the Boss, McGinty's unfathomable survival may suggest that arithmetic isn't ineluctable after all, nor the rule of the robber baron inexorable. I wouldn't go so far as to speak of an intuition of grace at the end of *The Great McGinty*; but the Boss's forbearance shows that the iron rule of logic was once suspended in McGinty's favor and might yet be suspended as well for the bank cashier, a character whom you can read either as a mere narrative convenience (an insufferable one at that) or as a stand-in for the younger Sturges.

The cashier has created failure out of a promising career, as Sturges did more than once. He wants to kill himself, but (like Sturges) doesn't pay enough attention to the job. And like Sturges, the cashier has lost a wife, about whom he doesn't care to speak directly. (He mumbles instead about the fake Tudor half-timbering of the family house.) Maybe the rumba dancer is correct at the end, when she urges this mope to go back to the United States, assuring him that his crime will soon be forgotten. The diagram might yet be smudged, allowing the cashier (like Sturges) a second chance, or a third.

But McGinty won't get away from arithmetic. As the movie ends—in yet another brawl, to William Demarest's cry of "Here we go again"—it becomes obvious that the Boss's mercy was only momentary, Catherine is gone forever, and McGinty (if that's his name) has reverted to the status of a mug. Once again, as the Boss gives out a roar, you feel the movie snap shut with unchallengeable logic. Once again, the imp of the amorphous tries to punch his way free—though not for love (too painful a subject) but merely for a chance to pocket two dollars left unattended on top of the bar: the price of one vote.

2

HE THINKS HE HAS IDEAS

Christmas in July

Of the ten major films that Sturges wrote and directed, six show what can happen when unmerited wealth or fame suddenly drops onto a person from on high, with the dangerous, drunk-and-disorderly grin of Dionysus. *The Great McGinty, Christmas in July, The Palm Beach Story, The Miracle of Morgan's Creek, Hail the Conquering Hero,* and *The Sin of Harold Diddlebock* all qualify in differing degrees as tales in which wild good fortune arrives, early or late, despite the protagonist's anonymity or obliviousness. Two important earlier screenplays that Sturges did not direct—*The Good Fairy* and *Easy Living*—also fit this category and helped set the tone for the later pictures.

These comedies of success amount to only a little more than half of Sturges's work as a writer-director, but they have exerted a dominant influence on critical opinion, which frequently characterizes Sturges as the satirist of a peculiarly American pursuit of the high life (despite *The Good Fairy*'s setting in a *Mitteleuropisch* fantasyland). The film that has done the most to establish this impression is the second he directed, *Christmas in July*.

It resembles the others in showing that solid benefits may flow from insubstantial appearances. The process is self-sustaining: once the protagonists are perceived to be winners, the world rushes to pour still more winnings into their hands. Where *Christmas in July* stands apart (with *Easy Living*) is in making this not-quite-perpetual-motion machine run within the domain of corporate America.

"The chief business of the American people is business," Calvin Coolidge had said in 1925, in a declaration that for millions remains an article of faith. Despite considerable evidence to the contrary, many Americans insist that entrepreneurship is the highest civic good, that average citizens are most likely to prosper when corporations are left to operate as they please, and that nothing is better for the government than to be put into the hands of expert business leaders such as Donald J. Trump.

Even more than *Easy Living*, *Christmas in July* takes us far from this belief system, and from the territory of Sturges's near-contemporary Ayn Rand, who in *The Fountainhead* (and the later *Atlas Shrugged*) codified the myth of the businessman-genius who forges ahead in splendid self-assurance, never caring about the opposition of a world of mediocrities. In stark contrast, the runt-sized titan who employs Sturges's protagonist Jimmy MacDonald (Dick Powell) in *Christmas in July* cheerfully admits he can't judge whether this youngish man's ideas will make any money. He bets they will, but only because other people already seem to have made the same wager.

Nor is Jimmy any better than his boss at forming independent opinions. Near the end of the film, when his girlfriend Betty (Ellen Drew) insists that he knows his own merits, a dejected Jimmy replies, "But I *don't* know. I never *did* know until I got that telegram this morning"—a prank telegram, as it happens, which fooled Jimmy and everyone around him into thinking he'd won the contest to write a new advertising slogan for the Maxford House coffee company.

Which brings me to the greatest distinction of *Christmas in July*. Alone among Sturges's films, *Christmas in July* is about the public use of words. His other films are as crammed as a fruitcake with boozy plums of political oratory, movie-studio puffery, legal doubletalk, gossip-column innuendo, and editorial-page pomposities. Only in *Christmas in July*, though, does the whole action turn on a phrase invented for a corporation's billboards and radio broadcasts: "If you can't sleep at night, it's not the coffee, it's the bunk." In its many iterations, most of them garbled, Jimmy's slogan for Maxford House coffee *is* the movie: a play of illusions, a tissue of misunderstandings, a sequence of words that might initially sound like they make sense but don't, or that maddeningly make no sense but *almost* bring an idea into focus.

In some ways, *Christmas in July* is as airy as the slogan on which it's built. At seventy minutes it is the briefest of Sturges's films. It has the fewest plot complications, narrative conundrums, and shifts of mood and the smallest population of memorable oddballs; and with its ready-made New York immigrant neighborhood, it exhibits the heaviest reliance on stock settings and types. If Sturges is to be seen above all as the filmmaker who punctured "the American myth of success"—whatever that means—then *Christmas in July* is perhaps too slight and peculiar a specimen of his work on which to base that reputation.

That's not to deny the film's role in his career. During Sturges's early years on contract at Hollywood studios, he repeatedly pulled two items out of his trunk in the hope of making a sale and getting an assignment to direct. One was the initial stage version of *Christmas in July*. The other, of course, was *The Vagabond*. But when transformed into *The Great McGinty*, *The Vagabond* proved to be a surprisingly personal film. *Christmas in July*, if watched attentively, might warn viewers not to imagine too direct a relationship between Sturges's life and art.

One way to complicate an understanding of that relationship is to look more closely at the development of a Sturges character type of particular relevance to *Christmas in July*: the American tycoon.

As the biographies reveal, Sturges always depended on the kindness of wealthy men.

First among them was his adoptive father, Solomon (1865–1940), a Chicago stockbroker from a large and locally prominent family who was forever Sturges's ideal of wisdom, generosity, and manly American indifference to artistic folderol. Second was Solomon's contemporary Paris Singer (1867–1932), an heir to the sewing machine fortune. As a lover and bankroller of Isadora Duncan—and through her an acquaintance of Sturges's flighty mother, Marie Desti, who was one of Isadora's close friends—Singer had the suspect habit of consorting with a European artistic set. Still, he was associated with an American industrial family (though a generation removed from its phase of capital accumulation) and was a large, forceful, munificent figure, who strode head and shoulders above his companions. As much as Sturges later mocked his mother's artsiness and complained of the neglect to which it had exposed him, he expressed nothing but warmth toward Singer, the one member of her crowd who always took care of him. From the age of eleven, Sturges looked up to Singer as if to a favorite uncle.

Many critics have proposed a link between these two guardians and the plainspoken, open-handed tycoons in Sturges's films. The cinematic lineage includes Edward Arnold's blustering financier J. B. Ball in *Easy Living*; continues with Eugene Pallette's equally vital and rotund Mr. Pike in *The Lady Eve*; and then, in *The Palm Beach Story*, yields the surplus of Robert Dudley's Wienie King and Rudy Vallee's John D. Hackensacker III: the first tiny and abrupt, the second gentle and corny, but both spraying eccentric fountains of cash and admiration just when the heroine needs them. To this list, I'd add Robert Warwick and Porter Hall as the Hollywood moguls LeBrand and Hadrian in *Sullivan's Travels*. These two are merely powerful and wealthy, as distinct from fabulously rich; but they do run a major studio along sensible commercial lines, from which they're smart enough to diverge for the sake of a valuable property.

In drawing these characterizations, Sturges himself diverged from the mainstream of Depression-era American comedies, which did not take for granted either the benevolence or the brains of the rich. Even though Hollywood productions of the 1930s and early 1940s assumed that social and economic mobility were facts of American life—for white men, anyway—movies were full of signs of class distinction, from the unbarbered heads and Noo Yawk accents of the Dead End Kids to the strings of pearls and semioperatic warbling of Margaret Dumont. Sometimes a tycoon in these films turned out to be a regular Joe, once you got to know him; and sometimes he would have a whimsical grown son who would run off with Carole Lombard. For the most part, though, wealthy men, whether they had inherited their money or were still piling it up, figured as overbearing bosses, vain socialites, the weaklings and cads of melodrama (who would be redeemed by a good woman, or else betray her), and stuffed shirts in need of a good untucking. Sturges was exceptional in presenting captains of industry and finance as likeable men—irascible at times, but also decent, indulgent, and deeply realistic.

No doubt Solomon Sturges and Paris Singer inspired these characterizations to some extent; but were Sturges's feelings for these two guardians a decisive influence on his writing, as is often assumed? If so, it seems odd that the personal associations kicked in so late. The figure of the kindly tycoon does not show up in the Sturges canon until the script for his fifth Broadway play, *A Cup of Coffee*, written as an exercise in self-discipline in summer 1931 (shortly before his thirty-third birthday) after the failure of plays three and four.

Even more strange: when Sturges at last got to make *A Cup of Coffee* into a film, *Christmas in July* (1940), the play's sympathetic magnate went missing. This was the only film with a business-world setting that Sturges would direct. Why would a character type who distinguishes Sturges's imaginative world—a type born in the original, stage version of *Christmas in July*—vanish at just this moment?

Despite a long experience with wealthy men—including Edward F. Hutton of Manhattan, Long Island, and Palm Beach, the not-so-kindly stepfather of Sturges's second wife, Eleanor—no hint of autobiography attended the birth of the wealthy tycoon character. We have Sturges's own word for that, in the stream-of-consciousness memo-to-self he wrote into the first pages of *A Cup of Coffee*. These middle-of-the-night ramblings clear the author of any suspicion of self-expression: "If I think of a good title this will be a fairly successful play. . . . It will be carefully constructed, will appeal to the simplest emotions and be very conscientiously (?) written. It will not be a smash because it is not going to SHOCK either the proprieties or the sense of justice. All great plays are SHOCKERS."[1]

It's also notable that the play's wealthy industrialist—Ephraim Baxter, founder of Baxter's Best Coffee—does not live up to Sturges's admiring image of Solomon Sturges and Paris Singer, let alone to the grand businessmen who will later bustle through the films. Aged, somnolent, querulous, and forgetful in the play's first act, Ephraim has to be roused from his torpor in the third to help the protagonists toward their happy ending. Stirred from a feebleness that has been imposed on him largely for thematic purposes—a younger generation can hardly step forward, if the older remains strong enough to stand in the way—Ephraim when awakened sounds a note of piratical generosity, which at this early stage in the development of the Sturges tycoon is not much different from the amoral benevolence that flows from George Bernard Shaw's arms manufacturers.

For the play itself, there was to be no happiness. Nobody would produce the conscientiously written *A Cup of Coffee*. A backer did step forward, to his own regret, for Sturges's sixth and final play, *Child of Manhattan* (also known as *Consider the Lily*). When it, too, flopped, Sturges concluded that Broadway was finished with him. He put the script for the unstaged *A Cup of Coffee* into his trunk and turned his energies toward making money in Hollywood.

But now that he'd set loose the urge to write about industrialists, Sturges kept going with *The Power and the Glory*; and this time, in contrast to the utilitarian attitude he'd adopted toward *A Cup of Coffee*, he took pride in authorship.

The Power and the Glory was the first important screenplay of Sturges's career, dreamed up on his own initiative (not at a studio's command) and sold on terms so favorable to the writer that they were virtually unprecedented in Hollywood. The story could perhaps be interpreted as a work of postdivorce revenge, enacted upon Eleanor through the image of her grandfather C. W. Post, the founder of General Foods. Marriage had provided Sturges with the gossip's version of the history of Post and his company—scandalous stuff, which included mental breakdowns, legal troubles, and suicide. But if the bitterness of divorce stung

Sturges into using this material, he took good care to disguise its origins.

The Power and the Glory is the tale of the rise and fall of the flawed hero Tom Garner (Spencer Tracy), a magnate not of corn flakes but of the railroad, narrated lugubriously after the funeral by his oldest and sole remaining friend. Apart from the occasional wry moment, the film is not at all a comedy—nor is Tom much of a life force, despite the physical strength and brutal audacity ascribed to him in the narrator's somewhat questionable memory. Affable only when Spencer Tracy exerts his innate charm, Tom appears in multiple, shuffled flashbacks as a hard man, bullying to colleagues and business rivals, murderous to striking railroad workers, and catastrophically distant from his wife and son. (The younger generation may supplant the older in *The Power and the Glory*, but not happily.) The narrator's suggestion that Tom was henpecked into success does little to soften the image of this frequently ruthless protagonist. Despite the innovation of the script's fragmented chronology (which was to influence any number of later filmmakers, including Orson Welles), Sturges's portrait of a self-made millionaire pretty well matched what audiences would have expected in 1933. Tom Garner confirms the idea that behind every fortune is a crime—or, in his case, two or three.

The Power and the Glory made Sturges famous as a screenwriter. But after it fizzled at the box office, he beat a tactical retreat, setting aside for a while the figure of the morally dubious businessman, as well as the use of jumbled chronology and morose, postfuneral narration. (He would return to all three in 1942 in *The Great Moment*, the darkest and most troubled of his major films.) For now, he went back to contract work—and soon enough, his labors at Universal yielded the opportunity to revive Ephraim Baxter, his more encouraging image of the American tycoon.

In 1934, Sturges sold Universal the rights to *A Cup of Coffee*. His letters record his elation; a script that he'd undertaken mechanically and for purely commercial ends—which he hadn't attained—now had fetched him thousands of dollars, as well as the increase in status that he desperately wanted. When *A Cup of Coffee* went into production, Universal promised, Sturges would get to direct.[2]

But the film didn't go into production. Instead, Universal scheduled Sturges to collaborate with William Wyler on an adaptation of Ferenc Molnar's play *The Good Fairy*—the first prestigious studio assignment for which he would receive credit, and the first of the existing literary properties that he would thoroughly rewrite. Then in March 1935, after *The Good Fairy* had enjoyed a successful opening, Universal asked Sturges to set aside *A Cup of Coffee* again to help on yet another project.

The studio had purchased the rights to a biography of Diamond Jim Brady, the gaudiest self-made millionaire of the Gilded Age, and now was distressed to discover that it shouldn't have hired the biographer himself to write the screenplay. After reading the first draft, the producers remembered, too late, that the biographer wasn't an author by trade but a jeweler.

So this somewhat true story of a down-to-earth, generous, flamboyant industrialist was thrust upon Sturges, just when he'd been thinking about reviving the shriveled tycoon of *A Cup of Coffee*. To the understandably impatient Sturges, the assignment of *Diamond Jim* might at first have seemed like a detour. In terms of the development of one of his most distinctive character types, though, it proved to be a course correction.

Diamond Jim plays in retrospect like a precursor of the film made from Sturges's first great comedy script, *Easy Living*, and not just because of the impeccable casting of Edward Arnold in both pictures. *Diamond Jim* also represents a shift toward vitality, celebrating its millionaire's unembarrassed, unconstrained enjoyment of life, in sharp contrast to the predominant feebleness of Ephraim Baxter and self-torture of Tom Garner.

As Sturges conceives him, Jim Brady builds a business career with the same high spirits that move him to eat for three men, wear enough jewelry for ten, and impulsively organize a wedding for himself on the scale of one of his adored stage musicals. Lucky in all things except love, Sturges's Brady bursts limits even in romantic misfortune. Having lost his heart early in the film to a sweet Southern belle (played by Jean Arthur), he insists on losing it a second time to a New York adventuress who looks just like her. When she turns out to be not just surprised but mortified to find herself cast as the lead in his impromptu marital production, Brady is so grand that he can laugh off the debacle—outwardly, at least.

Evolution of the Sturges tycoon: Edward Arnold with Binnie Barnes in *Diamond Jim*. Courtesy The Museum of Modern Art

Unlike Ephraim Baxter before him, or the J. B. Ball who was to come in *Easy Living*, Jim Brady is the protagonist of this story, not a supporting or enabling character. As such, he is subjected at the beginning and end of life to a morbid gloom, of the sort that had shadowed the margins of Sturges's portrait of Tom Garner. The film begins with boyish tears at the death of Brady's saintly mother. (Sturges's biographer Diane Jacobs notes that she was, in reality, a booze-swilling religious fanatic, whom the adult Brady committed to a mental asylum.)[3] It ends in a lonely, darkened mansion (Charles Foster Kane's Xanadu, you might think, realized before the fact), where Brady is preparing to carry out the grotesque project of eating himself to death. The producers at Universal objected particularly to this finale, and it's notable that Sturges fought for it and won. He apparently believed, at this stage of his career, that any subject worthy of full-length treatment required a few brushstrokes of doom.

Released in August 1935, *Diamond Jim* did good business and received some admiring notices; but it still did not open the way at Universal toward production of *A Cup of Coffee*. Pleading poverty, the studio assigned Sturges to write other projects—two of which brought him no credit, one of which went unproduced. By September 1936, he'd had enough. Sturges jumped to Paramount, where he immediately got the assignment that would bring to maturity his recently discovered character of the irascible but kindly tycoon who is full of life. He was told to adapt an original story, titled "Easy Living," that the freelance writer Vera Caspary had sold the studio.

At last the true Preston Sturges tycoon was ready to step into film history, right where he hadn't been anticipated.

Caspary's story is a morality tale about a poor working girl who steals a fur coat from a Park Avenue grande dame. The motive is the young woman's desperate desire to look like someone above her station; the instigating conflict is a disagreement between this social climber—a masseuse by trade—and the rich woman who is her client. How did the rich woman acquire the coat in the first place? Presumably, her husband gave it to her, as wealthy men normally did in popular fiction and Hollywood movies. That process and the man's character were of no great concern to Caspary.

But they were of enormous, amused interest to Sturges, who made the instigating conflict in *Easy Living* an extended, knockdown battle between the grande dame (now living on Fifth Avenue instead of Park) and her husband, no longer a neglected stock character but the highly particularized J. B. Ball: the third biggest banker in the United States (just ask him), known in the

Evolution of the Sturges tycoon: Edward Arnold with Jean Peters in *Easy Living*. Courtesy The Museum of Modern Art

tabloids as the Bull of Broad Street, and a primary focus of the story from the start. Righteously apoplectic over the extravagance of both his grown son and his wife (who has bought a new sable coat behind his back, despite having a closet full of furs), Ball sets the plot in motion by tossing the $58,000 offense off the roof of his apartment building.

The unwitting and unwilling recipient of this luxurious projectile, Mary (Jean Arthur), is first seen going to work on top of a double-decker bus. Unlike Caspary's protagonist, she does not seem at all to be an anxious social climber but is described in the screenplay as looking "serene" and enjoying the day. And, of course, she steals nothing (though later in the movie she will face all sorts of baseless accusations). The coat literally falls out of the sky.

"What's the big idea?" Mary shouts, glaring at the man sitting behind her as if he'd knocked her on the head.

The man—a Hindu wearing a turban—replies by pointing cheerfully to the book he's been reading and announcing *its* big idea, which also happens to be the operating principle of *Easy Living*: "Kismet!"

Mary is not yet prepared, though, to accept her personal kismet. In another shift from the letter and spirit of Caspary's story, she immediately tries to find the coat's owner and so comes face to face with J. B. Ball. From that moment, the Sturges magnate blossoms.

Already, in the opening scene, the character has exhibited his more common surface features: a gruff manner and sometimes rough way of turning a phrase, for example, and a watchful eye for practical details, such as the price of butter. Despite references to a privileged upbringing, Ball also lets slip a semiconfession of youthful wildness, long abandoned but apparently not forgotten. There is nothing stuffed about this man's shirt, despite all his money, nor do crime and tragedy darken the corners of his life, as they do Tom Garner's and Jim Brady's. He may seem punitive in throwing away his wife's sable coat (or rather *his* coat, since the bill came to him), but the absurd grandiosity of the gesture prevents the audience from suspecting that he might be mean-spirited. Ball feels people are taking advantage of him—it seems they are, too—and so he vituperates as anyone would, only more so, because he's a bigger man. He's also willing to undermine his own cost-cutting project to score a point. At 1937 prices, the coat he throws away would have bought 157,000 pounds of butter.

This is already a wonderfully rich portrait, made all the better, as it comes off the page and onto the screen, by the sly glint in Edward Arnold's eyes, the thrust of his shoulders behind his well-barbered boulder of a head, and the distracted mutter that he uses in alternation with howls of outrage. (The direction, by Mitchell Leisen, is not quite so lackluster as Sturges thought.) But it's only when J. B. Ball begins talking with Mary that the character's innermost traits emerge.

First, and most obvious, he can be susceptible to a young woman's charm—so long as she understands his feelings to be innocent. "Santy Claus," Mary calls him, a little sharply, when he refuses to accept the return of the coat and immediately tries to part from her—no phone number taken, no casual but meaningful caress attempted. It's crucial, for both this story and the character type, that sexual hunger is not one of Ball's defining qualities, despite his robust spirits. Crucial for the story because everyone in *Easy Living* is about to assume, wrongly, that Mary is Ball's kept woman. Crucial for the character type because Sturges (like everyone) knows that powerful men do pick up younger women along their route—as Tom Garner does, for example, and Jim Brady tries to. Ball does not. One of Ball's

Evolution of the Sturges tycoon: Eugene Pallette with Barbara Stanwyck in *The Lady Eve*. Courtesy Photofest

distinguishing features is the purely avuncular nature of his interest in the young woman before him—foreshadowing future characters such as Mr. Pike in *The Lady Eve* and the Wienie King in *The Palm Beach Story*.

With that established, Ball's outrageous high-handedness in flinging away the coat can take on the more pleasant coloration of an uncommon generosity, when he redoubles the original gesture by gruffly and knowingly making a present of the sable to Mary ("Happy birthday") instead of seizing the chance to recover a loss. At this moment, his impetuousness (apparently self-defeating in the opening scene) starts to look more like an executive's habit of decision-making gone momentarily into overdrive. And his respect for hard work comes to the fore. Practically the first thing he says to Mary, sizing her up, is, "You earn your own living?" Her ability to give an honest yes opens the way toward the rest of the exchange—including his imperious kindness in ordering her into his car, when he understands she's short of the dime she would need to reboard the bus.

Imperiously kind, and a lecturer on kindness. "Sometimes nice things do happen to people—*very* nice things!" he tells Mary, when she suspects there might be a catch to her receiving a fur coat out of the blue. As much as Ball knows about the harshness of the world—a lot, presumably—he rejects cynicism, insisting to Mary that she shouldn't "be *too* wise." But she shouldn't be played for a fool, either. When he realizes this decent, very pretty young working woman is liable to be gouged by unscrupulous merchants, Ball leaps to protect her—leading to an uproarious extended dialogue that only Sturges could have written, on the proper way to calculate compound interest.

The improbability of wringing comedy out of a bone-dry subject is perhaps this dialogue's smaller marvel. The larger one is its revelation of Ball's character. You see that he persists in his lesson partly out of male arrogance (mansplaining to her, as a later era would say), partly out of professional ethics and personal gallantry, but most of all perhaps because he cannot bear to let Mary win an argument through wrong-headed common sense. Her persistence in a frequently encountered error—that 1 percent interest per month amounts to 12 percent a year—affronts his meritocratically high status, which he hasn't stooped to announce but clearly would like to. ("Of course you don't know who I am, but I'm very good at computing interest.") If he were to let the argument drop, he would be complicit in the overthrow of the natural order, since Mary, in her simplicity, believes *he's* the simple one. ("I don't want to be rude," she says, "but I should think even a small child . . .") Trying with a single effort to help her and force her to admit she's wrong, Ball lowers himself to what he assumes is her level, proposing the kind of word problem that Mary would have been asked to solve in elementary school: "A farmer borrowed one hundred cows . . ." It's no use. Mary beats him again, at least in her own mind, and in the words of the screenplay is "almost embarrassed" to give him the self-evident answer to his puzzle: "twelve cows."

Why does Ball continue to harass Mary about compound interest in the face of such closed-mindedness, while showering her with an additional expensive gift? Let's say that Sturges has transmuted his earlier tycoons' appetite for sexual love into a simpler urge to have fun, innocently occasioned by the presence of a pretty young woman. And let's say that the ruthless competitive drive of Ephraim Baxter, Tom Garner, and even Jim Brady has been transformed into the more genial quality of quixotic stubbornness, tempered by the habits of practical thinking that any rational person can develop.

In making these changes, Sturges has abandoned his attempt at the slashing social analysis that theatergoers were used to receiving from Shaw; but that's no great loss. As evidence, here's the young hero of *A Cup of Coffee*, Jimmy MacDonald, explaining in act 2 why underhanded competition is not merely right but necessary: "every great fortune in this country was founded with methods that the word 'unfair' doesn't begin to describe. Big business was a hard game and a man's game. Look at Johnny Rockefeller, the elder Morgan, Hill, Fisk, Vanderbilt, Astor . . . what a fine upstanding bunch of pirates those babies were!"[14]

To which old Ephraim Baxter, momentarily stirred, says, "Hooray! That's the way I like to hear a fellow talk."

Though it's a dirty trick to play on the Broadway Sturges, quoting him back to back with Shaw, here for comparison is Andrew Undershaft, the vastly wealthy arms manufacturer of *Major Barbara* (1905)—a hair-raising man who is unashamed of multiplying the world's instruments of death—as he rebuts the charge that he rose by being "selfish and unscrupulous."

> Not at all. I had the strongest scruples about poverty and starvation. Your moralists are quite unscrupulous about both: they make virtues of them. I had rather be a thief than a pauper. I had rather be a murderer than a slave. I don't want to be either; but if you force the alternative on me, then, by Heaven, I'll choose the braver and more moral one. . . . Poverty and slavery have stood up for centuries to your sermons and leading articles: they will not stand up to my machine guns. Don't preach at them: don't reason with them. Kill them.[5]

To this tirade, "Hooray!" is not an adequate response.

For just a few moments in *A Cup of Coffee,* Sturges tried to imitate the Shavian manner by slicing world-historical forces into their immediate, personal dynamics; but he was using a borrowed razor, gone dull in the blade, to make perfectly conventional cuts. His judgment was correct; the play was not a SHOCKER. But by the time Sturges changed *A Cup of Coffee* into *Christmas in July,* he was prepared to equal or perhaps outdo Shaw at another game: stirring up delirious bustle, which he was almost uniquely good at thickening with odd nuggets of the mundane.

Sturges had gone beyond writing characters like Ephraim Baxter—pale imitations of Shaw's magnates. The problem was, his new model of the genial, generous, and effective tycoon simply did not suit the business world of *Christmas in July.*

There are, in fact, two competing settings for business in *Christmas in July,* each absurd in its own way.

Maxford House makes its headquarters in an office tower where everything is modern and impeccably gleaming, yet nothing seems to get done or be in working order. The polished corridors through which the boss hurries from one crisis to the next are forever unpopulated, except for the sight of his backside waddling into the distance. No one is available to occupy these halls—because behind the scenes, a dozen senior men who might have been useful elsewhere are wasting their days and nights smoking and bickering in a conference room piled high with cardboard boxes and teetering stacks of paper: the submissions to the slogan contest, for which this jury has yet to choose a winner.

The contrast between high-gloss façade and chaotic reality reaches its epitome in the Maxford skyscraper's radio studio, from which the company broadcasts the weekly program on which the winner is to be announced. Franklin Pangborn, the character actor most likely in 1930s and 1940s Hollywood to be cast as a proudly decorous hotel manager or shop clerk—the era's code word was "prissy"—applies his smooth baritone and rounded enunciation to the role of Don Hartman, the announcer who must maintain the sound of normality while everything around him is collapsing. As his celebrated sponsor, Dr. Maxford, hurries back and forth in consternation at not having a contest winner, Hartman mops his brow, chuckles mirthlessly at nothing, and lets the supposed elegance of his patter degenerate into antique puns and an apology for a "fox pass." Listening to this breakdown is like seeing him split the seat of his black-tie outfit. And yet the next day finds Don Hartman in the company's executive suite conferring alone with Dr. Maxford, who seems to have nothing better to do than converse with a radio announcer and occasionally shout into a thoroughly up-to-date intercom. That device, too, is probably kept around for appearance sake. Maxford is so loud that his secretaries must be able to hear him through the door.

The offices of Baxter's Best Coffee, by comparison, are a nightmare of drab regimentation. Sturges shows the clerks and typists punching the time clock, donning company-issued dusters in the locker room, marching in silent files to their desks, and taking their seats in unison to the starting bell. The furnishings of this workplace are as blandly uniform as the laborers' dusters, and the office manager, Mr. Waterbury (Harry Hayden), patrols the aisles to keep them that way, occasionally straightening an in-box so it aligns perfectly with the edge of the desk. There are to be no smiles in this place and no glamour—not even the phony glamour of a Maxford House broadcast—or any of the laxity that might allow an employee to challenge the boss, as Dr. Maxford's pig-headed shipping manager, Bildocker (William Demarest), dares to challenge him in the jury room.

Kindness and mercy in the Baxter offices can take the form at best of the moralizing speech that Waterbury delivers to Jimmy, after discovering him daydreaming on the job about the $25,000 Maxford House top prize. (That would be the equivalent, in current purchasing power, of almost $440,000.) As the dressing down begins, Jimmy clearly expects to be fired. Instead, Waterbury turns autobiographical—"Ah yes, I used to think about $25,000 too"—before advising the wayward clerk to be realistic, go back to his desk, and concentrate on eight hours of drudgery. For this encouragement, which might be summarized as "Abandon all hope," Jimmy actually thanks Waterbury.

Such are the twin poles of corporate America, as seen in Maxford House and Baxter's Best. Clearly there is no room here for gruff but high-spirited tycoons who can be both keenly practical and impulsively generous; and *Christmas in July* offers none.

Dr. Maxford (Raymond Walburn) is as formal as the honorific unaccountably attached to his name—a conspicuously old-fashioned man, round of face and body, who wears black tie to his radio broadcasts (though who would see him?) and even for his daytime duties insists on appearing in a wing collar, a broad waistcoat, and spats, with a monocle dangling to his tummy. He's like the bustling cartoon swell on the Monopoly box, except blustering and sarcastic. By the law of opposites that is integral to comedy, Maxford is the one element that's antique in his modern (yet secretly ramshackle) operation.

By the same law, Jimmy MacDonald's employer, Mr. Baxter (Ernest Truex), is the one ray of sunshine in a Dickensian sweatshop. With his sleek suit and snappy hat, Baxter cuts a far more dapper figure than Maxford. He's a bantam big shot, short, sharp-featured, lithe, and high-voiced. Though a bit yappy when provoked into screaming at his employees, he is more often pleased to croon at them, through the smile of a man who is easily flattered and quickly satisfied.

Very few hints of the real world of business, let alone of Sturges's experience of rich men, inform these contrasting stereotypes. If you had to discover a source for Maxford and Baxter, you'd do better to forget the likes of Solomon Sturges and delve instead into the old theories of humors and temperaments. On one side of *Christmas in July* is a fine specimen of the choleric type; on the other, an example of the sanguine (with a dash of excitability).

Sturges loved to deploy such traditional stock characters; but as I'll suggest in considering *Sullivan's Travels*, he was seldom content to leave them undeveloped. One of his greatest gifts was his knack for infusing old types with some of the messiness and circumstantiality of lived experience. He made no such effort, though, for Maxford and Baxter. You can't intuit an inner life for these characters (as you can, say, for J. B. Ball). They have no surprises in store.

All the more reason, then, to be astonished at the thickness of Sturges's portrayals of Jimmy and Betty, the young couple who in a lesser filmmaker's hands might have been little more than The Boy and The Girl.

When first discovered, huddling together on a tenement rooftop as movie lovers do on a summer night, Jimmy and Betty can sense possibilities hovering in the air around them: shining in the neon lights of midtown Manhattan, which they can see in the distance, and whispering in the radio waves that reach them from Maxford House. And yet the two spend much of the first sequence bickering like a husband and wife who have long since gotten fed up with each other. Some opening for a comedy: she belittles him for being gullible enough to think he can win promotional contests (which are rigged, anyway), and he hits back by belittling her intelligence. Not only does Jimmy accuse Betty of being incapable of understanding his unintelligible Maxford House slogan, but he also instructs her in how to calculate the shortfall they could expect in their finances if they should marry. It's like J. B. Ball's lesson in compound interest, without the kindliness and humor.

As Betty, Ellen Drew looks about right for a young woman of that era pushing for marriage before her chances dry up; she was twenty-four when shooting *Christmas in July*. But Dick Powell was thirty-five: manifestly old to be playing a man contemplating a first marriage (or stringing a young woman along while putting it off), visibly past the age when an office underling might have imagined a brighter future at his job. The costume he wears in this first scene only worsens the impression.

Sweatshirts are for college boys and athletes; by being dressed in one, an almost middle-aged Powell makes Jimmy seem like a case of arrested development.

And Sturges makes the most of the impression in the way he directs Powell. When Drew brings up marriage, Sturges has Powell look away from her almost brutally while snapping, "Nix." When Drew questions the aptness, or perhaps sanity, of the pun that makes Jimmy so proud of his Maxford House slogan, Sturges has Powell snarl, in close-up, "It's *funny*"—which is more than you can say for his response.

Sturges gets away with this bleakness by refusing to let it stick. In a series of swift edits that send this initial scene flying across Manhattan, he cuts from Jimmy and Betty to the Maxford House studio, to a sampling of diverse humanity listening to the broadcast, to the contest's jury room, and back to Jimmy and Betty on the roof. As Diane Jacobs writes, this opening sequence is six minutes of "breathtakingly terse exposition," presenting "characters so formally diverse their very coexistence disconcerts."[6]

Here, then, is some of the shock, or boldness, that was missing from *A Cup of Coffee*. Sturges risks beginning a comedy with a complex sequence that incorporates not only moments of broad satire, near-slapstick buffoonery, dizzying doubletalk ("it's the bunk—THE BUNK"), and a little Yiddish dialect humor from the neighbor downstairs, but also an extended conversation about the blighted hopes and bitterness that drive people to seek $25,000 prizes—or a few laughs at the movies.

Sturges touches on the reality of the youngish couple's predicament just enough to engage the audience's concern, meanwhile avoiding too heavy a pull of emotional gravity by keeping the whole sequence literally ungrounded. Except for the montage of people listening to the Maxford House broadcast, the settings in these first six minutes never come closer to the pavement than the tenement's roof, and often hover two or three dozen stories higher than that. The trick is pulled off so deftly, without calling the slightest attention to itself, that audiences may not realize just how much the movie owes its atmosphere of giddiness to being up in the air. When the sequence, at its conclusion, does begin a descent, with Jimmy helping Betty down a ladder and into her apartment building, the same prevailing giddiness makes possible an unexpected emotional change. Maxford and Baxter may not have an inner life; but in the scene's last moments Jimmy suddenly reveals the tenderness and protectiveness he nurtures for Betty beneath his hard-bitten, perpetual-adolescent pose. Betty, in turn, meltingly shows she's

Jimmy and Betty in their usual position, off the ground.
Courtesy Photofest

HE THINKS HE HAS IDEAS ⌘ 57

willing to pretend that he's not a fool—even if the audience knows it's utterly impractical to pin her hopes on him.

Having begun off the ground, the movie doesn't really set foot on the street until about three-quarters of the way through, when something wilder and riskier than giddiness takes over. Returning to the Paramount backlot version of a New York immigrant neighborhood, complete with front stoops, iron lampposts, and the standard Irish-Jewish ethnic mix, Jimmy and Betty create an uproar by distributing presents (which they don't rightfully own) to their entire block. (To get the ruckus started, Sturges focuses on a young girl in a wheelchair who weeps upon receiving the first nice new doll she's ever had. Once again Sturges touches, however sentimentally, on the grind of being forever short of money.) But despite this impromptu street fair's being the busiest scene in the movie—its high point of noise, crowding, and laughter, and also of audience anxiety about the trouble that is surely coming for the naïve but felonious Jimmy and Betty—the events that really matter in *Christmas in July* don't happen down on the pavement.

The film's general movement is upward—as when Jimmy (believing he's won the contest) leaps on top of a desk and pulls Betty up with him, or when the couple ascends to the executive floor. And even those offices, high above the avenues, are less important than the billboards that stand atop them, towering over Manhattan's skyscrapers. That's where the crucial action happens—in words that flash across the night sky and also in Jimmy's mind, as he fantasizes about scrawling his slogans over the city in insubstantial light.

Of course the $25,000 is important—essential, in fact—but the real excitement for Jimmy lies in being invited to pitch his ideas to the Baxter's Best advertising executives. It's so crucial to him that he goes to them first, even before visiting Maxford

House to pick up his prize money, so he can strut in front of Betty and the bosses and spout new ad campaigns. He improvises, with his eyes lifted toward an imagined skyline; he cups a hand and mimes setting his words in the ether; and all the people in the room, down to hard-headed old Waterbury, turn to stare at the nothing floating above them.

Is Baxter's really the blueblood coffee, as Jimmy brainstorms, its aristocratic superiority "bred in the bean"? This, too, is surely the bunk—but nobody cares. The important thing isn't the coffee but the invention of a phrase that sounds pretty good, and then the next one, and another. Jimmy tosses them out with much the same heedlessness that allowed his office buddies to revel in the practical joke they'd devised; much the same tireless enthusiasm that later inspires Torben Meyer, as a furniture salesman, to declare of the workings of a convertible sofa, "There is no limit to man's ingenuity!"

In the increasingly frenetic atmosphere of *Christmas in July*, nothing is so valued as the production of mental froth. As Betty argues to Baxter in the final scene, Jimmy belongs in the executive suite "because he thinks he has ideas." That being the main job qualification—thinking that you've had a thought—we shouldn't be surprised that ideas in this world can be churned very quickly and are impossible to judge by any objective standard, as the Maxford House jury discovers to its chagrin.

Looking back on these entrepreneurial charades from a twenty-first-century viewpoint, it's tempting to think of them as a critique of late capitalism, delivered on the early side. But if so, you can't generalize this critique across Sturges's films. It hardly needs saying that J. B. Ball, the Bull of Broad Street, would not base his business decisions on mere blather. (When confronted with a run on the price of steel company shares, Ball refuses to panic. He sees the fundamentals are sound.) Nor would the Wienie King be swayed by mere slogans, knowing as he does where to buy the meat cheap. And what about Mr. Pike, who has somehow remained wealthy all the way into 1940 despite his brewery's having been outlawed by Prohibition until 1933? Surely he's made of tougher, more corpulent stuff than any of the businessmen blowing about in *Christmas in July*.

The true Sturges tycoons, and Sturges's portrayals of business more generally, retain the practicality of their author, who in his spare time dabbled as the inventor of a vibration-free diesel engine. It seems more fitting to say that the business dealings of *Christmas in July*, like the figures of Maxford and Baxter, are throwbacks to traditional comic models. This is a film in which success in business has no more basis in reality than cunning Volpone's hints of a rich inheritance, or the vision of money that Jimmy's old-country mother superstitiously makes out in the bubbles of his morning coffee.

If any clinching evidence is needed, consider one more difference between *Christmas in July* and its source. In *A Cup of Coffee*, the type of business in which the characters engage is crucial. When Ephraim Baxter needs to be roused from his lethargy so he can help the young lovers, the solution is to serve him some of his own product, which the doctors have forbidden him for years. At the first taste of caffeine old Baxter wakes up, the young people win, and the premise of Jimmy's slogan is definitively shown to be false, all at the same time. However slight the play may be, its central joke and ultimate plot twist are well rooted in the setting. But *Christmas in July* literally has no grounds. The competing coffee manufacturers might as well be dealing in wing nuts, shoe lasts, saltwater taffy, or whoopee cushions. The nature of their business is arbitrary, and so too is the subject of

Jimmy's slogan, which becomes a free-floating brainteaser, universally recognized as false yet impossible to shoo away.

So should we say, amending Coolidge, that in *Christmas in July* the chief business of the American people is bullshit? Not quite—because Betty, at least, won't descend to doubletalk. Although she's nowhere near as strong-willed as Sturges's best heroines, she refuses in the opening sequence to soothe Jimmy with false praise for his slogan and, at the end, though fighting on his behalf for his new job, doesn't promise that he'll actually be good at it. In fact, her hardheaded argument runs the other way. In a gesture of encouragement even more deflating than Waterbury's, she predicts that Jimmy probably will fail—but he might as well be given a chance, now that Baxter has paid to have Jimmy's name painted on the door.

In short, Betty demonstrates a candor, stubbornness, and realism that might suit a Sturges tycoon, if one of them could exist in *Christmas in July*. As for the tycoon's natural high spirits, she doesn't have them—but Jimmy does. And the capacity for enjoyment, wed to kindness and outlandish generosity? Those traits emerge when Betty and Jimmy combine to rain presents on their whole block—down one side and up the other. When financial cares divide them at the beginning of the film, Jimmy and Betty live in tense semi-isolation from each other. When freed from want—and, in Jimmy's case, self-doubt—they merge, fulfilling as a breathlessly happy couple the functions that a Sturges tycoon might perform irascibly by himself.

This happiness, tellingly, does not throw off erotic heat. Like Ball, Pike, the Wienie King, and Hackensacker, Jimmy and Betty remain a little sexless, especially when compared with the Sturges lovers who gave such fits to the Production Code Administration. (This, too, is in part an effect of casting Dick

Powell.) You can't imagine these two crashing uncontrollably into each other's arms; they hardly even kiss. It seems, rather, as if the physical impulses that Jimmy and Betty have presumably had to suppress on the roof are now bursting out in the street as financial profligacy, to be sprayed across a cross-section of their peers instead of being innocently directed (in the manner of a Sturges tycoon) toward a comely individual.

The resulting democratic carnival is unlike anything else in Sturges's work. The one exception might be the episode in *Easy Living* where the Automat malfunctions, delivering free food to all. But in that scene, the bounty pours out mechanically, through nobody's generosity, and the needy people of New York respond by rioting. Here, for once in his career, Sturges imagines how wonderful it might be if Betty and Waterbury were wrong, wealth were abundant enough to go around, and failure were not the common lot.

He imagines such a world; but he doesn't pretend to believe in it for more than half of the street scene, or until outraged representatives of the merchant class roar into the neighborhood to repossess their goods, followed by an outraged representative of industrial capital demanding the return of his money. Considering the outbreak of shameless slapstick that ensues, you can't exactly call this reassertion of property rights a return to order. In its messy inevitability, though, the clampdown does suggest how little faith Sturges put in the principal civic creed of his era, which held that the common people, through self-government, would hold their own against riches and power.

Frank Capra, the cinematic St. Paul of this belief system, had preached its gospel to the nation in *Mr. Deeds Goes to Town* (1936) and *Mr. Smith Goes to Washington* (1939). By the time Sturges made *Christmas in July*, he wasn't prepared to challenge Capra by name—that would have to wait for *Sullivan's Travels*—but he was ready to counter Americanist sermons with parodic mockery.

Early in *Christmas in July*, when Dr. Maxford demands that his shipping clerk, Bildocker, fall into line with the rest of the contest judges, he gets this Capraesque retort, spoken (according to the screenplay) "with deep conviction": "I'm a member of this jury and I'm going to vote the way I think is right if it takes ten years! You can fire me out of the shipping department, but you aren't going to fire me off this jury because I don't work for you on this jury. I'm giving my services free."

Next, you'd suppose, would come something about being equal before the law in a government of the people, by the people. But Sturges has already undermined the effect by giving Bildocker's role to William Demarest, whose characteristically cranky, pugilistic tone is no better suited to civic oratory than are a bow tie and sleeve garters to his squared-off, back-street mug. A tough guy wearing the clothes of a mild-mannered clerk, a bar-room complainer seizing the dais on Independence Day, Bildocker cannot possibly lift this clash of wills onto the plane of democratic ideals. He's giving his services free, he continues, pointing to the hundreds of thousands of contest entries, "to the bunch of suckers who fell for this."

We the people. The next character to attempt a rousing, inspirational speech on behalf of all the Capraesque little guys really *is* a mild-mannered clerk—Waterbury, the Baxter's Best office manager—and he, too, is unconvincing.

"No system could be right where only half of one per cent were successes and all the rest were failures," Waterbury says, admitting to Jimmy that this is in fact exactly the result that the system produces. The solution? Instead of concluding that the system is wrong, Waterbury counsels Jimmy to cheer up, scrape by decently, and *call* himself a success.

Here, too, Sturges almost immediately undermines the speech. Knowing that no warm-blooded human would willingly follow Waterbury's advice, Sturges shows that Jimmy would still much rather have the money—but without the trouble of rising up to challenge the system. For Sturges, even to hint at such a desire for change would have been to imply an acceptance of redistributive schemes, including the Roosevelt administration's policy of "confiscatory" taxation, as he liked to call it. So, in a twist on Capraesque thinking, Sturges ignores Waterbury's praise for the common man and instead endorses the rhetorically delusional aspect of his advice. *Christmas in July* proposes that you *can* toss around $25,000 just by convincing yourself you've got it.

Unfortunately, though, you've got to hurry, because the method is good for a limited time only.

That's how Jimmy and Betty wind up less poor than before— the new, provisional job comes with a raise—but are still far from rich, and their spirits at the end are less than ebullient. It's once again nighttime in Manhattan, the action having taken place within twenty-four hours; and once again the lovers are about to descend, not down a rooftop ladder this time but in an elevator, taking them away from the Baxter skyscraper's executive floor. In an echo of the opening sequence, a black cat crosses Betty's path.

"Is it bad luck or good luck when they rub against you?" Betty asks the janitor, Sam, who is mopping up in the darkened office.

It's the sort of diverting lore that a white character in the movies would expect a Black character to know. Sam—played by Fred Toones, much put upon in the movies of the thirties and forties, in which he was known as Snowflake—gives a reply that provides the anticipated chuckle for the white people but does not reflect any superstition. "That all depends," he says, "on what happens afterward."

An eminently logical answer. Despite being confined to a menial job, and expressing himself in a dialect that white audiences took to signify ignorance, Sam wipes away magical thinking as efficiently as he cleans the floor. You get the feeling this man wouldn't let Waterbury or anyone fool him into thinking he'd be just as well off without an extra $25,000; nor does he seem likely to believe that one brand of coffee tastes better than another, just because somebody says its superiority is "bred in the bean."

But the film's last word does not go to the illusion-free Sam, or even to Jimmy and Betty in their disappointment. The kicker belongs to Bildocker, the hotheaded champion of democracy who proves at last to be democracy's prime chump. He's found the slogan for Maxford House—that is, he's browbeaten the majority of the jury into letting him have his way—and is so excited at his discovery that he demands to read it aloud: "It's what you call a pun—and believe me it's some pun!"

So the bunk triumphs, its final enunciation punctuated by the crash of a heavy object aimed at Bildocker's head. Up in the air, where people think they have ideas, insubstantial ambitions will continue to float without visible means of support or reason to exist. Down on the pavement, street fairs will continue to be whipped up from time to time as a lovers' mirage. And caught between the two, an old tycoon will go on sputtering and threatening, knowing better than to believe in gibble-gabble but nevertheless consenting to live by it, in great wealth.

3

I'M NOT A POET, I'M AN OPHIOLOGIST

The Lady Eve

The serpent was the most cunning of the beasts and tempted Eve to eat the fruit. She gave the fruit to Adam and he ate, too. Then their eyes were opened, and they saw they were naked.

Just so, a snake figures prominently in *The Lady Eve*—a Brazilian snake, called Emma—along with a woman who is sometimes called Eve; and after the woman "clunks" a man on the head with a piece of fruit (using the traditional though nonbiblical apple) he soon enough begins to fall, not once but six times. He's also conked on the head twice more (by a large hat box and an entire coffee service), gets a carving roast spilled over him with all its gravy, and is interfered with by a horse. It's a sophisticated comedy.

That unquestionable sophistication is apparent first of all in the settings of a luxury cruise ship and a Connecticut mansion—the sort of milieu in which Hollywood often placed its stories, but which Sturges, almost alone among Hollywood filmmakers, had known firsthand. (He lent his own silver service to the production, to ensure authenticity.) *The Lady Eve* is sophisticated, too, in its tone of wised-up elegance, which Sturges dared himself to sustain even while setting off ostentatious flurries of slapstick. I might talk about this peculiar merger of the elevated and the vulgar as central to Sturges's art; but that, for the moment, is not my subject. I am more concerned with another matter, though one that I think is related: why Sturges pressed a biblical text into the foreground of *The Lady Eve* and then made its meaning obscure.

One thing is clear: His mapping of the contours of Genesis onto the terrain of *The Lady Eve* accounts for some of his wised-up tone. A rube audience—to characterize such a group no more delicately than Sturges might have done—would have taken offense even at the opening credits, which reduce the instigator of Man's first disobedience to an animated cartoon serpent, grinning, top-hatted, and rattling a maraca in its tail. A more urbane audience soon notes that the overlay of scripture is not only irreverent but also noticeably uneven. In some places—sequences where physical indignities multiply, for example—the map seems to have bunched up, so that you witness the fall and fall and fall of Man. Elsewhere, the biblical features simply give out before the movie's borders are reached. There's hardly a snake to be seen or heard about in the entire second half.

Most puzzling of all are the inconsistencies between the Bible's characters and the movie's principal figures: Barbara Stanwyck as the adventuress Jean, or sometimes Eve, and Henry Fonda as the studious but none-too-bright brewery heir Charles, or sometimes Hopsie. A large body of critical writing has grown up around these two and the movie they inhabit, which is widely admired as one of the best ever made in Hollywood and one of the most thoughtful. As Stanley Cavell showed in *Pursuits of Happiness: The American Comedy of Remarriage*, you can even make philosophy out of *The Lady Eve*. Think about the typological parallels that Sturges forces on you, though, and you find that the most basic questions remain unresolved.

The fall and fall of Man: Hopsie listens as Jean discusses the future

If Jean is to be compared with the biblical Eve, why would it be such a waste of effort to tempt her? Not that anyone tries; she sees through all illusions right from the start and already knows plenty about good and evil. And yet, in a blatant departure from the Bible, this sinful trickster is the one who flees from snakes, while her gullible Adam professes that "snakes are my life." Charles is so mad about the creatures that another character calls him a snake. (This slur is uttered by Charles Coburn as Colonel Harrington, Jean's putative father and confederate in card sharping and con games.) How can it be that the film's Adam, after all his tumbles, should ultimately remain impervious to disillusionment, bouncing back up as the nickname Hopsie suggests? He does not end in chastisement but instead regains the state of innocence in which he began—only now (again to the likely discomfort of the rubes and the righteous) he is much, much happier.

I might put aside these questions and simply enjoy *The Lady Eve* were it not for the film's production history, which suggests that any discontinuities were purely intentional.

Sturges wrote the first version of the screenplay on assignment from Paramount from September through December 1938; responded to a detailed and highly intelligent memo sent in January 1939 by the producer, Albert Lewin; thoroughly revised the script from August through early October 1940; and then put that draft through another eleven-day rewrite to achieve the third and final version. By then, whatever may have seemed casual or offhand in the script was nothing of the kind, but rather a calculated pretense of randomness.

Why would Sturges want such an effect? Why did he ignore, for example, Lewin's objection that there was no compelling reason to make Charles an expert on snakes? (As a sign of Charles's pedantry, he doesn't call himself a zoologist or even a herpetologist. He insists on ophiologist.) These questions make me suspect that the mismatch between the Bible story and *The Lady Eve* may tell us something about the relationship in Sturges's work between writing and directing, text and image. I also suspect that the mismatch is intimately bound up with the film's interplay of literal-mindedness and imagination, wiliness and credulity, knowledge and innocence—even, perhaps, prose and poetry.

To trace the answers, I might begin with an anomaly. As Brian Henderson points out, *The Lady Eve* is unique among Sturges's major films in being based on the work of two other writers.[1] First came a short story titled "The Two Bad Hats" that Monckton Hoffe either wrote expressly for Paramount or else sold to the studio. Next came an adaptation of the Hoffe story by Jeanne Bartlett. Sometime in 1938, Lewin assigned Sturges to turn these materials into a screenplay. As Sturges usually did in such situations, he began by tossing out most of what he'd been given. All he kept was a high-toned British milieu (transformed in the finished film into mere imposture), a little intrigue involving card playing, and the outlines of a character: a beautiful young woman who fraudulently impersonates a nonexistent twin.

In the source material, the names used by this woman were Salome and Sheba, the first for the bad persona, the second for the good. This conceit of giving characters biblical names was something else that Sturges retained—but he changed his duplicitous woman into Jean/Eve and reinforced the associations of the latter name by giving the man who falls for her a professional interest in snakes. It remains to be seen what Sturges may have intended by these choices; but it's certain that whatever was original in *The Lady Eve*, whatever gave Sturges the right to call this story his own, had its roots in the Garden of Eden.

That's where *The Lady Eve* begins: in a tropical landscape that might indeed be Paradise, except for already having been tainted by lust, cash, and curiosity. Charles, with pith helmet and gun, is the agent of the latter two forces, having brought a scientific expedition "up the Amazon" with his father's money. As for the lust, that's evidently been the preoccupation of Charles's protector and sidekick Muggsy (William Demarest), to judge from his gruff dockside farewell to a mute, expressionless native woman. She hangs a wreath of flowers around Muggsy's neck— the chain of them big enough for a horse, their blossoms obscenely huge—while Charles, oblivious to this utterly emotionless sexual transaction, natters on to the research team about wishing he could live forever "in the company of men like yourselves, in the pursuit of knowledge." He apparently hasn't noticed anything impure in his version of Paradise; nor does he consider the implications of carrying a snake out of it, into a world where the men, and even more so the women, cannot possibly live up to his ideals.

The Lady Eve begins as the story of a man who not only believes he's found Eden but thinks he can leave it and come back later. The Bible says it doesn't work that way; and so Charles's willingness to leave the jungle—temporarily, of course—provides the first hint that his path will diverge from Adam's. By contrast, his failure to return to the jungle at the movie's end suggests that *The Lady Eve* might in some way conform to scripture. A moviegoer who wants to think about this story as carefully as Sturges did will need to follow a narrative that runs parallel with the Bible and also on the bias to it.

If that moviegoer is familiar with Sturges's other films, Charles's failure to return to the jungle will mark him as diverging from another model as well: the Sturges protagonist who comes full circle.

You see this pattern in the Sturges movies that start at the story's end (*The Great McGinty*, *The Miracle of Morgan's Creek*), or at a beginning that looks like the end (*Sullivan's Travels*, *The Palm Beach Story*), or on the occasion of a eulogy, when hindsight is at its most intense (*The Power and the Glory*, *Triumph Over Pain*). Despite the famously hectic pace of these films, despite the crowding of incident and stock players, their structures make it seem as if everything has already been decided in them; the audience just needs to discover how much bustle it will take, and how many surprises, to attain the foregone conclusion.

As with all good comedies, an undercurrent of disquiet runs through Sturges's films—an anxiety, in his case, about being stuck in an eternal return. The failed Marine who is the protagonist in *Hail the Conquering Hero* struggles to escape from his hometown and the imperative to live up to his late father's military fame but remains hopelessly trapped in both. Characters in *Easy Living* and *Christmas in July* go over mathematical calculations obsessively (if incorrectly), as if imprisoned by their logic. Events are recapitulated (*Christmas in July*, *The Palm Beach Story*), days are skipped and have to be revisited (*The Sin of Harold Diddlebock*), and characters conclude their adventures by resuming their old behavior (*The Great McGinty*).

Charles, too, might seem to fit this pattern. Tripped by a temptress at the beginning and end of *The Lady Eve*, he suffers the same fall in the same place, and the second time is restored by it to his keynote state of blessed ignorance. Now he and Jean are back where they ought to have started, prompting her to ask, in summation, "Why did we have to go through all this nonsense?" And yet, as one might hope from a comedy based on the story of Eden, the movie ends on a note of salvation. Charles has successfully broken the circle, or rather had it broken over him. Although he had thought he was going back to his false paradise on the Amazon, it's obvious at the finale that he's heading in an entirely different direction.

As Jean has done throughout the film, she concludes *The Lady Eve* by diverting Charles, in the full sense of the term.

Even before Jean has dropped the apple onto Charles's head—playfully, just to see if she can—Sturges has suggested her power to move him any way she likes. These hints come in the second scene as a prelude to her introduction, as Charles and Muggsy in their chugging little Amazon boat approach the cruise ship that will take them aboard. Sturges makes a gag out of the encounter, showing the smokestack and whistle of one and then the other vessel as they salute on the open sea. The puny whistle on Charles's boat chokes and boils over impotently, straining to achieve a mere piping ejaculation. The whistle on the other boat returns a blast that could knock a man backward. Not that you know yet that Jean is associated with this bellow. Only after Sturges has reviewed the faces of the cruise ship passengers at the rail, as they gossip about Charles Pike's wealth and marriageability, do a crane shot and a dissolve lift the camera to the deck above, where Jean and the Colonel are discovered standing in a position very superior to Charles, already plotting to cheat him.

At this introductory stage, the mistress of card games has not yet done much to show that she can toy with Charles; her abilities are merely implied, through the associative editing and construction of cinematic space. (These were Sturges's contributions as the director. In the screenplay, he made little of the ships' whistles and didn't think of an upper deck.) In the next scene, though, Jean asserts herself, demonstrating an almost magical command over Charles, her immediate surroundings, and possibly the movie itself.

In the main dining salon of the SS *Southern Queen* Charles sits alone, reading a book titled *Are Snakes Necessary?* while every eligible woman in the room strains to catch his eye. Jean, however, does not strain, nor will she stoop to compete. Instead, she amuses herself, studying everyone surreptitiously with the aid of her compact mirror. As many writers have noted, the image in the mirror creates a frame within the frame—in effect, a secondary movie. The events that play out in it provide Jean with the material for a self-delighted satirical commentary, in which she voices the unspoken thoughts of the people she's watching, supplies lines of their unheard dialogue, mockingly advises them on the attitudes and actions they're adopting, and even predicts what they'll do next. In her omniscience, she might as well be a writer-director creating a film.

I would go so far as to say that the film in question is a Preston Sturges movie, since the combination of her running remarks with more-or-less silent images replicates the widely touted method of "narratage" that Sturges had claimed as the great innovation of *The Power and the Glory*. As a writer who was then only beginning to make his way in an industry that gave directors precedence, Sturges may be said to have invented narratage to serve as both a tool and a weapon; it gave his words equality with the director's images, and even dominance over them. Although Hollywood failed to recognize the potential of this modern breakthrough and sent him back to contract work, he reintroduced narratage for Jean, who is unmistakably tickled by the powers it gives her.

She also knows the limits of these powers—perhaps better than Sturges did, to judge from a memo to himself that he inserted into the final script. Just before a passage of Jean's commentary, he wrote: "Only enough of this dialogue will be used to match the action."[2] His plan, evidently, was to shoot the images first and then record the words, trimming and adjusting them so the timing would come out right. This would have been the sensible way to proceed, or at least to explain his intentions to the supervising producer; but in the finished film, the entire block of words remains intact, suggesting that the images were instead timed painstakingly to the dialogue. Sturges the screenwriter had won out, at the cost of some trouble to Sturges the director.

Jean, however, shows she prefers action to words. Having thoroughly enjoyed her seeming ability to control people and events through her language, and having had a good laugh at the contrivances of every other woman in the dining room, she triumphs at the end of the scene by deploying a direct, physical tactic that none of the rest had considered: she sticks out her foot and trips Charles.

Then she stands and speaks for the first time to the abashed and disheveled prey she's brought down. At this moment, as James Harvey notes in *Romantic Comedy in Hollywood*, familiar points of reference snap into place for the audience. Jean abruptly takes on the well-established aspect of a Barbara Stanwyck character, while the banter shifts into the known, reassuring channels of screwball comedy.[3] Harvey's comment is astute; but it's worth remarking that the moment is not only funny but also stunning because of the violence with which Jean wills herself into the action. Like an actress who hurls herself out of the wings and onto the stage, she has just committed herself in the flesh.

For the remainder of the first half of *The Lady Eve*, she will rely less on her words than on her body, and on the physical skills (not least of them sleight of hand) that are ingrained in it. She won't return to her verbal wiles until the film's second part, when she transforms herself into Eve. For now, the flesh comes first, while her use of language proves to be remarkably honest, even if her purposes are not.

She is a con artist who gives fair warning. She joins Harry in directing Charles's attention to a sign in the lounge advising passengers to beware of professional gamblers and informs him that Harry is a good card player. At the end of her first game with Charles, when she and Harry have baited their victim by allowing him to win, she all but announces the swindle ("How much do I owe the sucker?" she asks across the table), assures Charles that she will get her money back, and promises that, if losing will salve his conscience, he will soon feel a lot better.

Even more important, she speaks honestly about the power of her body and how she uses it. Early on, Jean patiently explains to Charles that she's flirting with him (he's been too dazed to understand). In the most candid question ever whizzed past the enforcers of the Production Code, she asks him, eye to eye and nose to nose, "Don't you think we ought to go to bed?" (All she means is that it's too late at night to go dancing.) Later, she advises Charles that it's dangerous to trust people he doesn't know well, or to plunge into a shipboard romance. At a critical point in her relationship with him—very soon after he's learned that she's a crook, but immediately before he reveals that he knows—she even recalls the wiles she'd used to get him sexually worked up and confesses, from the heart, that she hadn't expected to fall for him.

By the time Jean gets to this point, her words and her body are saying the same thing and meaning it. There is no distance between them—nor is there any distance in this revelation scene between Sturges's words and images. The rest of his movie will depend on the audience's believing that the deceitful woman is speaking plainly, that the powerful woman can be hurt and is owning up to her weakness. So after Jean's secret has been laid bare, Sturges cuts from a wider view that shows some of the surroundings to a close two-shot that admits into it nothing except the characters and their emotions. He positions the actors so that the focus is on Jean, who faces the camera, with Charles in profile, a little bit out of the light, on the right side of the frame. Under this scrutiny, Jean begins to weep. (The script merely called for her to bite her lip before exiting—but Sturges, as director, understood the resources he had won for *The Lady Eve* by securing Stanwyck, who specialized in tears.) Most important of all, Sturges the director ordains that Charles will refuse to look at Jean. If he would only turn his head, he would recognize at once what the audience understands, that she's pouring herself out to him. But the image now confirms what the plot and dialogue had been telling us: Charles literally cannot see when someone is telling him the truth.

Earlier, Jean's truth-telling had been an amusement, for her and the audience; she could indulge in it safely, knowing that Charles wouldn't believe the plain meaning of her words. Now her truth-telling is desperate; she needs him to believe her words, and he's incapable of it. Her remedy, in the second half of the film, will be to give him the deception he deserves. She will take on a biblical name—Eve—and put on an imposture in which almost every word that comes out of her mouth will be a lie, even in its British pronunciation. In this guise, Jean will be much more like the temptress of traditional scriptural interpretation, a figure so closely associated with the Father of Lies that you can't tell, looking at the pictures by Dürer and Lucas Cranach the Elder and Titian, whether Eve is receiving the fruit from the serpent or feeding it to him. In Blake's picture, where Satan coils around her, it's even difficult to see where her body ends and the serpent's begins.

But that's not Jean in the movie's first half. I would argue that Jean, unlike the Eve she calls up, is more tempted than tempting, and speaks the truth more than is good for her. Charles is the serpent-bearer—and even though he is the most guileless character in *The Lady Eve*, his way of talking proves to be a slippery cheat.

When does Jean fall in love with this man? When does she go from playing him for a sucker to working to protect him?

It must happen sometime after he springs the snake on her. Until then, Jean is effortlessly in control of Charles, keeping him dizzy with her perfume and the proximity of her flesh. She makes him stare at her legs, hangs on his arm, sits shoulder to shoulder with him at the card table, and at last, just by coincidence, guides him to the door of his cabin, where Charles, as a gentleman, will be all but required to invite her in. What Jean intends to do with him once he's got her inside is anybody's guess; but I don't accept the suggestion ventured by some critics that beneath her bravado, she is afraid of sex and flees the cabin because Charles's snake, once it has been exposed, reminds her of something else.

Sturges does associate the snake with intimate articles found in and around a bed—a set of pajamas in Charles's cabin, a stocking and a water bottle (cold) in Jean's—but he scarcely insists on the standard Freudian interpretation. Charles calls the snake Emma and speaks of her as if she's a baby ("I don't want to wake her up"), which is hardly a contribution to phallic symbolism; and Jean, in any case, is being played by Stanwyck. No doubt the passengers who see her run screaming from Charles's cabin assume that she has been subjected to a brutish sexual advance. The audience knows better. She's simply succumbed to the stereotypical female panic at the sight of a snake—the first stereotypically feminine thing she's done.

It will pretty much be the last as well. Eventually, in the guise of Eve, she will play the conventional role of a bride, with all the trappings; but for now, she quickly returns to her atypical manner, once Charles has followed her to her own cabin and has calmed her. She recovers her superior position (stretching out on a chaise longue, above the spot where she's dumped Charles on the floor) and resumes something like the air of omniscience she'd enjoyed during her narratage in the dining room. Once more she's the one who's composed—mussing his hair and toying with his ear, as she keeps his head firmly in her grasp—while he licks his lips, sweats, and strains to choke out his words. (In a foreshadowing of the later revelation scene, he almost never turns to look at her.) Nevertheless, something has changed. "You don't know what you've done to me," she says with a tremor in her voice; and although her breathy tones of arousal are phony, the words, as usual, are true. Charles doesn't understand that he's made her body respond, if not through lust then through fear.

And she hints that she likes it. When she meets the man she consents to marry, Jean says, she doesn't want a predictable type but someone who will "sort of take me by surprise." "Like a burglar," Charles stammers, filling in a space that she hadn't really left blank. Until now, Jean hasn't shown any predilection for being a crime victim, but it's his suggestion, and she'll go along with it. "That's right.... All of a sudden I'll hear a step behind me and somebody breathing heavily . . . and then . . ." And then she cuts short this rape fantasy and, fully in charge, sends Charles out the door, laughing at him as he goes.

The scene fades out on Jean reclining alone on the chaise longue, obviously feeling pleased with herself. But her self-assurance must have been shaken, because the next time she appears—lying alone in bed the following morning—she wakes up screaming. What's disturbed her? "That slimy snake," she tells Colonel Harrington, who has rushed to her in alarm. "I've been dreaming about him all night."

She doesn't mean Charles, she goes on to explain, but his "reptile." Then something very strange happens. Having sounded dismissive, or even disdainful, when speaking of Charles and his enthusiasm for snakes, she goes on to sound pitying ("the poor sap . . . that card trick!") and finally tender. Not that she mentions Charles at the latter moment. But the scene ends with her saying dreamily to the Colonel, "Harry, tell me my fortune," and the audience knows it has just watched a woman fall in love.

What's curious is that nothing within the scene triggers this change, unless it's a bit of business that has no obvious connection to Jean's feelings, or even to the progress of the plot. The Colonel, keeping his fingers limber, is idly practicing a crooked card deal while talking with Jean—a deal so improbably difficult that she challenges him as a liar when he says he's doing it, and is rapt with admiration when she sees he's telling the truth. These two passing emotions, of skepticism and wonder, are the only transition between Jean's pity for Charles (a man to whom she and her father are knowingly superior) and her first implied expression of warmth toward him. It's all the transition needed. Considering the novelty of what she's going through, right before the audience's eyes, nothing could be more appropriate for Jean than skepticism about her feelings for Charles, followed by the onset of wonder at them.

This happens in less than a minute—a span during which all of Jean's emotions shift and she is visibly transformed, from a hardened crook dragging on a cigarette to someone "smiling like a little girl" (in the words of the screenplay). And yet the motives behind the shifts go unmentioned; the nature of the ultimate change is unnamed; and nothing happens of immediate consequence. A viewer might be excused for forgetting the scene even took place—there are no astonishing one-liners, no memorable outrages to convention—except that the most complex and subtle emotional alchemy is accomplished in it, quietly, swiftly, and entirely beneath the surface.

If poetry differs from prose in its degree of concision, rapidity, and allusive power, then Sturges is a poet in this passage about Jean's awakening. It's a distinction with which he's seldom credited, despite the high regard in which he's held. People who value visual pizzazz above all else commonly speak of Sturges as a workmanlike director, while people who prize cleverness and daring in plot and dialogue regard him as an engineer of genius, who had an engineer's coldness. Yet the awakening scene is all intuitive form and emotional fluidity; and at its core is a densely packed contradiction in Jean's attitude toward the snake and Charles. She associates him with an unclean animal that might harm her; she despises him for the association; she experiences her contempt for him as a natural expression of her superiority; she melts.

She is, in short, nothing like the biblical Eve—unless Colonel Harrington is right to guess that the snake who might beguile her is Charles himself. Hopsie will indeed lie to Jean and bring her low, eventually; but for now, both she and the audience may assume that the only slimy creature Charles truly resembles is a bookworm. The man is harmless, clumsily playful, puerile—the same traits, oddly enough, that he has imputed to Emma, much to Jean's disbelief. Still, he has taken her by surprise; and still, she's afraid of Emma. All too soon, this mixture of emotions will make sense to Jean; Charles, in his pride, will turn on her and bite. But at this point, it hasn't yet happened. Until Jean is wounded, she will not make herself into Eve.

So there are contradictions both in Jean's character and in the parallels Sturges draws to the Bible story. There is also a solution to them. It lies in the way Sturges goes quietly, allusively, like a poet, beyond the text of Genesis.

According to a legend found nowhere in the Bible, Adam had a mate before Eve was created, just as Charles initially has Jean. This first woman's name was Lilith. Although discussions about her were confined for a long period to Jewish literature, European writers and painters in the nineteenth century began to take an interest in Lilith and to elaborate on her image. She was said to be proud of her hair (which flowed loosely over her shoulders like Jean's, rather than being put up like Eve's) and enjoyed looking into mirrors (as Jean does, too).

Did Sturges covertly use this myth about Adam's two wives as a model for *The Lady Eve*? I would hesitate to suggest it, if not for the glaring discrepancy between Jean in the first half of the movie and the character she impersonates in the second. By this point, I hope it's apparent that the texture and details of the film all but force the viewer to deny Muggsy's literal-minded conclusion that Jean and Eve are "positively the same dame." They are, and they aren't; and because the film itself tells us so, I think it's relevant to point out that Sturges could very well have known about the myth of Lilith, long before a typescript of "The Two Bad Hats" landed on his desk.

The legend was current in New York City when Sturges was living there in the late 1920s and beginning his career in the theater. John Erskine, a Columbia University professor and popular author (the two were not then considered mutually exclusive),

Jean as Lilith, with flowing hair and mirror

Jean as writer-director, narrating an unfolding scene

had just published the latest of his novels retelling ancient tales, *Adam and Eve: Though He Knew Better*. In it, he provided a full account of Lilith, making this first woman as substantial a figure in the story as her successor, and a more attractive one. It's possible that Sturges read the book, and likely that he at least heard about it. In 1927, the year of its publication, Erskine also had another success, when one of his earlier novels, *The Private Life of Helen of Troy*, was made into a hit movie.

It's also possible that Sturges reencountered the legend the following year, upon the posthumous publication of the autobiography of Isadora Duncan—a book that would have interested him greatly, given Duncan's influence over his early life. Sturges could easily have run across a review of the book in *The*

Century Magazine—by then declining in circulation, but still considered smart and popular—which ran under the title "A Modern Lilith."

In writing about Duncan's way of narrating her love affairs, the reviewer, Joseph Anthony, gave a useful summary of the contrast between the healthy, generous Lilith and the scheming, scolding Eve in Erskine's version of the story (though not, as we'll see, in Sturges's): "she [Duncan] speaks on the subject with the voice of John Erskine's *Lilith*, as one too innocent to grasp ordinary conceptions of wickedness, honest because she couldn't begin to see the point of being otherwise, and regretting only the affairs she never had. When she explains the reason for her many loves, however, it is no longer *Lilith* who is talking, but *Eve*—for her reason is the fickleness of men."[4]

All this proves nothing, of course, except that references to Lilith were common enough in 1928 Manhattan that men-about-town like Sturges were expected to grasp them immediately. I don't think it's farfetched to imagine that when Sturges was given "The Two Bad Hats" a decade later and read about the "twins" Salome and Sheba, he was able to think of a better pair of biblical names.

But if so, why didn't he use them? Why, instead of calling his first woman Lilith, did he name her Jean—Eugenia, actually, meaning "well-born"? (Lilith was equal to Adam in birth, having been created at the same time and out of the same earth, rather than being a product of surgery, like Eve.) I suppose Sturges was covering his tracks and had more than one reason to do so. He might not have wanted people to think he was cribbing from Erskine—that would have diminished the impression of wild originality that was his stock-in-trade. He especially might not have wanted to flaunt a familiarity with any legend so high-toned (or, as he would have put it, deep-dish) as to have entered mainstream European culture through Goethe, Rossetti, and Browning. Sturges always insisted on presenting himself as an entertainer, out to do nothing more than please an audience; when he made a sophisticated comedy, it overflowed with slapstick.

A third possible reason comes to mind as well, one that is less focused on protecting Sturges's image and concerned with advancing his art. A filmmaker capable of conceiving and executing the scene of Jean's awakening would also have been deft enough to keep the Lilith theme unstated, so that it could do its work under the surface. Let the audience catch onto the Eden references early on and then be thrown off balance when they apparently drop away. Let contradictions and discontinuities build up around Jean, so that their tension can be released with all the more energy in the film's second half. Most important of all, let Jean be something like Lilith, but don't make her the antithesis of Eve. Draw attention to the contrast, overemphasize it, and you would spoil the most important lines of dialogue in *The Lady Eve*, the words that everyone rightly quotes: "You see, you don't know very much about girls, Hopsie: the best ones aren't as good as you probably think they are, and the bad ones aren't as bad—not nearly as bad."

On one level, these words are so unchallengeable that they can only be a platitude—mere prose. Coming from Stanwyck's lips, however, their charged connection to well-submerged allusions and half-hidden poetry makes them feel deep, touching, and true. Charles, who won't turn his head, cannot see that truth. He will go on refusing to see it until Jean makes him, all but rubbing his face in it, using the cruelest means at her command—after which he will tacitly own up to something else that he's steadfastly denied. He will accept the fact that he, too, is at least halfway a poet.

As James Harvey points out, Charles is a much less attractive figure in the second half of the film than in the first, and he comes in for much rougher treatment.[5] Yet he's positively the same guy. It's even possible to think that the Charles Pike who sailed on the *Southern Queen* would have behaved throughout his voyage exactly like the utterly conventional, self-regarding man you later see in Connecticut, if Jean hadn't diverted him. Charles is a man at risk of willfully, blindly trapping himself in the eternal circuit that is Sturges's special horror. This tendency becomes obvious, and Charles becomes blameworthy in yielding to it, in the scene where he repeats to Eve, almost verbatim, the words he had spoken when proposing marriage to Jean.

The self-plagiarism seems unconscionable (to Eve/Jean, no less than to the viewer) in part because it's so unnecessary. "I'm not a poet, I'm an ophiologist," Charles had said during the original proposal, excusing himself for sounding, as he imagined, "as dull as a drugstore novel." But it's been evident from the outset that words come easily to him.

On his first time alone with Jean in her cabin, when her perfume made him so "cockeyed" that her face swam before him out of focus, erotic wooziness didn't prevent Charles from letting loose a stream of language, spoken for him by Henry Fonda in forceful but charmingly unaffected tones that were less blue-blood Connecticut in accent than middle-class Nebraska: "It's funny," volunteered the brewery heir as he changed Jean's shoes, "to be kneeling here at your feet and talking about beer. You see, I don't like beer"—meaning, apparently, that he did like fondling her ankles. But that wasn't a safe topic; so, having gotten started on his dislikes, Charles kept going: "bock beer, lager beer or steam beer. . . . And I don't like pale ale, brown ale, nut brown ale, porter or stout." Jean could talk as if she'd been peeking into Sturges's dictionary of slang, but Charles ran on like a thesaurus.

If his flow of vocabulary could be unstoppable, so too was his fount of metaphor, which made up in volume what it sometimes lacked in novelty. "You've got the darndest way of bumping a fellow down and then bouncing him up again," he told Jean at breakfast; and when she laughed and said, "And then bumping him down again," he continued the chain of contrasts without hesitation: "I was just going to say that I could imagine a life with you being a series of ups and downs, lights and shadows, sometimes irritation, but very much happiness."

"Why, Hopsie," Jean replied, perhaps more moved by this outpouring than she let on. "Are you proposing to me so soon?"

He was not—but when the moment came, not very much later, Charles burst out with the most remarkable flood of all. Standing with Jean at the ship's bow, feeling the wind blow past and hearing the keel cut through the waves, Charles suddenly elaborated on a comment he'd made in that previous scene, when he'd said he felt he'd known Jean for a long time. "Every time I've looked at you here on the boat it wasn't only here I saw you. You seemed to go way back. I know that isn't clear, but I saw you here and at the same time further away, and then still further away, and then very small—like converging perspective lines. No, that isn't it, more like figures following each other in a forest glade." These figures he proceeded to describe in detail, until a close-up of Stanwyck, shown in the softest, most melting light, revealed just how little Charles sounded for the moment like an ophiologist.

Notice the fluency of Charles's invention in this speech. He evaluated his words as they emerged, thought of their history, changed their course, amplified them at will. A man with such abilities has no excuse for resorting to a canned speech, especially at a moment that's supposed to be one of high emotion—and yet, in his proposal to Eve, it's obvious that Charles has dull-wittedly rehearsed every syllable. (The only events to elude his planning are some welcome interruptions from a horse, which provide the only evidence of animal impulse in these proceedings.) Sturges called in his screenplay for Charles to speak "passionately" by the end of the proposal;[6] but when he directed the scene, he had Fonda drain himself of everything spontaneous, let alone ardent. Charles is now stilted and proper in speech, while Eve, who here faces away from him (as he'd faced away from Jean during the revelation scene), is cool and surreptitiously amused. She registers a flash of quickly suppressed anger only when first realizing that Charles is offering her the rewarmed leftovers of another woman's proposal.

This is a new way to take a woman by surprise. It's unpleasant, too—even compared with the alarm that Charles had inadvertently set off in the first half of the movie when exposing Jean to the snake. That imagined physical threat at least had made her heart jump and her skin crawl; she knew she was alive. Now Charles himself might as well be the cold-blooded snake, trying with a forked tongue to tempt Eve into a marriage that would surely be a living death of convention and routine.

Evidently, the snake in *The Lady Eve* has tacitly taken on new connotations, just as Jean has changed into Eve without ever having been explicitly acknowledged as Lilith. The snake at first appeared to be the plaything of a curious, overgrown boy, who could be sexually eager and awkward in equal measure. It is now the symbol of the proud, creeping, earthbound mentality of a passionless man, who turns out to be less interested in exploration and research than in clinging to whatever knowledge he thinks he possesses.

It must be a shock to Jean that the man she had loved can shut off his imagination this way, condemning himself (and some unlucky woman) to a life lived by rote. And yet, as I've suggested, Charles's character has been consistent throughout. Despite being played by an actor who was associated with Abraham Lincoln and Tom Joad, Charles has given evidence all along that he's not such a nice guy.

Jean herself had seen it in the ship's dining room, when she covertly studied Charles in her mirror. "Not good enough," she had said—meaning that every woman on board was inferior in his eyes. "He feels they're just a waste of time." It turned out that Charles felt that way about a lot of people. There was a touch of arrogance in the way he spoke of a deck steward in the third person, as if the man wasn't present: "He doesn't understand." (This, after Sturges had taken care to show that the ship's crew are watchful, clever people and not a little judgmental.) Worse still, Charles was dismissive of Muggsy, belittling him to Jean as a "very bad valet"— an ungenerous thing to say about a man, especially while admitting in the same breath that "he saved my life one time in a brawl." As for the source of the wealth that entitled Charles to get into fights that somebody else had to end for him, he was openly contemptuous. Not only wouldn't he drink ale and beer, he sneered at the people who did. "Every time the clock ticks," he told Colonel Harrington, "fourteen people open a bottle of Pike's, I don't know why."

In its first half, the movie went so far as to hint at an element of brutality in Charles. As in the awakening scene, very little of this feeling broke the surface; and yet Sturges suggested it both in the dialogue (when Charles unaccountably decided that, if Jean wanted to be taken by surprise, she must have wanted to fall into the hands of a criminal) and in the way he directed Fonda. "I hope I didn't hurt you," Fonda said after changing Jean's shoes, as he knelt at Stanwyck's feet. "Of course you didn't," she replied—at which point Fonda, one of the subtlest of actors, looked down momentarily and came up again with a look that could be read as strained sexual self-control, but also as disappointment or even petulance. You could see, very quickly, that Charles felt a little insulted by that "Of course not." He ought to have had enough power to hurt Jean. At the end of the first half, he certainly tried his best.

He succeeded, too, well enough to make Jean want to fashion a new woman out of herself, in an all-female analogy to the creation of Eve from Adam's rib. This second woman—sparkling in her white gown, furnished with a feathered wrap like angel's wings, delivered into Connecticut as if from thin air (the passenger boats from Europe having stopped because of the war)—looks good enough to overcome all of her Adam's doubts and exists solely to hurt him back, as the ostensibly sinful Jean cannot.

Although Eve's plan of punishment is mysterious for much of the second half, it clearly entails making Charles stumble about and bang into things; and each time, as with that passing glance in the shoe-fitting scene, Charles gazes upward while betraying more emotion than he'd like. The smile he pastes on his face isn't broad enough to cover his anger at being humiliated; Fonda's artfully bared teeth make him look simpering, sick, or snarling by turns. This series of grimaces reaches its culmination during the honeymoon scene, when Charles (knocked about by the motion of a speeding train, and by Eve's lurid revelations) extends his "sweet forgiveness" (an offer shouted into

The continuing fall of Man: Hopsie, upon meeting Eve

her face) and proposes, "Let's smile and be as we were." The screenplay specifies that, after speaking this line, Charles "smiles like a gargoyle"[7]—an effect that in this case is achieved precisely as written, with Fonda and Sturges giving new meaning to the term "awfully funny."

Then even the fake smile drops away. For the remainder of the scene, Eve relentlessly fills Charles with the knowledge he'd rejected: that a good woman isn't nearly as good as he'd supposed. And since the ophiologist had claimed during his original proposal to be as dull as a drugstore novel, she now metes out fitting justice to the snake by retelling a series of dime-store plots.

She knows he's susceptible. Eve's purported uncle, Sir Alfred McGlennan-Keith, RFD (or rather Jean's associate in con games,

Pearlie), already has successfully explained the striking resemblance between the two women by feeding Charles the story of "'Cecilia, or the Coachman's Daughter,' a gaslight melodrama." ("You mean," she asked in awe upon being told, "he swallowed *that*?") Now, with Charles trapped beside her in the train's bridal compartment, she confesses her past participation in the full repertoire of Edwardian pornography.

Not that we hear much of these stories. In the first place, the Production Code would have forbidden it, and in the second, Sturges now wants to deny his characters their eloquence, their imaginative flights, their double-edged truth-telling. He shreds their language. Past the halfway mark of the scene, little comes from their mouths but fragments—cries of outrage, expostulations, reproofs, shouted names—with scarcely a sentence to be heard.

At this crisis point, Sturges by and large replaces words with images and sounds appropriate to the situation. Wanting to evoke, and mock, the emotions of worn-out melodramas, he turns for a model to the cartoon animators, who were better at this sort of thing than anyone else in 1940s Hollywood. They were the ones who specialized in patching snatches of Wagner and Rossini into scenes to poke fun at the action, as Sturges does now. They were the ones who reduced speech to sputtering, posted on-screen commentaries on signboards ("Pull In Your Head—We're Coming to a Tunnel"), and fractured scenes into a rapid series of views, mostly focused on pantomime gestures. Elsewhere in *The Lady Eve*, Sturges had imitated a different cinematic tradition when he speeded up the images of Jean fleeing down a staircase and Charles tripping over a sofa, making these moments look as if they'd come out of a silent slapstick comedy. Now he out-vulgarizes himself by putting Eve and Charles into the aural and visual equivalent of a Looney Tune.

The result is a double paradox. During the confession, subject matter that would then have been called highly sophisticated is narrated (or rather concealed) through a type of filmmaking that would then have been called low and cheap. After the confession, the racket stirred up by the cartoon commotion subsides abruptly into silence, and even solemnity. Charles falls again, this time into the mud, but it's a mirthless tumble. Eve watches him through the window of the train but does not gloat. She slowly, quietly lowers the shade as the train pulls out of the station. We don't even see her face.

Jean, or Lilith, had tried to tell Charles that good and evil are not absolute in women, but he hadn't wanted to listen. Now Eve has tempted him into tasting the knowledge of good and evil—snake that he is—and nobody feels better for it.

Like a master of sleight of hand, Sturges has reached this critical moment in *The Lady Eve* by forcing some aspects of his story on the audience's attention and concealing others. He has taken explicit references to Genesis, combined them with covert allusions to biblical legend and his own history of narratage, and mixed them with elements of screwball, romantic melodrama, old-fashioned slapstick, and even animated cartoons. In many cases he elides the emotional and thematic connections among these disparate elements, or makes them pass almost too quickly for the viewer to notice. At the same time, though, he makes *The Lady Eve* as a whole play like an almost seamless example of a genre that producers and audiences could recognize, the romantic comedy.

As a romantic comedy, *The Lady Eve* demands a happy ending—so Sturges supplies one. With a showman's flair, he insists on doing it in record time, bringing the characters from their deepest heartache to their highest elation almost instantaneously. With a poet's grace, he quietly exceeds the demands of convention and makes this happy ending a liberation from the past: Jean's, Charles's, Adam's, Lilith's, everybody's.

Within a scene that looks at first like a mere recapitulation—the solitary man's stroll through the *Southern Queen*'s dining salon, his pratfall over an extended foot—Charles takes Jean by surprise for the third time, and takes himself by surprise as well. He bolts forward and gives her the full-blooded kiss that was missing even from his original marriage proposal. It's pure impulse, action instead of words: the triumph, you might say, of Jean's preference for the physical, and of the image-maker over the writer. But *The Lady Eve* has set itself against such antithetical thinking, and no sooner does Charles act than his flood of words resumes, more joyously than before. He might not be much of a poet in his immediate chatter, but he's not at all an ophiologist, or a prisoner of the snake's certitudes. "I don't want to understand," he cries out to Jean between hungry kisses at her cabin door, when she seems at the point of explaining why she might want forgiveness. "I don't want to know. Whatever it is, keep it to yourself."

With these words, and the kiss that backs them up, innocence and experience, ignorance and knowledge, forgiveness and fresh sin all win out together. (Fresh sin, because Charles thinks he's about to commit adultery and doesn't intend to be stopped.) This conclusion goes beyond the satirical reversal of accepted values, or their reversal and subsequent reaffirmation. *The Lady Eve* finishes by exploding the very categories that make such reversals possible. The "dull round," as William Blake would have called it, has been broken, and something new can come into the world.

Where in the world it will appear, we don't know. The final mystery of *The Lady Eve* is its location. Unlike other Sturges films, which take place in New York City, Chicago, Los Angeles,

Palm Beach, or the small-town America everybody knows from the movies, *The Lady Eve* is a film perpetually in transit. Only in its middle section does it settle down, in and around the Pike mansion in Connecticut; but that setting, for all its marble, silver, and household staff, seems as insubstantial as a wood outside of Athens on a midsummer night. The Pike mansion is clearly nothing more than a stage set (especially to Mr. Pike himself), where illusions come and go. The only true homes in *The Lady Eve*, if you can call them homes, are the ship and the locomotive. Where will Jean and Charles live together, after the movie ends, if not on the *Southern Queen*?

The wised-up viewer understands that the redemption granted Jean and Charles at the end isn't valid for our use—and not only because the characters in this fantasy of unlimited luxury have been freed from the logic of wages and salaries. More generally, they have been liberated within a world of Bible stories, legends, and Hollywood filmmaking—which is to say, a world of imagination, or, at its best, poetry (to use the word Sturges would have resisted). We in the audience cannot live in this world. But we can feel grateful, all the same, to have been excluded not from a garden but from a voyage, where surprises are possible along the way.

4

AS YOU ARE, SO SHALL YOU REMAIN

Sullivan's Travels

For all their volubility, Sturges's first three films as a writer-director are exercises in concealment. One covers up the stinging experiences of failure that lay at its root. Another takes the vitality and generosity that Sturges liked to imagine in wealthy men and displaces them, none too convincingly, onto the democratic parade. The third, while gleefully flaunting the ruses of card sharps and grifters, carefully disguises the depths of its art, while making a case for the blissfulness of the audience's ignorance.

The principal deception in Sturges's fourth film, *Sullivan's Travels*, is the pretense of self-revelation. A famous man by the time of the film's release in January 1942, Sturges encouraged the audience to think of the main character as a stand-in for himself and to understand the concluding moral (it's a very moral movie) as his *apologia pro vita sua*. To this day, suckers are swallowing the bait, and for understandable reasons. *Sullivan's Travels* is Sturges's only major film about a man who can be identified with him by trade, the rest of his protagonists being con artists and politicians, office clerks, inventors, military dropouts, a runaway wife, an orchestra conductor, and a rich ophiologist. Only John L. Sullivan, who wanders like a modern Gulliver through strange and satirical locales, is a successful director of movie properties, and a valuable property in himself to the studio that employs him.

Many previous Hollywood pictures, from Chaplin's *Kid Auto Races at Venice* through the likes of *The Last Command*, *What Price Hollywood?*, and *A Star Is Born*, had self-reflexively shown the methods and professional mores of filmmaking. Sturges had written such a picture himself in 1935, when Universal had wanted a vehicle for the opera star Marta Eggerth, and he'd responded with a studio back lot comedy with music, never produced, titled *Song of Joy*. What distinguishes *Sullivan's Travels* from these others is its ostensibly confessional spirit, combined with a willingness to stray as far as possible from Hollywood and change tone radically while doing so.

Sturges had always shifted among moods and styles. Think again of the note of menace in *The Great McGinty* when the Boss returns; the interruption of the carnival atmosphere of *Christmas in July* to show an image, shot almost as a street photographer would, of the poor girl in her wheelchair; or the slapstick assaults on Hopsie in the midst of silver-tongued romance in *The Lady Eve*. In none of Sturges's previous films, though, had these mash-ups been as radical and prolonged as in *Sullivan's Travels*. At times the picture plays like *Hey, Hey in the Hayloft* or another of the rustic laff riots that Sullivan is ashamed to have made. At other times it resembles the serious social problem movie that he longs to direct, while including (as he admits) "a little sex." Not content to leave the kitchen sink untouched, Sturges also throws in some screwball comedy, a biting subplot about divorce and taxes, and a scene of Black church life so dignified and respectful that it is almost un-assimilable within classic American film and attracted a thank-you letter from Walter F. White, executive secretary of the NAACP.[1]

Some eighty years after the fact, it's hard to do justice to the daring of this mélange. The industry, then as now, depended on its being able to tell exhibitors and audiences exactly what kind of product was on offer: a Western, a horror movie, a comedy, a musical, a woman's picture, a costume epic, a searing drama ripped from today's headlines. But in making *Sullivan's Travels*—the first movie he'd directed from a screenplay that was entirely new and intended for himself alone—Sturges risked puzzling everybody with something that could not be neatly characterized, except as the tale of the education of a filmmaker ostensibly like Preston Sturges.

For all the film's faults, of which there are plenty, viewers at the time recognized and applauded both the ambition and the supposed candor. Ever since, despite occasional critical carping, the picture has remained Sturges's best-known achievement. But what exactly is the movie being ambitious about? And how candidly does it reflect its author?

As if to explain *Sullivan's Travels*, Sturges tacked a dedication onto the opening credits, in the florid, semiantique style he favored when making pronouncements as a great man: "To the memory of those who made us laugh: the motley mountebanks, the clowns, the buffoons, in all times and in all nations, whose efforts have lightened our burdens a little, this picture is affectionately dedicated." This notice matches the spirit of the concluding speech that Sturges puts into his protagonist's mouth, when the wised-up Sullivan, thinking of the poor and suffering men he's gotten to know better than he ever intended, declares that the making of dumb comedies is a worthy endeavor, since the laughter they provoke is "all some people have." The dedication also accords with the explanation that Sturges gave at the time for having wanted to make *Sullivan's Travels*, and that he later expanded upon in his memoirs. He wrote, with prideful humility: "After I saw a couple of pictures put out by some of my fellow comedy-directors, which seemed to have abandoned the fun in favor of the message, I wrote *Sullivan's Travels* to satisfy an urge to tell them that they were getting a little too deep-dish; to leave the preaching to the preachers."[2]

But if *Sullivan's Travels* can be reduced to that moral, then it, too, is a message movie. And it would be a little too self-contradictory, even for Sturges, to claim to be a happy servant of the mass audience while devising a film to address a handful of Hollywood directors.

Who were these directors, anyway? I can think of Capra, who is name-checked in the first scene of *Sullivan's Travels*, and whose *Meet John Doe* certainly deserved a good razzing—but it was released in March 1941, a month *after* Sturges began writing *Sullivan's Travels*. The only other comedy director who might have fit the description was Chaplin, in *The Great Dictator* of 1940— which in its final monologue preached the brotherhood of man (as did *Sullivan's Travels*, for that matter) but which, on its way to this conclusion, provided more and better slapstick than Sturges could offer.

I have to conclude that the project of sending a message to other comedy directors was a subsidiary program, perhaps hit upon in the midst of writing *Sullivan's Travels* or even after the fact. On the other hand, Sturges does seem to have decided from the first to use Sullivan as a mouthpiece, and to set up the audience to understand the character's final words as the credo of Sturges himself. But to believe that Sturges is fundamentally the same as Sullivan—to take the credo literally—would be to fall for a case of mistaken identity, similar to the one that advances the plot of *Sullivan's Travels* on credible but misleading evidence. Sturges may plant his business card on Sullivan's body, so to speak; but he is not the author of *Hey, Hey in the Hayloft*—nor can *Sullivan's Travels* be viewed, with open eyes, as making a case for fun, pure and simple.

As soon as the movie begins you notice two novelties for Sturges, the first of which is an air of moneyed importance. Unlike his previous films, this one makes a show of being a deluxe production—just like the book, titled *Sullivan's Travels*, that's unwrapped and paged through to present the opening credits. The picture on the book's padded cover is fit for a library of illustrated classics. The paper inside is weighty, with a visible rag grain; the typeface that's impressed on it, a mixture of italic elegance and Roman solidity. The music that accompanies the printed list of names throbs and swoons with late-Romantic grandiloquence.

Then Sturges dumps you out of this languorous, bubble-bath mood into the new, breakneck tempo that from now on will be a defining trait of his style. The pace in his first films had been brisk, but not unusually so, and he'd taken the Hollywood director's usual care to establish each location before proceeding to significant action. Now, as an orchestration of the last movement of the Moonlight Sonata pounds away on the soundtrack, a locomotive comes roaring through the night (going where?), while two men (who?) wrestle with all their might on the unsteady roof of a boxcar (why?). As they tumble off into a watery abyss, a title card floats to the surface, haunting the opening of *Sullivan's Travels* with the doom-laden words: The End.

You don't understand what's happened; you don't even know where you are. And when a cut reveals that this nightmarish struggle has in fact taken place on the screen of a Hollywood studio's projection room, your delight in having been fooled is maybe mixed with a suspicion that you've been had. The deluxe motion picture you thought you'd paid for, and that seemed to have been in progress, has suddenly been snatched away.

This hint of chicanery will hang over much of what's to come in *Sullivan's Travels*; but you don't have time to dwell on it, because Sturges continues to force the tempo. As soon as the death-train movie is over, Sullivan (Joel McCrea) leaps to his feet and launches into an argument about it with two studio executives (Robert Warwick and Porter Hall); or, rather, he resumes a dispute, as Sturges throws you into an action in medias res for a second time, when the movie isn't yet three minutes old. The rattling pace of the lines that Sullivan tosses back and forth with his interlocutors is matched by the movement of the camera, which follows the three men as they step out of the screening room and into an adjacent office, jabbering all the while. Sturges's supervisors were worried about his wanting to shoot this scene—more than nine pages' worth of dialogue—in a single mobile take, thinking it would be botched and throw the production behind schedule.[3] They protested; but he sped forward and won. So much (for the while) for Sturges's bosses.

As for what Sullivan's bosses are trying to prevent: they want to keep him from spending a million dollars of their money on the screen version of a social protest novel, *O Brother, Where Art Thou?* Mr. LeBrand (whose name, I suppose, is prominent in the studio's logo) and Mr. Hadrian (who evidently is responsible for administering the entertainment empire) try every argument they can think of but clearly won't dissuade their physically large and righteously hot-headed director. Unable to deny that the doom-and-gloom movie they've just been watching—a precedent for the one that Sullivan wants to make—has just been held over for a fifth week at Radio City Music Hall, they claim that nobody goes to the Music Hall except communists. When that doesn't wash, Sullivan presumably having heard that the Rockettes don't kick to "The Internationale," the executives change tactics, suggesting that the project might seem imitative of the work of a director already famous for message pictures (with a little sex). Another failure. They have no rejoinder to Sullivan's gruff retort, "What's the matter with Capra?"

But despite *Meet John Doe*, that's another red herring, in a movie through which several have already been dragged. The appropriate comparison—as LeBrand, Hadrian, and the audience of *Sullivan's Travels* all would have known in 1942—is not to Capra but to another director, who only recently had turned a best-selling social protest novel into a hit movie that won two Oscars. Surely an awareness of *The Grapes of Wrath* would have floated somewhere in Sturges's consciousness, so soon after he'd put John Ford's innately dignified Henry Fonda through a course of pratfalls. As for LeBrand and Hadrian, they might prefer a session of root canal surgery to an hour spent reading *O Brother, Where Art Thou?* by Sinclair Beckstein (note the travesty of John Steinbeck's name). Even so, they must know this material need not be box-office poison if put into the hands of the right director. More likely—and this is the one objection they don't dare make—it would be poison *for Sullivan*. He's so good with comedies and musicals, despite that hulking demeanor. He'd be so bad with *O Brother, Where Art Thou?*[4]

And so, in an exchange of dialogue that Sturges directs like a three-sided ping-pong match, the bosses remind their prized director of his great good fortune, rapidly bouncing at him the escalating sums he's made at the studio: two thousand a week, three thousand, four thousand. (As context: Sturges's weekly pay at Paramount, not counting bonuses, was $3,250, reportedly one of the highest salaries in America.)[5] "What do you know about trouble?" Hadrian asks, challenging Sullivan's ability to make a movie about the characters in *O Brother, Where Art Thou?* "What do you know about hard luck?" At last the executives seem to have found a winning argument. Sullivan, in a moment of humility that will prove anomalous, admits he's led a sheltered life. Unfortunately for Hadrian and LeBrand, he at once reverts to type, deciding to *seek* trouble by going on the road as a hobo, so he can learn firsthand about suffering.

With that, *Sullivan's Travels* announces its theme. This is going to be a movie about knowledge—and not just any kind, but the deep knowledge that condenses from lived experience, becoming inseparable from identity.

The assumptions inherent in Sullivan's educational project are so widespread, persistent, and dubious that I'd better pause.

"Write what you know"—or, in Sullivan's case, "Direct what you know"—is unchallengeable advice in our era; but it would have been a puzzling instruction to most authors from the time of Homer to, let's say, Goethe. (Goethe knew just about everything available to a person of his era; but of the ocean that he poured into *Faust*, only a few drops had been personally verified.) It was only in the eighteenth century that a general appetite took hold for artworks that incorporated the robustness, variety, and urgency of current circumstances and personalities—works that were, in a word, full of "life," as Samuel Johnson put it. Even a century later, though, when readers were profoundly moved by Dickens's hard-pressed characters and knew these figures had a source in the harshness of his childhood, people understood the author could not vouch with his own life for the entire sweep of his portraiture and social pleading, let alone his great swaths of satire, fantasy, and romance.

Today, by contrast, it's an article of faith that artworks ought to be rooted in the artist's experience. Sometimes this doctrine of authenticity serves a perfectly valid descriptive function, drawing attention to qualities of vividness and nuance that would not have been present without personal observation. At other times the doctrine becomes entangled with political concerns—legitimate ones—having to do with the desire of long-silenced people to make themselves heard, which again is perfectly valid, so long as the focus remains on the merits of opening the world to more voices. But the demand for authenticity can also become prohibitive, reserving entire realms for those who by birth or heritage are said to have the exclusive right to explore them. Hand in hand with this idea comes the "you wouldn't get it" defense: the argument that a work can be appreciated properly only by a member of the group from which it emerged.

Taken to its logical conclusion, this way of thinking implies that identity is absolute, and that people from one walk of life have no legitimate way to enter imaginatively into the minds of people from another. In which case, society is nothing but a complex of mutually impermeable prisons blocks, where the arts are incapable of telling the inmates anything they don't already know.

Sturges worked years before this aggravated version of "write what you know" became codified, years during which, I might add, he didn't have to compete for jobs against Black or female filmmakers. The fully developed doctrine of authenticity might therefore seem irrelevant to *Sullivan's Travels*—except that here, too, the insistence on authorial experience is phrased prohibitively. Instead of warning Sullivan that his otherwise marvelous skills are inadequate to the kind of film he wants to direct, Hadrian and LeBrand tell him he's the wrong type of *person* to make *O Brother, Where Art Thou?* He didn't grow up knowing poverty. It isn't long before someone else goes further and warns him that he has no right to this material.

Here is Sullivan's butler Burrows (Robert Greig) explaining why his employer should abandon the project of trying to learn about the poor by impersonating a hobo:

You see, sir, rich people and theorists, who are usually rich people, think of poverty in the negative, as the lack of riches, as disease might be called the lack of health. But it isn't, sir. Poverty is not the lack of anything, but a positive plague, virulent in itself, contagious as cholera, with filth, criminality, vice and despair as only a few of its symptoms. It is to be stayed away from, even for purposes of study. It is to be shunned.

Of course it's funny that a portly man in impeccable costume should pronounce this orotund anathema in calm British tones. It's a double twist that the speaker is a servant instructing his wealthy boss. But the message comes through with conviction, despite this droll incongruity: the poor occupy a realm of their own. Sullivan should not venture across its border—the inhabitants, says the butler, would resent the intrusion—nor should he try to learn about conditions in the interior. That knowledge isn't for the likes of him.

I believe most viewers feel that Burrows gets the better of Sullivan, with the added merit of doing so on the grounds of experience. When Sullivan objects to being warned away from research into poverty—"Well," he says, "*you* seem to have made quite a study of it"—the butler replies, "Quite unwillingly, sir."

That ends the discussion; and yet it doesn't quite clinch the argument. If Burrows is to be believed, then there must be at least a little traffic across the border from the realm of poverty, because here he is, well fed, well housed, and predictably more conservative than the man who employs him. The butler even has a taste for knowledge, though of a different kind. When Sullivan remarks, in Burrows's absence, that "He gets a little gruesome every once in a while," the valet (the even more exquisitely British Eric Blore) explains, "Always reading books, sir."

So *Sullivan's Travels* admits some give-and-take in social and economic identity, despite giving the impression that people generally are what they are. As further demonstration of this proposition, as well as its elasticity, here is Sullivan about three sequences later, reflecting feverishly (he's got a terrible cold) on his repeated failures to get onto the road: "It's a funny thing the way everything keeps shoving me back to Hollywood, or Beverly Hills. . . . Almost like, like gravity, as if some force was saying, Get back where you belong. . . . Maybe there's a universal law that says, 'Stay put. As you are, so shall you remain.'"

In other words, know your place. If you're a comedy director (as Sturges said in his memoirs), then stick to directing comedies. If you're a girl in a movie (like Veronica Lake in this one, going through the proceedings without the benefit of a name), then be The Girl. All the rattling, complicated machinery of *Sullivan's Travels*, from "The End" at the beginning to the concluding "The End," is geared to nothing else but reconciling Sullivan to the life he already has, with the single improvement (not inconsiderable) of substituting a younger, prettier, less demanding romantic partner for his unloved, estranged, and expensive wife.

And yet Sullivan speaks almost with horror of the universal law that says, "As you are, so shall you remain." That's what makes the rest of the movie possible and makes him a character worth following. Even in his fever, he remains determined to break out of the closed circle. He eventually does it, too. He just hasn't reckoned what the knowledge will cost.

To tote up the account, it helps to note the stages of Sullivan's education, and also the movie genres through which he passes to get his lessons. Sturges is not nearly so virtuosic in shifting styles as Vincente Minnelli would later be in *The Bad and the*

Slapstick, with a little sex: Margaret Hayes, as the secretary, gets bounced about in the land yacht

Beautiful (1952), but he is no less determined to proceed through different types of films to tell his story of a filmmaker.

Slapstick comedy. The journey begins with a sample of the crude, effective, entirely standard stuff that Sullivan, Hollywood's "Caliph of Comedy," probably could have dreamed up on his way to the commissary toilet. Unhappy about being followed on his travels by a trailer full of movie studio personnel—a bickering lot, given to spritzing dialogue at cross-purposes—Sullivan escapes by hopping a ride with a young farm boy, who is driving a makeshift hot rod that he's decorated like a Whippet tank. (The Whippet was a small, light British tank of World War I. The boy is evidently looking forward to action in the current war, a hint of which intrudes into *Sullivan's Travels* for the first time.) In the ensuing high-speed chase, a motorcycle cop gets muddied, a pretty secretary is flung upside-down with her legs and panties exposed, a Black cook is humiliated with the whiteface of pancake batter, and a team of horses is put to flight, all to a frenetic light-classics medley that Carl Stalling might have composed for Looney Tunes. When Sullivan is satisfied that he's got his minders thoroughly shaken up with this prank, he tells them to stop shadowing him and wait down the road, a suggestion they take up without protest. From this easy success, he can conclude only that he was born to direct these people. He's learned nothing.

Small-Town Comedy. Once embarked in earnest upon his adventures as a hobo, Sullivan immediately finds himself trapped in the sort of humorous small town that was a staple of 1930s Hollywood. According to the movies, America was dotted with little enclaves of people who were dependably warm, quirky, and wise, whether the filmmaker depicting them was Capra in his *Mr. This or That* movies, George B. Seitz in the Andy Hardy series, John L. Sullivan in *Hey, Hey in the Hayloft*, or Sturges himself as screenwriter for *Remember the Night*. In exceptional cases, filmmakers worked against this cozy image, for the sake of protest (*Fury*), satire (*Nothing Sacred*), or (in the present instance) mean-spirited fun. Sturges tortures Sullivan—and, inadvertently, a twenty-first-century audience—by turning the Hollywood small town into the setting for a prolonged, unpleasant joke about a sex-starved middle-aged woman. A vain widow (the cooing, eye-fluttering Esther Howard) takes in Sullivan as a hired hand and then tries to lock him up. Worse still: as part of her campaign to seduce and sequester, she treats him to the movies, where he's exposed (seemingly for the first time) to the horror that is his audience. He sits appalled in a suffocating crowd of bored children, wailing infants, and people stuffing their faces mechanically while staring ahead as if blind.

Screwball, with a little sex: The Girl and Sullivan meet cute in the all-night diner

Sullivan's lessons from this stage of his journey: women are despicable—again, something he already knew, or thought he did—and so too are the dimwits to whom he thought he'd deliver his socially useful film.

Screwball comedy. Having hitchhiked to the exact spot he didn't want—back where he started—Sullivan steps into a more sophisticated, up-to-date comic genre when he enters an all-night diner at dawn and encounters Veronica Lake as The Girl. Suddenly *Sullivan's Travels* is full of arch banter, misconstrued identities, madcap run-ins with the law, and high-class trappings, whether in the diner (where The Girl is discovered in an incongruously glamorous outfit and sultry pose) or at Sullivan's mansion. These are among the hallmarks of screwball, including mockery of the spendthrift rich, fantasies of joining them in tossing away money, and a promise of easy sex. (For the latter, Sturges implies that Sullivan and The Girl might have tumbled into bed after their first dip in his swimming pool but doesn't leave them enough time to have been anything but chaste. In a single gesture, he teases both the audience and the Production Code Administration.) Through these screwball experiences, Sullivan finally absorbs a lesson or two. He learns something about tact when he's shoved into his swimming pool for having "made fun of a poor girl"; and he learns something about responsibility when The Girl cajoles him into taking her on his research expedition. He had been arrogant enough, or sufficiently aroused, to have offered her temporary protection. Now he'll have to keep her.

Romantic adventure on the road. Capra's great hit *It Happened One Night* must have made a deep impression on Sturges, because he copied it twice—the second time in *The Palm Beach Story* (as we'll see) and the first time here, when Joel McCrea and Veronica Lake go off on an intimate, rough-and-tumble journey. Their positions of authority are reversed, compared with those of Clark Gable and Claudette Colbert; this time it's the big, gruff man who's naïve and unprepared, and the spunky young woman who is wised up (or at least claims to be). Still, despite this change, audiences would have recognized the premise of this section as almost a genre in itself: attractive, mismatched couple carries their high spirits through a Depression-era landscape.

What audiences could not have expected was Sturges's jarring break with convention at the beginning of this section, in a pair of extended tracking shots filmed on location in harsh sunlight. First, the camera stays with Sullivan and The Girl as they walk silently through a shantytown: a mobile panorama, you might call it, crowded with men who look convincingly idle and despondent, and who include a high number (for 1940s

Hollywood) of unsmiling, unmusical African Americans. Then, as a freight starts out of the yard, the camera looks down from the top of a boxcar onto an unfolding vista of Sullivan and The Girl almost lost amid dozens of men pouring and staggering down an embankment, so they can run beside the tracks and hop the train.

Sullivan's Travels had begun within a parodic movie, set on a freight train. Now, with the introduction of this second train, the picture seems momentarily to burst out of its succession of film genres and into the world. This first rupture is brief; very soon, Sullivan and The Girl are again playing cute, in a Capra set-up. But the intuition of larger, scarier possibilities has emerged, and the shock of it seems to have affected Sullivan himself. At the end of this section, he's lying helpless in bed with a fever, having been taught another lesson: he's vulnerable. Unfortunately, he hasn't yet learned it well enough.

Documentary. John L. Sullivan would flub the direction of *O Brother, Where Art Thou?*—but Sturges, betraying the difference between himself and his presumed alter ego, devotes the next section of *Sullivan's Travels* to a successful imitation of *The Grapes of Wrath*, or at least of its near-documentary visual style. Commentators in 1940 had praised the images of John Ford and cinematographer Gregg Toland as having the stark, uncompromising strength of the photographs of Dorothea Lange and Walker Evans or the actualities footage of Fox Movietone News.[6] Striving to approximate them, at least for a while, Sturges now resumes his earlier, brief illusion of breaking into the real world and maintains it for seven wordless minutes, sometimes with the mixture of pity and disgust that is common in lower-depths documentaries, sometimes with the touches of sentiment and humor that soon would be a part of De Sica's neorealism.

Documentary: the railyard hobo encampment

This montage sequence was shot in the studio (as was much of *The Grapes of Wrath*); the camera never ventures out to a location. But as in the railyard scene, Sturges establishes the tone with traveling shots that track Sullivan and The Girl as they wander through a shantytown. The difference now is that it's night, and the camera goes by slowly enough to study the faces with their signs of woe; and this time the faces turn upward, again and again, as if to return the gaze of Sullivan and The Girl, and so look back through them at the movie's viewer. As if to close that distance, Sullivan and The Girl go missing from half the shots. All you see of them is their shadows passing across the scene, leaving no one to mediate between you and the homeless wretches.

As the sequence continues, Sturges interrupts the mood now and then with narrative touches (images of the movie studio's photographer capturing publicity shots of Sullivan) and bits of comic business (such as Sullivan and The Girl jumping from flea bites). Sturges also inserts the film's second image of an audience, one that contrasts remarkably with the earlier crowd of small-town moviegoers. This audience comprises rows of silent, still, weary people in a rescue mission, waiting for a sermon to end so they can get a free meal and a place to sleep on the floor.

Many aspects of these seven minutes—through-composed music, expressionistic lighting, well-timed moments of comic relief—might remind you that the images you're seeing are products of movie artifice. And yet a reality effect holds, achieved in part by a chatter-happy filmmaker's sudden withdrawal of all dialogue. This section of the movie seems struck dumb by the suffering to which it makes you a witness, a misery that Sturges even tries to get you to smell. The lesson for Sullivan, as he looks at the effect of all this on The Girl: His butler was right. Poverty is something to flee.

Which ought to be the end of *Sullivan's Travels*.

The argument has been settled, the firsthand knowledge acquired, the studio satisfied with a publicity campaign, and The Girl brought into the picture. As Sullivan himself says, "Here we are at the end of the adventure. I'll go down tonight and give 'em a little money"—"them" being the poor on the streets, to whom he intends to hand out five-dollar bills—"and that winds it up." There is no longer any material reason why Sullivan can't make *O Brother, Where Art Thou?* and settle down to a happy ending with The Girl.

So Sturges invents impediments.

The Girl first. Despite having bedded down repeatedly with Sullivan on the road—despite strolling into his bedroom now in her dressing gown—The Girl learns that Sullivan is married, a detail he hadn't bothered to mention during those nights of holding her close. He assumed she knew; "everybody" does, says the great man. The topic comes up now only because Sullivan is offering options for how he'll send her away.

Any number of reactions from her would be plausible—shock, anger, self-blame, heartbreak, hard-bitten resignation—depending on who you think The Girl might be. At various times, Sturges has characterized her as a disillusioned vamp, an almost childish ingénue, a canny striver, and a survivor of hard knocks. Which is to say, he's hardly characterized her at all, except as convenient; whatever the plot might need at the moment, that's what she is. So she remains now, as she reacts to Sullivan's revelation of his marital status and its retrospective implications about how he's treated her. She's surprised, briefly; she's mildly disappointed. After a few vengeful expostulations, she's also rather quickly satisfied with Sullivan's explanation of why he can't get out of a marriage to a woman he loathes. It seems the wife was in cahoots with his crooked business manager, and Sullivan, though rich, famous, and supposedly inventive, can do nothing to escape their trap.

The best you can say for this narrative excuse—"complication" would be too big a word—is that it passes quickly. The Girl agrees with unconvincing complacency to continue a relationship with Sullivan that the audience can imagine only as adulterous (though to the Production Code Administration it would necessarily have been a warm friendship). Is she being tricked by Sullivan, as he's apparently been cheated by his wife and former business manager? And is the audience in its turn being shortchanged by Sturges? The film's pace gives you no time to ask. The first impediment to a happy ending having been posited, the movie hustles off at once to establish a second, as

Sullivan heads back to Skid Row, truly alone this time, with a very large wad of cash in his pocket.

Has he really learned so little?

The answer is yes, according to Sturges's shooting script from May 1941. It contains more of the speech about "the end of the adventure" than is heard in the film; a lot more. As originally drafted, the speech has Sullivan continue:

> And the funny part is I don't know any more about trouble than when I started.
>
> I mean about how to cure it, and what's wrong with the world and all that stuff. It's like Shaw said: The trouble with the poor seems to be poverty—and what we're going to do about it I don't know.[7]

It's only after he's dragged Shaw into the affair that Sullivan concludes with the next sentence heard in the finished film: "I'll go down and give them a little money tonight."

We've known since the first scene that Sullivan was educated at a boarding school and college (advantages enjoyed by relatively few Americans in the 1920s and 1930s), and we've heard him speak with exquisite pedantry when asking hobos how they "feel about the labor situation." Of course he'd be familiar with Shaw. By this point in the movie, though, the name-drop had to be cut. It would have been too "deep-dish" even for Sullivan, which is perhaps why the shooting script makes him deflate himself, unconvincingly, by becoming inarticulate all of a sudden, as he talks about "what's wrong with the world and all that stuff."

But the strongest reason to delete the reference to Shaw is to avoid spelling out in advance the next stage of Sullivan's education. He is about to try doing exactly what Shaw recommended: cure poverty by giving the poor money. That was more or less the method that Andrew Undershaft practiced in *Major Barbara*, one of the plays that I suspect haunted Sturges when he was writing *A Cup of Coffee*.* That was also the method that the Roosevelt administration had been pursuing since 1933, to Sturges's disapproval. It would not be plausible for Sullivan to quote Shaw in one breath and say in the next that he didn't know what "we" were going to do about poverty. "We" had already committed to a remedy, on stage and in Washington.

Shaw's name never made it into the movie; but the trace it left in the shooting script is enough to reveal why Sullivan's adventure cannot yet be over. Before he can embrace his identity as a privileged director of comedies, he has to learn that he can't end poverty. He has to be punished for even trying.

Searing Drama, Ripped from Today's Headlines. So Sullivan steps into the final movie genre through which he will travel, and from which Sturges again breaks unexpectedly in mid-narrative.

Warner Bros. had established the genre definitively in 1932 with *I Am a Fugitive from a Chain Gang*, whose precedent glimmers darkly throughout Sullivan's term of penal servitude in the South. The shooting script, too, betrays Sturges's reliance on that source, and others. After specifying one of the images that Sturges wants—"THE HANDS OF A BLACKSMITH—FORGING THE ANKLET ON SULLIVAN'S ANKLE"— the script adds in parentheses, "Check research for correct way of doing this."[8] From this, a student of the arts may learn that in practical terms, the injunction to write or direct what you

---

* The Theatre Guild's production of *Major Barbara* ran for a healthy six weeks in late 1928, exactly when Sturges was trying to break onto Broadway with his first play, *The Guinea Pig*.

know comes with the addendum, "or what you can copy from others."

But the film's pedagogical scheme permits no such leniency. *Sullivan's Travels* never questions the doctrine that experience is the great teacher, whose lessons constitute one's identity, which means that, if Sullivan's curriculum has failed him so far, it's not because he learned no method to change the world (such methods being inconceivable, in Sturges's view) but because *he* hasn't changed. He came back from a short season on Skid Row as the same man who set off: sarcastic more than humorous, cocksure more than principled, a little hot-headed, a little gruff, and still determined to make *O Brother, Where Art Thou?* Which is to say, Sullivan continues to know his place. He may sometimes want to get away from it (and feels frustrated when he can't), but if he does break away, he believes he can always return.

If he's truly to learn, then, his ties to home must be severed, and the man himself wiped away.

So here comes an engine of destiny and narrative complication, rumbling through a railyard: the film's third locomotive. While implicitly signaling to the audience that the movie must be getting into part 3, the locomotive carries Sullivan into something deeper than a predicament from which Sturges can cleverly rescue his hero at the last moment. It delivers him to perdition. Sullivan loses his place in the world, his freedom, and (for a while) the memory of his name. According to official records, he even loses his life.

Sullivan's sense of self dies hard, though, despite his abrupt legal demise. As we've seen, he is used to brushing off run-ins with the law. With a butler and valet to back him up, he has even felt free to insult cops to their faces. Now, when he is dropped beyond the reach of normal society, his response is to point out that his situation is irregular: "They don't sentence people like me to places like this." True. It's telling, all the same, that in his eyes the injustice has less to do with the brutality of the prison farm system than with the lapse of protocol that has assigned him to it, as if to a B-list table too close to the kitchen door. The Mister in charge of the prison farm (Al Bridge) has his way of correcting such vanity. He locks Sullivan in the sweatbox, reducing him to a state of pure animal need. Only when Sullivan has in effect died to himself, having been taken out of the sweatbox in a pose reminiscent of the deposition from the cross, can he be reborn as a new and better man, who is capable of laughing at a Walt Disney cartoon.

This resurrection takes place, appropriately, in a church. Its immediate effect is to unite Sullivan for the first time with an audience. He has suffered stiffly among small-town moviegoers. He has waited out a sermon at a rescue mission, amid the bums from whom he held himself aloof. Now, attending this third spectacle, he at last lets himself melt into a crowd of fellow nobodies: the chain-gang prisoners and rural Black people who dwell at the bottom of American society.

"Leave the preaching to the preachers," Sturges wrote in his memoirs; and yet he delivers this turning point of *Sullivan's Travels* into the hands of a Black minister (Jess Lee Brooks). Deep-voiced and bespectacled, with a fringe of white around his hair and an old-fashioned frock coat garbing him in dignity, the pastor makes his way with deliberate steps up the church aisle, first chuckling with his congregants over a mild joke about their evening's entertainment, then exhorting them to welcome the "guests" who will be coming, and who are "less fortunate than ourselves," then lifting his voice in a rousing sermon on the equality of all people before Heaven's eyes and the deliverance promised by God.

118 *So* AS YOU ARE, SO SHALL YOU REMAIN

By this time the pastor has walked part of the way back down the aisle and is ready to lead the congregation in a song of welcome: "Go Down, Moses." During its first verse, Sturges concentrates your attention on the fervent, upraised faces of the pastor and his flock; they are the reality, while the chain-gang prisoners, seen in cutaway shots, are mere silhouettes, tramping across the screen in front of a view of the distant church (which itself seems insubstantial, since it's obviously a matte painting). As the second verse begins, though, a view from the altar shows the church doors opening and the prisoners shuffling inside in double file. You get a few glimpses of faces, including Sullivan's as he slides into a pew; but mostly the screen is crowded with filthy, patched trousers and manacled feet, seen as if by a penitent prostrate on the floor, as they trudge endlessly toward the camera. As the last of the trousers move off to the left and right, the

Redemption: Jess Lee Brooks as the preacher

aisle clears at last, and there, magically returned to the back of his church, stands the pastor, bringing the song to its close.

As Penelope Houston once wrote, Sturges throws everything he's got at this scene, "and a curious everything it is."[9] The repertoire includes expert gradations of pastoral rhetoric (delivered exactly as written in the screenplay), the pathos of the spiritual that Sturges has selected, the candid portraits he delivers of the congregants as the camera passes across the pews, and the expressionism of his exterior process shot and forced perspective up the aisle. What's clear amid all this fuss is that the scene is taking its sweet time to build up a mood of solemnity and expectation, and the figure who seems to be calling it up is the minister.

That Jess Lee Brooks goes uncredited in this crucial role may count as just another instance of classic Hollywood's disregard for Black supporting players; and yet more than mere neglect seems to be at work here, since the omission helps prevent audiences from thinking of Brooks as an actor. Indeed, most moviegoers would not have identified him as anyone they'd seen before; though active in the movies from the early 1930s, he had worked mostly in pictures produced expressly for Black audiences.[10] Here, though, in a striking anomaly, Brooks dominates an entire scene in a major studio picture, doing so with a gravity that Hollywood had almost never permitted a Black actor, made all the more intense by the suggestion that the man you see is a genuine minister. Once again, Sturges seems to break out of recognizable movie fiction—this time in the midst of flagrantly aestheticized shots—into a mode that resembles documentary.

All this, so Sullivan can laugh with everyone else at Pluto the Pup's misadventures. A deep change is happening within Sullivan; but instead of trying to make that process play out gradually across the face of the actor (a tough job, with Joel McCrea), Sturges cannily works an emotional change in the audience, moving his viewers with an experience entirely outside the Hollywood norm. White people's depictions of Black church life had appeared before on mainstream stages and in the movies—*The Green Pastures* was one notable example, and in about a year *Cabin in the Sky* would be another—but with an emphasis on the charm of African Americans' supposedly naïve, folkloric thinking. In the mainstream, only Sturges (with the possible exception of King Vidor, in *Hallelujah!*) showed a Black church service without condescension, as a matter of life or death; and through this break with convention he prepared the audience to identify with Sullivan's conversion experience. Life on a chain gang was not enough to push Sullivan into his moment of spiritual liberation, if only because moviegoers were already familiar with stories about that sort of misery. For the miracle to happen, Sullivan (and the audience) had to be immersed in something new that spoke of sorrows even deeper than the chain gang's, and hopes cherished beyond any individual's lifespan.

But to be clear: the change toward which this scene is driving happens only within Sullivan. On behalf of the Black characters in the scene, Sturges neither calls for a change—spiritual, material, social, political—nor implies the need for one.

As hard as it is to imagine after the civil rights movement, the minister's cry for all people to be understood as equal in God's eyes does not amount to an argument by Sturges for Black Americans to be treated equally when using water fountains, going to public toilets, eating at lunch counters, or applying for decent housing, schools, and jobs. You will search in vain through Sturges's films and writings for any hint of outrage at the status of African Americans, or any notion that their condition, after

Emancipation, could be other than what it was. Sturges was too full of good ideas as a writer, and too proud of his skills, to supply a Black character with dialogue that was less than witty and memorable, and he was too fascinated by the challenges of directing not to take up the test of imbuing a Black church service with depth of feeling. That said, he still cast Charles R. Moore and Fred Toones as eternal menials and assumed that Jess Lee Brooks, or someone like him, would forever preach before a congregation resigned to its lot in life.

Which is neither to accuse Sturges of racialist thinking (although he certainly indulged in it, like so many then and now) nor to charge him with bigotry (of which he seems to have been innocent). My point is that Sturges felt most comfortable working in a long-standing tradition that based dramatic characters on types, each with a fixed social status.

A Study of the Drama by Brander Matthews, the scholarly work that Sturges chose as his textbook when he decided to become a playwright, includes a useful, brief survey of the history of stock characters, with particular attention to the way *commedia* actors specialized in types.[11] The game, which had persisted from the time of the Roman theater to the Elizabethans and beyond, was to pour vitality into these standard figures. That's what Sturges famously did with his stock company of Paramount bit players, such as Frank Moran (the gravel-voiced bruiser who's smarter than he sounds), Jimmy Conlin (the friendly, nervous little fellow), Torben Meyer (the functionary with a foreign accent and brusquely officious ways), Al Bridge (the fount of drawling sarcasm), and of course William Demarest (the inveterate hothead, voluble, cynical, but good-hearted). The same process of bringing fresh life to ready-made types held true even with the treatment of leading actors—for example, Joel McCrea, who in Sturges's films is always the enterprising monomaniac, stolid, self-serious, and not quite as bright as he ought to be. There could be shortcomings to this method, as with Veronica Lake in *Sullivan's Travels*, whose namelessness betrays how little was invested this time in the spunky, seductive dame; but in general, Sturges devoted an abundance of wit and observation to fleshing out his repertoire of traditional figures. He sparked his invention with these types and so assented to their implication: that society is a static hierarchy.

This is where Sturges departed from the message-delivering filmmakers. Writers and directors working in that vein showed their characters struggling within a society that could change and *had* to change—a notion that was extraneous to Sturges's art and inimical to his sensibility. He was conservative in politics, after the fashion of moneyed people who resent paying taxes, and proudly cynical. (Recall how the Boss, in *The Great McGinty*, explains that he runs all the political organizations, including the Reform Party. "You think I'm goin' to starve every time they change administrations?") To Sturges, such expectations about the ways of the world were merely practical and accorded well with his interest in the price of everything. From *Sullivan's Travels*, you can learn that at the end of 1941 a cup of coffee and a donut sold for ten cents. Ham and eggs: thirty-five cents. Marriage of convenience to an unloved woman: $12,000 a year (or half of Sullivan's projected income-tax savings). Expression of joyful wonder on the face of a homeless person: $5 in alms. Precise and relentless, this attention to dollars and cents is more than just another facet of Sturges's reality effect. It's a testament to the inescapable primacy of material need and therefore to the relative inflexibility of social relations, as his preferred mode of dramaturgy conceives them—a reminder that even if Jimmy MacDonald gets a provisional windfall in *Christmas in*

July, he's still fundamentally an office clerk, and if John L. Sullivan temporarily loses everything, he still was not born and reared for the prison farm. When Manny Farber collaborated with W. S. Poster in 1954 on what remains the best single essay about Sturges (not to mention the gaudiest), he feinted in the direction of this view of an unchanging, hierarchical society but did not hit it on the nose.

> What Sturges presents with nervous simultaneity is the skyrocketing modern world of high-speed pleasures and actions . . . in conflict with a whole Victorian world of sentiment, glamour, baroque appearance, and static individuality in a state of advanced decay. . . . From McGinty to Harold Diddlebock, Sturges gives us a crowded parade of courtly, pompous, speechifying, queerly dressed personages caught as they slowly dissolve with an era. . . . Nowhere did Sturges reveal his Victorian affinities more than by his belief in, use, and love of a horde of broken, warped, walked-over, rejected, seamy, old character actors. . . . They are very much part of the world of Micawber and Scrooge but later developments—weaker, more perfect, bloated, and subtle caricatures—giving off a fantastic odor of rotten purity and the embalmed cheerfulness of puppets.[12]

But it's not individuality that's static in Sturges's films (while somehow also being in decay), nor is Sturges's imaginative frame of reference peculiarly Victorian, except by virtue of the gaslight era's being for him an accessible version of the bygone past. To Sturges, *every* previous era survives intact in the "skyrocketing modern world" as a structure of generally immovable class and caste relations, whose dramatic types (the genteel pauper trying to keep up appearances, the aged and embittered miser) might wear the costumes of a Micawber or a Scrooge but might equally well be dressed in togas, Renaissance doublets, or business suits from Schindel's department store. Perhaps this persistence in an age-old mode of characterization, accompanied by unquestioning acceptance of a society imagined as unalterable, was what James Agee had in mind when he repeatedly complained that Sturges was "rejecting half his talents."[13] Agee never specified which half that might be; but he made clear his conviction that artists should not be content with displays of exuberance but must also *think*—about what their exuberance is good for, and how much truth remains to be discovered about people, and what the battles raging overseas might mean for everyone (except perhaps for Sturges, who in *Sullivan's Travels* refers to World War II only for the sake of giving Sullivan something else to be pompous about). Other critics also detected something inadequate, or perhaps cowardly, in Sturges's attitude, as it was revealed in the film's happy ending. Bosley Crowther and André Bazin both wanted to know why there was no bitterness, no irony, in Sullivan's final decree, handed down when he remounts his four-thousand-dollar-a-week Hollywood throne, that the only hunger he need try to satisfy among the world's suffering people was their need for laughter.

By contrast, consider the worldview of the showman who has tacitly been shadowing Sturges from the first page of this book.

"Do you think Orson Welles is crazy?" asks The Girl in one of the lines cut from the shooting script. "In a very practical way," Sullivan replies.[14] An astute judgment from Sturges, who knew something himself about building a career on shows of flamboyant eccentricity and an air of independence. Indeed, contemporary newspaper and magazine articles frequently linked Sturges and Welles as the geniuses who were revolutionizing Hollywood.

Unlike Sturges, though, Welles aligned himself with actual revolutionists.

That was hardly the only difference between the two. So far in my comparison I've elided matters such as age (Welles was almost a generation younger than Sturges, though he liked to play at being twenty years older), fundamental temperament (an actor and visual artist, more than a man of words), and preferred method (a brilliant adapter of existing repertoire, versus a tireless spinner of new works). For the present purpose, though, the most telling divergence was political.

A fervent public supporter of the Roosevelt administration and a prominent member of its Federal Theatre Project—the sort of government make-work program that Sturges detested, and that Republicans frequently characterized as an outlet for socialist propaganda—Welles devoted a large portion of his career in the late 1930s to making an eclectic roster of historic works speak to his moment. *Macbeth* in his hands became a foray into the legacy of slavery and rebellion in the Caribbean, and an opportunity for Black performers to erupt into the theatrical mainstream. His *Julius Caesar*, with its trappings reminiscent of a Nuremberg rally, attacked European fascism at a moment when much of the American public wanted to leave Mussolini and Hitler undisturbed. In adapting *The War of the Worlds* for radio, Welles turned H. G. Wells's political parable into a lesson about the power of mass communications in an era of demagogues. Collaborating with Marc Blitzstein, a loyal member of the Communist Party, Welles staged the union-versus-bosses oratorio *The Cradle Will Rock* and participated in its now-legendary bootleg production.

Welles continued in this Popular Front vein when he stormed Hollywood and made *Citizen Kane*. Much of the excited commentary about that film focused on its formal daring, and on the scandal of its thinly disguised dramatization of the career of William Randolph Hearst—still a public figure when *Kane* came out in 1941, though old and weakened, and widely known for his editorial attacks on Roosevelt and forbearance toward Hitler and Mussolini. Somewhat lost in the discussion, perhaps because the point seemed obvious at the time, was the affinity between *Kane*'s review of contemporary history (however baroque in style) and the topical plays of the Federal Theatre Project's Living Newspapers.

Welles's next film, which went into production right after Sturges completed *Sullivan's Travels*, lacked the immediacy of *Kane* but was concerned in a much deeper way with historical process as experienced across the generations. *The Magnificent Ambersons* looked back explicitly, not just by implication, on a bygone America of bustles, high collars, horse-drawn carriages, and formal balls. It was the very opposite of a Preston Sturges picture. Lavish, brooding, and heartfelt, it traced the transformation not just of its characters' circumstances but of their emotions—their sense of who they were in the world—over the course of decades of social and economic change.

Continuing to respond to the historical moment, Welles postponed editing *The Magnificent Ambersons*—a catastrophic decision for his Hollywood career and film history alike—so he could go to Brazil on a mission of cultural diplomacy, intended to counter the influence of the Axis powers. In the aftermath of Pearl Harbor, other prominent filmmakers—among them John Ford, Frank Capra, and Sturges's good friends William Wyler and John Huston—volunteered to serve their country in uniform. Sturges, meanwhile, declined to be bothered, writing phlegmatically to an old friend that "this war has not been as well advertised as the last one."[15] When *Sullivan's Travels* was released in January 1942, Sturges was contributing nothing to the

war effort except for a quickie instructional film, using Paramount personnel, about *Safeguarding Military Information.*
But then, he didn't have to do anything more. In February 1942, the government ruled that movies were "an essential industry"—the same decision that had been made during World War I—and exempted film studio employees from the draft. In effect, the Roosevelt administration concurred with the conclusion of *Sullivan's Travels.* Entertainment was a service to the nation.

And so, with the circularity that is characteristic of so much of Sturges's work, this discussion has come back to the questions with which it began. If laughter, pure and simple, is enough to justify a movie's existence and its filmmaker's life, then why does Sturges put himself through so many deluxe contortions in *Sullivan's Travels*? How candid is he being about himself? Who is he arguing against so fervently, other than some semi-imaginary filmmakers who had supposedly grown too serious, and the Roosevelt administration, which wasn't disagreeing with him? What kind of education does this movie offer, and what kind of a fast one does it pull?

"Make 'em laugh" is clearly not an adequate answer to any of these questions. Indeed, the parts of the film that Sturges sells most strenuously as comedy are the ones that are least satisfying. The slapstick chase uses up its chuckles before it's half over, the small-town flirtation embarrasses the audience as much as it does Sullivan, the dawn encounter with The Girl splinters into irritating fragments with every reaction shot of the counterman mugging at her arch jokes, and the tumbles into the swimming pool don't get any more uproarious for happening twice too often. I assume John L. Sullivan would have handled these scenes better, or he wouldn't have been worth four thousand a week.

One of the most striking aspects of *Sullivan's Travels*, in fact, is the mirthlessness of the clowning that the film claims to defend.* But what if you were to understand *Sullivan's Travels* not by its intentions, stated or implied, but by the effect of what's actually on the screen? Or, to put it differently: What if Sturges as a director manifestly contradicts the meanings that Sturges the writer put into the script?

In that case, *Sullivan's Travels* becomes less of a paean to movie comedies in their run-of-the-mill aspect than an attack against them. Slapstick, rural Americana, and screwball comedy pass painfully before you, straining for effect and ringing hollow. If you should enjoy this mediocre fare, wretched viewer, then take a look at what you're like: one of the witless yokels in the small-town movie theater where Sullivan is held captive.

I'm distinguishing, of course, between the deliberately generic patches of comedy in the first half of *Sullivan's Travels* and the brilliant exchanges of banter that bear Sturges's stamp, and his alone. (These seem to become more hilarious as the actors delivering them are more tightly compressed. The members of the stock company, pressurized within the "land yacht" trailing Sullivan, remain a marvel, so long as they're talking instead of being battered.) My point is that *Sullivan's Travels* itself keeps making this distinction, fracturing into moments of dancing wit that carry you along with them and moments of lead-footed tomfoolery that try to bully you into laughing.

---

* Out of deference to the historical record and Diane Jacobs's research, I note that the slapstick scenes were especially well received when Paramount previewed *Sullivan's Travels* in Inglewood and Long Beach. My only response to this fact is to paraphrase Sullivan himself: "If they knew what they liked, they wouldn't live in Long Beach." I have yet to meet anyone whose first reaction, when *Sullivan's Travels* comes up, is to chortle about the chase scene.

It's a movie divided against itself, in not just one way but two. On one level it keeps venturing into reality effects and then retreating from them, as it carries to a foreordained conclusion a polemic about art versus life, or more precisely light entertainment versus the trials of poverty. But the film undermines this argument—the quasi-realistic scenes being the most memorable and affecting—and at last all but confesses the emptiness of its thesis by closing on the weakest line of dialogue Sturges ever wrote. When Sullivan is moved to awe and wonder by the memory of his experiences, with ghostly, laughing faces gathered about him, you are to gauge the power of the vision he's been granted by the way he utters an astounded, summarizing, "Boy!" Some revelation, to inspire him to rise even higher than "Gee!" and "Gosh!"

By announcing, with such hypoarticulation, the triumph of the comic spirit over grim reality, *Sullivan's Travels* debunks itself. And all the while, on the second level, it's been carrying out another self-debunking, by exposing the shabbiness of generic filmmaking in the very act of seeming to celebrate it.

It's clear what kind of movies Sullivan has been directing and doesn't want to make anymore. He may condescend to name Lubitsch to The Girl when she asks if he, an apparent bum, could give her an introduction; but despite this moment of surreptitious pride in his circle of acquaintance, nothing suggests that the author of *Ants in Your Plants of 1939* has ever directed anything so glorious as *Trouble in Paradise* or *The Shop Around the Corner*. Although Sullivan's movies are wildly lucrative for his studio, and their mere memory is enough to make The Girl laugh out loud, she's never heard of the man who directed them. In that sense, Sullivan's disguise matches his reality. Compared to Lubitsch, he *is* a bum.

Sturges knew how it felt. While working his way up at Paramount, always pushing to be made a director, always hoping for his own stories to be put on the screen, he'd banged out scripts for bread-and-butter projects such as *Hotel Haywire* and *College Swing*; a Jack Benny vehicle titled *Never Say Die*, which somehow misplaced Benny along the way; Cecil B. DeMille's *The Buccaneer*, from which Sturges was summarily fired; and a couple of romantic comedies, *Next Time We Love* and *Love Before Breakfast*, for which he went uncredited. The elaborate machinery of *Sullivan's Travels* labors to reconcile its protagonist to a life of making such stuff; but it also enacts a revenge against the mediocrities that Sturges had spent years grinding out, without knowing if he would ever get to do anything better.

Despite what *Sullivan's Travels* says aloud, in its secret heart it doesn't resent Capra, Ford, or any other director who had become too preachy. It rages against the Preston Sturges who once had been stuck turning out product, and against the alternate-universe Sturges who might yet flop, be abandoned by the producers, and return to anonymity. That had happened to Sturges on Broadway; it could happen in Hollywood, too. I can almost imagine that the allegorical figures of Capital and Labor who wrestle on top of the train in the first scene of *Sullivan's Travels* are Sturges struggling with himself: the momentarily celebrated writer-director desperately hanging on to his good fortune, while grappling with the perennial left-behind who lashes out in frustration.

Sturges knew what it meant to be blocked, belittled, passed over. He'd had that experience ground into his identity—unlike Welles, who in 1941 hadn't yet made time for failure. Welles had burst into the ranks of elite radio actors by age twenty, had made himself the wonder of the New York theater by twenty-one, and at twenty-three was world-famous. It wasn't until he'd returned from his Brazilian sojourn at twenty-seven that he took his first steps into a career shadowland that would engulf him for the rest of his life, as it would soon enough consume Sturges.

To the person who thinks in a grand sweep of time—someone like the young Welles, who regarded Shakespeare as his contemporary, and his audience as a democratic public mobilized to create its own future—an awareness of the dynamism of society across the generations may provide solace in adversity. But to the person who thinks as an individual, knowing that after a term of seventy years (or, if granted strength, eighty) the story is over, nothing can salve a consciousness of stasis. In his earlier travels, Sullivan doesn't fully confront that reality—not because he is merely dipping in and out of poverty, but because he expects the "adventure" to advance him to a new stage of his career. Only when he gets trapped in the last of his travels does Sullivan truly learn the terrible lesson of being stuck in one's condition.

Until then, he is necessarily the butt of the movie's joke—because even if you credit Sullivan for his conscience, how seriously can you take the man's troubles when he lives in that mansion? It's only when he's lost the way home that an audience can feel at one with Sullivan in his horror at the thought "As you are, so shall you remain." The chain gang is a good, clear choice of image to represent that likelihood, understood not as a rule of social hierarchy but as an existential fact. The pastor and congregants of a Black church provide the model—surprising in the context of classic Hollywood, but entirely appropriate at that time—of abiding with grace and dignity amid a situation that feels as if it will never change.

You could argue that if Sturges is projecting his own disappointments onto that church, his own dread of being consigned to the fate of making lousy movies, then he's indulging from a position of privilege in the most stingy-hearted self-pity.

But then, Sturges asks for no indulgence, for either Sullivan or himself.

Sullivan sits in the church not as a victim but as a witness, seeing himself at last as one among the multitudes who wait their way through brief lives that go nowhere. His reaction to this knowledge is prompted less by Pluto the Pup than by the people around him, at whom he keeps glancing; and as in the film's earlier Skid Row documentary section, his response to his ultimate place in the world lacks words, even a single "Boy." All Sullivan can do is laugh.

5

TOPIC A

The Palm Beach Story

Even after Sturges wrapped *Sullivan's Travels* in late July 1941, he continued to push his luck on that risky picture, resisting the suggestions made to him after the first preview by Paramount's new head of production, Buddy DeSylva, who wanted him to tone down the misery and cut the Black preacher. Sturges hoped that when the movie went into release, months in the future, the box office would prove that he'd been right and his boss wrong—although that wouldn't be such a safe position for him, either.

Meanwhile, rather than wait to see what fortune might bring, Sturges hedged his bet by starting to write a new comedy, one that would give Paramount and its audiences all the frothy fun they could want. *The Palm Beach Story* would turn out to be the airiest of Sturges's movies, the most flagrantly madcap and least susceptible to obvious biographical interpretation (despite the traces of smashed personal history that litter it like debris from the Ale and Quail Club). It would be as seemingly uncomplicated as *Sullivan's Travels* is thorny, with no ostensible ambition other than to entertain. And yet, on its face, it would also be exactly what Sturges had disavowed years earlier, when the need for a hit had moved him to write *A Cup of Coffee*. This movie would be a SHOCKER.

He began the screenplay in an interrogative mood, choosing as his working title *Is Marriage Necessary?* He'd already proposed a related question in *The Lady Eve*, when he'd had Hopsie dine alone on his first evening aboard the *Southern Queen*, fenced off from a roomful of avid young women by a book titled *Are Snakes Necessary?* Hopsie knew they were; snakes were his life. As for the sacred institution into which the encompassing women wanted to tempt him, he wasn't so sure. He did come to feel that matrimony, or a tumble into original sin, would be worth the trouble so long as his wife was Jean—or maybe Eve. But nothing in Hopsie's behavior implied an endorsement of marriage as such.

For his part, Sturges seemed even less convinced: "A young woman works her way to Palm Beach [he wrote in an early draft] to see what life holds for her: a husband or adventure. She has left her husband because together they could not succeed. She chose Palm Beach because it contains more wealth in the shape of rich men per square mile than any other locale."[1]

Already, Sturges was flirting with a portrayal of matrimony as legalized prostitution. The Production Code Administration did not yet know what sort of outrage he was contemplating; but by early September 1941, when he wrote the preceding note, the Hays Office had already decreed that he could not offend popular sentiment by titling a movie *Is Marriage Necessary?* Sturges backed off, a little, by reframing the question as *Is That Bad?* Merely to ask, though, was to imply an answer: maybe not, but it sure looks it.

In an extensive and witty examination of the notes and drafts for the film, Brian Henderson has determined that Sturges spent about two months, from early September through early

November, laboring over the problem of why the young woman decides to take off when she does, how explicitly she ought to market a pretty face and long legs, and whether her husband, before or after the break, should knowingly allow himself to profit from her talent at beguiling men. That is to say, Sturges assessed more and less severe degrees of "bad" while calculating what his audience and the Hays Office might let him get away with. Remarkably, most of this two months' work went into the first twenty-five or thirty minutes of *The Palm Beach Story*: the setup. Sturges dashed off his draft for the other two-thirds, including the majority of the film's funniest, most memorable scenes, in a couple of weeks in late October, while continuing to rework the opening.

I take nothing away from this Mozartean feat by observing that Sturges must have had that last two-thirds sketched out in his head all along. Maybe he'd had a plan in mind even before he put the first words on paper. The possibility gains substance from an anecdote that Claudette Colbert recounted to Diane Jacobs, recalling a preview screening of *Sullivan's Travels* that she'd attended with Sturges. As the lights came up, Colbert had said to him, "I want you to write a picture for me."[2]

Why wouldn't he have leapt at the proposal? Colbert was the biggest star at Paramount. And Sturges was friendly with her; they shared a background in the New York theater and would playfully cut others out of their conversation by switching to French. I can easily imagine Sturges mulling over her request, meanwhile thinking back to Colbert's best-known roles to get a sense of what he might ask her to do. By early September 1941—the date of the first extant drafts for *The Palm Beach Story*—he certainly would have wondered how to toy with the audience's memories of her performance as the runaway heiress in *It Happened One Night*.

It would be hard to exaggerate the popularity of that movie, or the degree to which it defined Colbert, who would from then on be known as the woman who hitchhiked by baring her legs. As the young heiress in Capra's film, she escaped an impending marriage by diving off her father's yacht, and then made her way overland from Florida to New York without money or luggage. I doubt it's a coincidence that in Sturges's movie, Colbert escapes from an impoverished marriage she no longer wants by running out of a Park Avenue duplex, and then makes her way overland in the opposite direction, from New York to Florida, without money or luggage, finishing the trip by yacht. In *It Happened One Night*, Colbert needed help from a large, sexy man, Clark Gable, to manage her journey. In *The Palm Beach Story*, Colbert tells a large, sexy man, Joel McCrea, that she can very well travel on her own and makes good on the boast.

Assuming that Sturges conceived *The Palm Beach Story* as a vehicle for his star—an assumption that approaches certainty, when you consider that the shooting script's introductory sequence refers to the heroine not as "Geraldine" or "Gerry" but "Claudette Colbert"—you might say the movie is a continuation of Capra's film.[3] It shows what life might have brought Colbert had she married her original large, sexy man: a drudgery of unpaid bills and jealousy. Sturges frees her from that trap, in effect by running *It Happened One Night* backward.

Was marriage to Clark Gable necessary, when after a few years he would turn into Joel McCrea? (To quote the title at the end of the introductory sequence to *The Palm Beach Story*: "And they lived happily ever after. Or did they?") Was it bad of Colbert to want not only to dissolve that marriage but to make as much money as she could on the next halfway suitable man to cross her path? As Sturges imagined what these questions might imply for a teasing, rambunctious comedy, he worked in a few scraps of autobiography.

McCrea's character, Tom Jeffers, vaguely resembles Sturges during an earlier period in his life, as an inventor struggling to persuade people to bankroll his projects. Gerry's sudden departure recalls how both of Sturges's first two marriages ended. As for Gerry's destination for divorce and fortune-hunting: Sturges's surrogate uncle, Paris Singer, had done more than anyone other than Henry Flagler to establish Palm Beach as a town of oversize mansions for the staggeringly rich, and Eleanor Hutton had kept Sturges there as a house guest no one else wanted, back when Mar-a-Lago was her mother's winter home and not yet a site of national disgrace.

The personal associations are evident; and yet, in a departure from Sturges's previous films, they add no emotional depth to *The Palm Beach Story*. Pursuing an ingenious plan to deliver shocks while seeming to provide only light comedy and a little sex (or, rather, as much sex as the industry would permit), he built *The Palm Beach Story* on a foundation of movie-house experiences. The central figure steps out of another film. Her journey reverses that picture's narrative, and so overthrows its conventional faith that legally enforced monogamy is the sole route to happiness. Even the names that Sturges chose for his troubled couple suggest that *The Palm Beach Story* is inhabited by fictional characters rather than human beings. Tom and Gerry (or Jerry): the cat and mouse who were the most popular new cartoon duo of summer 1941. The smaller and slyer of the pair always won.

Almost the last the audience sees of Colbert in *It Happened One Night* is the image of a woman in a wedding gown, dashing away from the altar and running flat-out toward her future with Gable. At the beginning of *The Palm Beach Story*, Colbert is again in a wedding gown, this time dashing flat-out *toward* the altar and a future with McCrea. The most striking difference is not that the first man has a raffish screen image, and the second is unfailingly upright. It's that the two-minute wedding sequence at the start of *The Palm Beach Story* plays like a complete screwball comedy, run at forty-five times normal speed. It's all fainting housemaids, disrupted phone calls, careening vehicles, disarrayed costumes, and mysteriously trussed-up women, as if Sturges were giving you the high points (and only the high points) of a story about Colbert's progress toward marriage. Also, the sequence is inexplicable—or at least it won't be explained until the very end.

And so the first thing you learn about *The Palm Beach Story* is that this movie might not make any sense. The second is that the film's characters will behave as if in a game.

After the credit sequence, Colbert vanishes as mysteriously as she'd appeared, and three new characters step into the story spouting mutually confused dialogue. These are Franklin Pangborn, typically fussy as the manager of a Park Avenue apartment building; Esther Howard (the principal female member of the Sturges stock company) as a trilling grande dame with a house in Yonkers; and Robert Dudley, dwarfed by a cooking pot of a black Stetson lowered onto his head and an unnecessary wool overcoat drooping off his frame, as Howard's husband, the old, deaf, braying, unnervingly direct Wienie King. Admitted into an apartment that his wife might want to rent, the Wienie King wanders off on his own and so intrudes into the quarters of the current tenant, Colbert (that is, Gerry). What does she do? Play hide-and-seek.

She has no good reason to make sport of this meeting. Strangers are being permitted to pry into her home because she's

Gerry plays hide-and-seek with the Wienie King

facing eviction for nonpayment of rent—a humiliating circumstance for someone who is fully adult. In late 1933, when Colbert had filmed *It Happened One Night*, she had just turned thirty and was playing a character who was meant to be younger. She wore her hair short, sucked in her cheeks to produce a kewpie-doll pucker, and often kept her face to the camera while peeking sideways at Gable, so her big eyes looked bigger on their upward roll. With her quickness of gesture—she moved more abruptly than anyone else in that picture—the impression of juvenile impulsiveness was complete. "A brat," Gable had called her; and a brat might have been forgiven for insouciance in the face of being kicked out of her home. But the Colbert who filmed *The Palm Beach Story* was thirty-eight, and her character is discovered in a Park Avenue boudoir as a mature, lush-haired sophisticate in lipstick, false eyelashes, and a form-hugging wrapper. So why does she slip silently from room to room, improvising places from which to spy on the Wienie King? Why are the two of them going around in circles?

Not only deaf but also (on the evidence of the big eyeglasses) half-blind, the Wienie King uses a dog's senses to track the female presence he picks up, tasting her lipstick and toothpaste and sniffing her perfume. Gerry is manifestly disgusted at being made into an implied object of delectation—though she may also be amused, to judge from the way she slinks about, chasing a man who has not yet realized she's near enough to be caught. There will be another scene of pursuit in this movie, a much more threatening one; but for the moment, Gerry has no reason to fear. She knows the little old man who is doddering after her is harmless, as she shows when she at last throws back the shower curtain to confront him.

I suppose Gerry must have been playing this game for fun—which turns out to be the Wienie King's primary motivation, too, and a source of almost immediate understanding between these characters. In the blink of an eye—the standard Preston Sturges unit of time—they're making each other laugh, trading confidences, and exchanging an astonishing sum of cash, $700, which the Wienie King pushes into her hands (with a concluding "Yippee!") simply because "it makes me feel young again." Despite a lingering awkwardness to which Gerry sometimes returns, the two of them are bound by a mutual desire for amusement. He wants to feel he can once more plunge ahead experimentally with a beautiful woman, and also put one over on his wife. She wants to be entertained by the "funny old man," and also regain a sense of freedom.

Which she does, at once. Now that Gerry has so much cash, her apparent problems have been solved at a single, whimsical stroke and the movie can end, much as *Sullivan's Travels* could have wrapped up with the return from Skid Row. But, of course, Sturges now has an even more acute case of premature termination than before; *Sullivan's Travels* was two-thirds done when it reached its false cadence, whereas *The Palm Beach Story* has scarcely begun. What keeps it going after the initial fake resolution is the sense of unease—dread, in fact—that keeps breaking through the characters' fun and games.

The most famous expression of this dread is the podium speech that the Wienie King recites, apparently from memory, upon meeting Gerry: "Cold are the hands of time that creep along relentlessly, destroying slowly but without pity that which yesterday was young. Alone our memories resist this disintegration and grow more lovely with the passing years. That's hard to say with false teeth."

Indeed it is—an observation that deflates the oration's pomp while confirming its truth. But even though the audience is invited to laugh with Gerry at this utterance, whose incongruous, ornate splendor flows unprompted, the speech is not that much of an anomaly. Sturges has already set loose an equally grim thought, which whizzed past the audience when the Wienie King began his tour of inspection. To his wife's complaint that the apartment needed cleaning, the Wienie King had declared, "Dirt is as natural in this world as sin and disease and storms and twisters." Some inventory; some reason for equanimity.

Now, having raised a shiver with the image of Time's cold hands, the Wienie King rubs in his message of fatality (in the most reassuring way possible, of course) by telling Gerry she'll get over the shame of being broke: "You'll get over bein' young too. One day you'll wake up and find it's all behind you. Gives you quite a turn. Makes you sorry for a few of the things you didn't do, while you still could." As the Wienie King approaches the conclusion to this warning, Sturges cuts to a close-up of Gerry. The script doesn't call for the shot. Sturges the director has inserted it, to show that Gerry isn't laughing anymore. Softly, with an expression that seems to reflect inner worries even as her gaze goes out in sympathy toward the old man, she asks, "Are *you* sorry?"

To which the Wienie King does not respond. Instead, in a non sequitur, he shoots back, "How much rent do you owe?" Rather than linger on the hint of sadness, Sturges uses it as a springboard, vaulting the plot forward. Meanwhile, though, the close-up of Gerry has done its work, establishing her motivation without the need for a word of explanation. You've caught her thinking about lost opportunities and vanishing youth.

As soon as she phones Tom at his office, the deepest of all her causes of disappointment leaps into view: she's married to a man who can't share her joy. She wants to tell him about "the most exciting thing" that's happened; and like many a self-serious businessman before him, Tom cuts her short, reasonably, distractedly, dully. You see at once that he lacks Gerry's talent for fun—and yet, apparently, he spends his days playing with toys.

That's his notion of business: pulling little wooden airplanes up and down on strings, so he can demonstrate his design for cable-suspension airports to be strung over city centers. He never cracks a smile about this boy-hobbyist way of trying to make money, and neither does the potential investor in his office, a gentleman who shares the Wienie King's candor about age and futility but has none of his humor. When Tom, frustrated, insists on starting the sales pitch again from the beginning, the prospect replies, "Go ahead, my time ain't worth anything. I'm retired."

Tom plays with toys as his business

There is, in fact, only one type of fun that Tom is good for, as you see a few minutes later when Gerry settles on his lap, late at night in their now paid-up apartment, so he can help unhook the back of her dress. She is stuck in the first of her many wardrobe malfunctions—as a rule, Gerry either can't remove her clothes or has no clothes to put on, fails to get naked or narrowly avoids being laid bare—and the proximity of her rump to Tom's crotch is sending her into some of the most convincing wriggles of arousal in Hollywood history. "Hold still," Tom tells her, with a hint of self-congratulation breaking through his stolid façade, as he gives an order that he knows she can't obey. She wouldn't squirm so helplessly if he weren't so completely and proudly a stiff, who now asserts the one claim he can still make on Gerry.

Topic A: Gerry squirms in Tom's lap

By this point, after many paragraphs of bickering that Sturges has cleverly spread for variety's sake across two scene changes and a transition to drunkenness, she's told him she wants a divorce—and not just because she intends to enjoy what's left of her youth. Gerry has also complained that Tom ought to have let her work on bankers and company presidents for his benefit, the way he's now working on her as she sits on his lap. It's a matter of self-respect, as she sees it. The marriage might have succeeded, had Tom recognized that her skill in using her sexual allure is just as worthy, and economically valuable, as his entrepreneurial ideas—more valuable, if anything, considering his record of business flops. (Like his near-namesake, the sage of Monticello, Thomas Jeffers is a great improver. He's just not much good at pursuing happiness.) Now, though, the personal asset that Gerry had been wanting to deploy for financial gain is being used against her, to draw her half-unwillingly back into Tom's arms. But it's only for one more night, as she knows and he doesn't. The postcoital smile that plays over Tom's sleeping features the next morning, in a rare exception to the grumpiness of McCrea's performance, proves there's *something* that Tom enjoys, and suggests that he feels he can rely on it, too. He's like the women in more conventional stories who try to bind spouses to themselves through their sole resource—while Gerry is like the men, who take what they want and tiptoe out at dawn.

She tries to tiptoe out—but instead, with a misdirected straight pin, she stabs the movie into the frenzy it will maintain for the rest of its running time. As Gerry makes her dash toward freedom, amid shouts, tumbles, an abortive police intervention, and a brief episode of indecent exposure, the film resumes its air of being a game played in a nonsenscial, made-up world. Witness Gerry's first act upon escaping from Tom's clutches, though for the moment by only a few inches. She asks a cabbie where to go for a divorce, accepts his remarkably knowledgeable recommendation of Palm Beach, and gets a well-omened response when she explains she's broke and would like a free ride to Penn Station: "Why, certainly. Hop in, babe."

Viewers at this point are likely to be as happy as kids at a party when they've been spun around to make them dizzy. They will have neither the capacity nor the inclination to look back and assess everything that's happened so far in *The Palm Beach Story*, and if presented with documentary evidence about Sturges's creative decisions will rightfully crumple it and toss it on the ground. Nevertheless, a lot of emotional and thematic groundwork has been laid leading up to the straight-pin stab. This was the part of the movie that Sturges labored over in his writing, and it's worth examining—even though, as usual, he's taken care to distract you from its import.

What's evident, going back to the earliest drafts for *The Palm Beach Story*, is that Gerry's motivation is much more complex than Sturges originally sketched out, and her relationship with Tom far trickier.

Recall that Sturges wrote, "She has left her husband because together they could not succeed"—that is, make scads of money. In his earliest drafts, he tried developing this idea using the well-worn materials of marital comedy. The marriage couldn't "succeed" because Gerry was unsuited to the role of helpmeet, cooking disastrous meals and the like. (Imagine the heiress from *It Happened One Night* stuck in the kitchen, trying to fix breakfast for a Gable who is no longer so amused.) A few traces of this standard stuff remain in *The Palm Beach Story*, with Gerry lightly mocking herself for her lack of the expected domestic skills, and Tom sadly agreeing. But in the finished film, Sturges isn't at all satisfied to get by with a superficial explanation for the breakup. The film's early scenes concentrate instead on what the relationship between Gerry and Tom has been—and it's nothing ordinary.

It's not just that Sturges has reversed the conventional sexual roles of women and men, making Gerry the rover and Tom the homebody. He's also reversed the economic stereotypes of gender, doing so on grounds that might seem immoral to audiences today, let alone in 1942. Sturges floats the idea that a woman who peddles her body as Gerry wants to do (set aside for the moment the question of how far the peddling might go, and under what legal cover) is engaged in a business activity like any other and deserves to be praised if successful—unlike the passive Tom, who seems to be waiting for people to come to him with money, and who might be worthwhile to Gerry as a kind of trophy husband, to be prized so long as he keeps his looks.

The force of these reversals, of course, depends on their contrast to commonly accepted notions of the relationship between women and men. Sturges acknowledges these norms with a sting, giving Gerry several paragraphs of dialogue about what we would today call sexual harassment. She calls it "the look," which starts just after childhood, she says acidly, when your girlfriends' fathers become "arch all of a sudden." From then on you get the look constantly, "from taxi drivers, bell boys, cops, delicatessen dealers, visiting noblemen . . . it gives you a fine opinion of men on the whole." That, as we know too well, is the reality, which Gerry describes as being no less unrelenting than the Wienie King's dirt, sin, disease, and decline.

The catch is that the look is supposed to result in fun—for men, of course, but sometimes for women too, especially those who snag the occasional Joel McCrea. And so Gerry tries to change how she manages her own sexual desires. Until now, she has been their vehicle. From this time on, she hopes, they will be her instrument. She responds to the reality of the look not by yielding to bitterness (though it's a close call, considering the edge in Colbert's line readings) but by deciding to pursue financial profit from it—profit being the surest guarantor of the fun she wants. Her husband having turned out to be an unreliable provider, she will now provide for herself, through an exploit that weds a lowered expectation of sexual pleasure to a heightened chance at other kinds of enjoyment. And all this had better happen fast, because the cold hands of time creep onward.

She will have fun, at a record pace—and so, from now on, will *The Palm Beach Story*. But as the movie careens along, it will occasionally strike a passing undertone from the setup: a remembrance of Gerry's hint of contempt for her husband, her economy of disillusionment (in which she balances sex against life's other pleasures), her sense that time is running out. These darker notes don't slow the movie or suddenly alter its tone, as the Boss's return changes *The Great McGinty*. They merely give you a hunch that Gerry might be playing nonsensical games for real stakes.

That said, she's taken the field without a game plan, which makes *The Palm Beach Story* something new in Sturges's work.

Jean in *The Lady Eve* knows at all times how she wants to steer the game. She needs to adjust when Hopsie's pride and her emotions interfere with the strategy, but she always has a scheme and the skill to carry it out. McGinty's Boss is a great schemer, too, who controls an entire city. Jimmy in *Christmas in July* follows a plan for acquiring riches (though a bad one); and Sullivan, a born director, devises an entire scenario to enable him to make his chosen film. In all these movies, the characters must cope with the unruliness of circumstance, but they at least have a step-by-step process they can follow while it falls apart.

Gerry is different. She's more like Mary in *Easy Living*, who spends the movie puzzling her way through events—except that Mary responds to a situation that's fallen out of the sky, whereas Gerry knowingly flings herself into the need for improvisation.

This type of premise, which sets in motion a train of seemingly spontaneous complications, must have appealed to Sturges, because he used it for all but one of his subsequent comedies. *The Miracle of Morgan's Creek*, *Hail the Conquering Hero*, and *The Sin of Harold Diddlebock* all make their protagonists cope moment by moment with events no one had intended or foreseen. Among the films released from 1944 through 1948, *Unfaithfully Yours* is the sole throwback to the earlier comedies about people who plan; and there the whole point is that the protagonist's brilliant schemes dissolve upon contact with reality, leaving him to scramble through failure after undignified, absurd failure.

Gerry suffers reverses, but she is not undignified, and for the most part she succeeds. In fact, the need to improvise brings out talents in her that she didn't know she'd had. When she loses all her clothes on the train to Florida, she ingeniously scissors a Pullman blanket into a chic ensemble—even though she'd told Tom, earlier in the film, that she isn't someone who can "cook or sew or whip up a little dress out of last year's window curtains." Having boasted to Tom that she could be an adventuress who makes her way through the world in style, on other people's money, Gerry discovers she actually can be that person, and more.

When she manages to board the train to Palm Beach without a ticket, traveling as the guest (or "mascot") of the "rich millionaires" of the Ale and Quail Club, she proves that her charm is as potent as she's imagined. ("I'm sure that my ticket will come," she quavers within earshot of one club member after another while standing at the platform gate, her eyes fixed vaguely on the middle distance where a nonexistent savior might appear. Though it's a poor bit of playacting, it's good enough for an audience that's eager to be persuaded.) But as the club absorbs her into the most riotous episode in Sturges's films—an uproar as extravagant as the poor people's carnival of *Christmas in July* but with almost his entire stock company packed into the confines of a private railroad car—Gerry discovers that wealthy suitors can be a trial.

By the time the club's members break into her sleeping compartment to serenade her, Gerry is smiling in a way that recalls Colbert's forced gaiety toward the end of *It Happened One Night*, with the difference that she and Sturges allow her misery to show through for a moment. It's clear that she can't imagine providing sex to any of these men, who are more insistent than anticipated; she can't even bear the task of keeping them aroused while fending them off. Nor, for what it's worth, can she claim the right to take refuge in her sleeping compartment. The members of the Ale and Quail Club feel perfectly entitled to enter. The place belongs to them.

And still the sequence rattles and blasts along, its humor becoming hectic until it's almost frightening. Maybe audiences in 1942—white audiences, at any rate—laughed without a second thought at seeing two members of the all-white Ale and Quail Club terrorize the private car's bartender (Fred "Snowflake" Toones) by using him in effect for target practice. Then again, maybe some viewers, perhaps including Sturges himself, felt the rumpus at this point was still funny but had taken an ugly turn. All I know is that Gerry is soon fleeing in fear from the club's members, who eventually reconstitute themselves as a drunken posse and pursue her with shotguns and baying dogs. With the bartender's justifiable panic having set a precedent for Gerry's reaction—and with the chain gang sequences of *Sullivan's Travels* having established that Sturges knew of America's less genteel traditions—it does not seem too far-fetched to say that once the collective sexual hopes of the Ale and Quail Club have been frustrated, the members turn into a parody of a lynch mob.

There's that much of a darker side to Gerry's improvised adventure, even as she's succeeding in it. She learns something disturbing about the men who might be enticed to pay an attractive woman's way: they can be more demanding and dangerous than they look. She also learns something dark about herself: that a woman who wants to be bought but not used may need to be callous toward a man, and even cruel. That's what Gerry finds out, symbolically at least, during the sublimely funny meet-cute with the man who will be her almost-perfect meal ticket: John D. Hackensacker III (Rudy Vallee).

Love, which John D. apparently has never known, is blind; and Gerry is the one to strike him sightless, stepping on his face not once but twice and grinding his eyeglasses against the lids both times. ("Just pick off any little pieces you see, will you?" he asks, smiling with faultless courtesy.) While at it, she also manages to crush his hand, which he gallantly excuses, telling her she's as light as a feather. At this point, as she hides out in the sleeping berth above John D.'s, Gerry has no idea who she's just abused to such favorable response. She ought to feel grateful toward him for having helped her escape the Ale and Quail Club. And yet the following morning, when Gerry accepts his badly needed invitation to breakfast, she feels free to tease this mild-mannered, slightly stuffy, apparently tight-fisted man, with his old-fashioned pince-nez and hair parted in the middle—"tease" being a nicer way to say "belittle." She laughs at him, among other reasons, because he copies her in ordering a prairie oyster and then, in his innocence, is startled to find it's a drink. Pleased at what she imagines to be her superior sophistication, Gerry doesn't enlighten him about its being a hangover remedy.

It isn't until John D. has treated Gerry to an impossibly extravagant shopping spree and then welcomed her onto his yacht that she understands who he is and stops mocking him. Just in time. He's one of the world's richest men (in the shooting script, he's *the* richest). He's also pleasant enough to look at (though he's no Joel McCrea), is obviously smitten with her, and unlike the members of the Ale and Quail Club shows no aggressive tendencies. What's more, as Vallee plays him, John D. is immediately likeable.

Except when straightening up to deliver one of John D.'s stern ethical pronouncements ("Tipping is un-American"), Vallee gives the character a blithe smile, through which he filters unembarrassed remarks about the scandalous family history; a melodious tone, in which he keeps up artless conversation (he has, as Gerry later observes, "a nice little voice"); and a posture that was presumably molded into gentlemanly form in the Yale gym, so that the torso stays upright when not tempted to perform polite little bows. In all this, Vallee is the opposite of scowling, hulking, sulking McCrea, as John D. instinctively understands without ever having set eyes on Tom. "That's one of the tragedies of this life," he declares, abandoning his stated desire to punish Gerry's husband for presumed brutality, "that the men who are most in need of a beating up are always enormous."

Another of the tragedies is that a woman might still ache for the hulking, sulking type, even if he's poor, and even if the available fellow is harmless and immediately likeable and has all the money in the world. By the time Gerry has realized she shouldn't be overtly cruel to John D., Sturges has shown her misty-eyed in that upper berth—no doubt feeling alone, perhaps still feeling frightened from the posse's pursuit, but (as the cross-cutting to Tom suggests) certainly missing the body she's decided she has to live without.

She's so stuck on Tom that when he shows up in Palm Beach, having hurried down with the idea of reclaiming her, she improvises an adhesive alias for him: Captain McGlue. The movie by this time has flown into uninhibited gibberish, having just introduced natty little Sig Arno in the role of the linguistically indeterminate gigolo Toto ("Grittinks!"), so the name McGlue somehow seems plausible, if unfortunate. (It's perhaps less humiliating than the nickname that's simultaneously been revealed for John D.: Snoodles.) Still, dark implications lurk here, too, beneath the silliness. If Gerry feels sexually inseparable from Tom but won't abandon her chance at the unstirring John D., then she's presumably heading for adultery, and beyond.

This solution is simply not possible in classic Hollywood comedy, and not just because of the Production Code. The Hays Office used to forbid such behavior not out of prudery alone but in deference to a belief that had predated the movies and was an article of faith to much of the audience. The myth of romantic monogamy is not exclusive to America; but to a degree that is uncommon in history, and that has reflected as much as influenced the stories we like to tell, Americans believe they marry not for purposes of economic exchange or clan solidarity but for love of a uniquely appropriate partner.

Outside the realm of fiction, most people understand that what they call "love" represents a balance struck between sexual dreams and other needs, such as companionship and financial security. For situations in which the balance is off, and a person is perceived to have given up too much of the sexual ideal, Americans have coined a less pleasant term: "settling."

Within American studio movies, though, the exclusive love that leads to marriage figures predominantly as sexual desire, experienced by actors who may be described as normatively gorgeous. Which is to say, stars do not settle. They attain their sexual ideals, on big screens set up in public places, so the rest of us may find it easier to believe in our compromised version of marriage for love. This is the bargain that audiences make with screen illusion—a bargain that *The Palm Beach Story* is now threatening to rip into confetti.

Claudette Colbert thinks of giving up her sexual ideal—her marriage to that one special man who can make her wriggle as no other—precisely with the aim of settling. No matter that she'll get a high price. If committed, Colbert's violation of the standards of movie love would be almost as unforgivable as Gerry's projected crimes.

I come to Topic A, as Tom Jeffers calls it. But before I talk about Sturges's Three Bears treatment of sex, with John D. having too little interest in it, his sister Princess Maude (Mary Astor) too much, and Gerry and Tom just enough, I want to add a bit of context about the degree of seriousness with which *The Palm Beach Story* threatens cinematic order.

You needn't look far to find other films that jest with their own conventions. At Paramount, *The Palm Beach Story* was sandwiched into the 1941–42 production schedule between *Road to Zanzibar* and *Road to Morocco*, in which Bing Crosby, Bob Hope, and Dorothy Lamour joke about being actors in a movie, comment on their own shtick, and sometimes give up on the action altogether to wisecrack directly to the audience. Compared to these comedies, *The Palm Beach Story* is almost sedate in exposing its movieness.

Take the scene in which John D. totes a full orchestra to the lawn outside Gerry's window to serenade her with "Goodnight, Sweetheart," and Rudy Vallee suddenly comes to the surface of the character he's playing. In 1942, when Vallee was still famous as a radio crooner, almost everyone in the audience would have caught the gag; and yet the moment of double vision is voluntary. If you prefer to continue thinking of the figure before you as John D., Sturges leaves you free to accept the scene at its goofy face value.

You might say that Sturges is being tactful, to use a term that Richard Wilbur suggests in one of his essays. That is, he provides a second layer of meaning for those who can appreciate it but doesn't ruin the fun for those who can't.[4] As an artistic virtue, "tact" sounds rather gentlemanly (a word that meant something to Sturges). But the paradoxical effect, here and elsewhere in *The Palm Beach Story*, is to ratchet up rather than relax tension. Instead of knocking down the Tinkertoy edifice of movie conventions, in simple *Road* movie style, Sturges leaves it teetering in place, and so lends a sense of suspense, or substantiality, to the thought of an impending crash.

In much the same way, he gives you the impression that the characters are continuing to play for real stakes, although the game they're in gets progressively sillier. John D. remains a puppyishly ardent man, even when the actor who underlies him pops into plain view. He has set his heart on an indifferent woman, and like saps before him, in the world as in the movies, he will be unhappy if he doesn't get her and unhappy if he does. As for Gerry, she still needs to prove her cleverness (to herself and Tom both) and have fun before it's too late. More than that, she's coping thoughtfully with a problem that many women face when their employment opportunities are limited and monogamy is enforced. She needs to cash in on her principal economic asset without either too grossly devaluing herself or too sorely squelching her desires.

Unfortunately, John D.'s voice sets loose physical longings in her, even though his face and body don't. As Gerry gives up the struggle, lapsing back into Tom's arms, there can be no doubt of the strength of her primary urge. Topic A is costing her millions. But as she abandons herself, a question remains: What has Tom done to deserve her?

Granted, he's taken the trouble to fly to Palm Beach. His behavior, though, has not improved with the climate. Before John D. unwittingly helps the cause by singing in the moonlight, Tom makes no effort to win Gerry back, other than to crush her in a bear hug that's more possessive than seductive. Proud instead of remorseful, angry instead of accommodating, he continues to stamp around (as Gerry puts it earlier) with the wounded, unyielding magnificence of "Sitting Bull in a new blanket," still broke and still no fun.

But as it turns out, he doesn't need to do anything else. As the movie resumes its earlier joke of reversing gender roles, Gerry bustles about generating income while Tom continues to be passive, recommending himself to people through nothing but his physical allure. The difference is that now, with the Princess hotly pursuing him, he involuntarily proves to be as powerful and potentially profitable a sex magnet as Gerry had expected herself to be. For the first time in the movie, she echoes his jealousy. She also becomes piqued at Tom for a second reason—because instead of striving to show himself worthy of Gerry, he's casually showing her up.

I wish I could say this friction leads to deeper emotions or a more complex situation, but it's not that kind of movie. Sturges does nothing with the emerging rivalry, other than externalize it through a careless subplot about Tom and Gerry's decision to leave a ceramic sculpture sitting on the guest room mantle, as a sign that neither has yet given in to a suitor. The audience may be forgiven for forgetting about this tchotchke. Sturges almost does, introducing the prop half-heartedly and then abandoning it the same way.

But then, that's how Sturges handles all the incidents in the film's final act, which has a remarkably high ratio of surface frivolity to plot. Almost nothing consequential happens before Gerry and Tom's reconciliation, except for her improvising an additional way to extract cash from John D.—why sucker him for a hundred thousand dollars, more or less, when she can get two?—and Tom's smashing the ceramic sculpture in a fit of absent-mindedness. Other than that, act 3 is all fluting banter from the Princess, fashion statements from a ridiculously well-outfitted Toto, and leisure activities in sets so lavish that the Princess's boudoir mirror looks as big as the parlor fireplace at Xanadu.

Perhaps this atmosphere of utter meaninglessness is the secret reason why Gerry decides to return to Tom, despite his inability to change. Although jealousy at the Princess's lust for him might have revived her own appetite, and his bumbling success at gold-digging might have spoiled her pleasure in exercising her skills, maybe Gerry softens toward Tom because she takes him more seriously now, given the chance to compare him to the people in Palm Beach. He may spend his office hours playing with toy airplanes, but at least he does *something*.

Another convention of studio comedies: when the rich waste this much money, a character must eventually confront them on behalf of the audience's moral sense, whether he speaks with the smooth disdain of a live-in butler (*My Man Godfrey*) or the stammering anger of a desperate intruder (*Mr. Deeds Goes to Town*). You might expect the writer-director who had made *Sullivan's Travels* to fulfill this expectation, too, or at least acknowledge that the advantage the Hackensackers enjoy over the great majority of people is, if not grossly unfair, then at least disproportionate. But except for having Charles Moore, as a Pullman porter, complain wittily about John D.'s idea of a tip, Sturges allows the rich in *The Palm Beach Story* to go on heedlessly. Or, rather, he lets them indict themselves.

Witness Toto, who gives no evidence of being able to survive if not awash in other people's money. Spry, slim, small, and presumably lubricious, he capers incessantly around the considerably larger Princess, who condescends to him as one would to a pet that's grown tiresome. "She goes out with anything," John D. says of the Princess when Toto first comes into view, as if disparaging not the social classes with which his sister consorts but the species. Given that no one can identify the language Toto speaks—it might be Beluchistan, the Princess speculates—this uncanny little person might just as well have originated outside normal human realms. Yitz. Nitz. Spegoglu. As far as the other characters are concerned, these are the piping, gurgling ejaculations of a domesticated stray the Princess has had the heart to take in but won't keep.

I think most viewers enjoy Toto and would perhaps feel a little sorry for him if he had any virtues beyond persistence. He's always being ordered off on disagreeable errands, forgotten in the rumble seats of cars, or left alone to play solitaire in evil-looking Beluchi style. Then he invariably bounces back, once again cheerful, springy, and spouting further nonsense.

His keeper is a different story. Accounts of the production record that Mary Astor disliked the way Sturges directed her as the Princess and felt uncomfortable chattering at top speed in her highest vocal register. The resentment shows in the brittleness of the performance, which subtly clashes with the Princess's habit of finding hilarity in everyone around her and pretending to youthful insouciance by trying to talk like Cab Calloway. (What's buzzin', cousins? What's knittin', kittens?) An absurdly wealthy, man-eating sybarite would presumably be a little more relaxed than Astor seems in the role. But that's part of what keeps Tom safe from temptation, while signaling to the audience that something must be wrong with these idle spendthrifts. John D. at least has a heart, as well as an aptitude for corny puns. The Princess's behavior suggests that the members of her class are cold, and for all their incessant laughter lack a sense of humor.

Tom Jeffers articulates no principled reasons for standing apart from the society of the Hackensackers; but both Gerry and the audience see that he's aggressively aloof and presumably credit him for having at least a little common decency. When Gerry at last goes back to him, she therefore does more than reestablish a domestic order that the audience knows can't be overthrown in the movies. She also completes the standard Hollywood process of ushering the audience into a fantasy of great luxury, then assuring them that they're better off among their own good kind.

With that, *The Palm Beach Story* accomplishes everything that might be wanted of a high-gloss screwball comedy, and achieves it with superior élan. But if the film did nothing more than that, it would be nothing more. Instead, *The Palm Beach Story* is an unmistakably singular eruption within the tradition of movie comedy, today as much as in its own era. It separates itself from the others, first of all, by maintaining that hint of desperation beneath the lightness and frivolity, and (more important) by refusing to cheat its way out of the dilemma that Gerry has posed. With or without Tom Jeffers, she has the same problem as every other woman who feels that her abilities are greater than the economic value assigned to her by marriage. When John D. carefully jots down the cost of every item he buys her, he doesn't bother to add up the total, because even if love matters a great deal to him, money means nothing. But for Gerry, the total is crucial, and so is the problem of managing to pay it while still married to Tom.

Is marriage necessary? In a few years, while making *Unfaithfully Yours*, Sturges would have a very superior character mock the afternoon he'd wasted at the movies, saying he'd watched a feature that questioned the necessity of marriage for eight reels "and then concluded that it was essential in the ninth." *The Palm Beach Story* makes no such retreat. For eight reels, it acknowledges that sexual desire is no respecter of persons. Eros plays where it will despite monogamy's genteel fiction that each

Colbert must have been made for her particular McCrea (even if she's been made for a Gable before him). And in the ninth reel, with stunning consistency, it reveals that there are *two* Colberts and *two* McCreas: enough to go around. Snoodles attains his sexual ideal (though he might not know what to do with her); his too-much-married sister gets her ideal, too, in the extra McCrea (and will probably tire of him within the month); and the original, sexually compatible pair remains together. Here they all are, spread across the screen for your inspection in one of those horizontal arrays, just a little behind the picture plane, that I might call Sturges's buffet shots, after the paired images of the breadline and the Boss's election-night spread in *The Great McGinty*.

This final shot of the three couples at the altar might also bring to mind the conclusion of a fairy tale, which neatly wraps

The marriage buffet: interchangeable partners, presented for inspection

up all options for the characters, good and bad. But if the Colberts and McCreas are multiple and interchangeable, there can be no fairy-tale ending. This time, when we read "And they lived happily ever after—or did they?" we know the answer. They did not, because we've been at this altar before, at the start of the movie. The story has turned out to be another of Sturges's circular narratives, and dissatisfaction must come around again.

Colbert, doubled, gets to have both her choices, which means that neither is uniquely right for her, and the ideal of sexual exclusivity is nonsense. More than that: this high-handed conclusion demolishes the notion of choice itself. For viewers who still recall, however vaguely, *It Happened One Night*, the final shot might revive a memory of how Colbert in that picture claims in a moment of demoralization that it "really doesn't matter how—or where—or with whom" she settles down. That story proves her wrong, of course; and speaking those lines for Capra, she looks fatigued and puts a note of huskiness in her voice. Here, with Sturges, the story proves her right, and there's finally no voice at all. Colbert exercises both her choices at once, and neither is likely to prove satisfactory.

There are more convivial, optimistic ways to arrive at the same conclusion. As Molly Bloom puts it at the end of *Ulysses*, "and I thought well as well him as another." For all the laughter that the conclusion of *The Palm Beach Story* provokes, it doesn't convey Molly's affirmation. It's jeering, discordant—a trick played on the characters and audience alike. It makes *The Palm Beach Story* not a comedy of remarriage (in Stanley Cavell's terms) but a comedy of disillusionment.

But that's a grim way to characterize the sleight-of-hand rescue that ends Sturges's most madcap comedy. It would be truer to the tone of *The Palm Beach Story* to say that while the movie doesn't guarantee anyone wedded bliss, it does endorse the pursuit of happiness by Mrs. Thomas Jeffers. Starting out broke, with nothing to lose but her husband and nothing to peddle but her good looks, she sets off to live as an adventuress, and somehow the world is crazy and complicated enough that she stumbles into success, temporarily, more or less.

Sturges had every reason to cheer on a woman who risks this course. That's what his mother had done.

Mary Dempsey grew up in poverty in Chicago, living with her widowed mother and multiple siblings on the charity of an uncle by marriage, who kept a saloon near the stockyards. A brief marriage to a drunken, abusive ne'er-do-well named Biden produced a child, Preston, and much unhappiness. Sometime in 1900 or early 1901—Mary's command of facts was flexible—she scraped together enough money to take off alone with her somewhat frail, two-and-a-half-year-old son, going to Paris, where she had a notion to take singing lessons. She was about twenty-nine; but though encumbered by a child and no longer in the first blush of youth, she almost immediately got herself invited to an opera ball, danced with everyone while a chambermaid kept an eye on little Preston back in the cheap hotel, and when recovered from her initial whirl went apartment-hunting, a task that led her to a Mrs. Duncan. So she met Mrs. Duncan's daughter Isadora, immediately became inseparable friends with her, and under the fanciful name of Marie d'Este (later Desti, when some people in Ferrara objected) tagged along with her famous companion on a breathless career of artistic tours, romantic alliances, and fitful entrepreneurship, interrupted only slightly by marriage to the astonishingly indulgent Solomon Sturges.

She died in an apartment in New York in 1931, of leukemia, attended by her son, who had scoured the city for a bed she might find comfortable in her final illness. In his memoirs, he recalled that a few days before her death, she spoke to him of the extraordinary childhood she'd put him through, dropping him here or there for months at a time when she'd felt the need, filling his time with opera performances and museum visits when she picked him up again, and frequently having a strange new man to introduce. "I know there were things you didn't understand," Sturges recalled her saying, "but I'm sure they don't bother you anymore. I was only trying to find happiness."[5]

He understood the part about trying, as he also understood that for sixty years his mother had managed, against great odds, to run a foot or two ahead of sin and disease and storms and twisters. She did it by staying light on her feet. When ten years after her death Sturges invented the character who was most like her, he let Gerry Jeffers run full-out after happiness, and kept her world as bright as Marie Desti believed it ought to be.

6

HOMO SAPIENS, THE WISE GUY

Triumph Over Pain

Unlike formula-movie characters, who advance toward victory or defeat at points as well marked as highway exits, Sturges slewed into his downfall in a slow-motion skid. Facing the wrong way half the time, he couldn't even see where he'd crash. In this, he was not unlike the protagonist of his nonformulaic lost film *Triumph Over Pain*: a man who stumbles through a period of darkness, enjoys a few weeks of glory, and then grinds through twenty years of frustrating reversals.

Because it's possible to see only Paramount's botched edit of *Triumph Over Pain*, released as *The Great Moment*, let me hold off for the moment on an attempted reading of the film and begin instead with an account of how Sturges insisted on this debacle. He had a chance to cut his losses and would not, even though the movie at first had nothing to do with him.

The catastrophe was supposed to befall Samuel Hoffenstein. In 1938, amid a small wave of enthusiasm in Hollywood for tales of crusading scientists—*The Story of Louis Pasteur* (1936), *Dr. Ehrlich's Magic Bullet* (1940)—Paramount bought the rights to a history of surgical anesthesia, *Triumph Over Pain*, by René Fülöp-Miller, and hired Hoffenstein to work up a biopic. He was a former contract writer for Paramount who most recently had done some uncredited work at MGM on *Marie Antoinette*. The intention was to cast Gary Cooper as one of the book's principal figures— W. T. G. Morton (1819–68), the Boston dentist who developed and demonstrated the use of ether—with Henry Hathaway to direct. As Sturges's biographer James Curtis notes, the picture was a little odd for Paramount; it would have fit more comfortably on the slate at Warner Bros. After Cooper and Hathaway became unavailable, the Paramount executives might have let the project wither—but Sturges kept it alive. He'd become aware of *Triumph Over Pain* and asked to take over from Hoffenstein as screenwriter.[1]

According to Brian Henderson, Sturges began work on *Triumph Over Pain* in mid-March 1939. Proceeding as he usually did with adaptations—throwing out almost everything he'd been given and starting over—he finished three complete drafts of the script by mid-December. To judge by the timeframe, the subject matter must have meant something to him. He wrote these drafts just when he was preparing *The Great McGinty* for production, and he kept tinkering with the script for several days into his inaugural shoot as a director.

Then came the success of *McGinty* (soon to win the Academy Award for best original screenplay), followed by the whirlwind of *Christmas in July*, *The Lady Eve*, *Sullivan's Travels*, and *The Palm Beach Story*. By the time Sturges had that last movie in the can, the script for *Triumph Over Pain* had lain in his drawer for more than two years.

He might easily have left it to die of suffocation. Instead, he lobbied Paramount to green-light *Triumph Over Pain* and began revising the script again in February 1942—which was, by coincidence, the month in which Orson Welles and Herman Mankiewicz followed him in winning the Oscar for screenwriting. With *The Palm Beach Story* in postproduction, Sturges began shooting *Triumph Over Pain* in April. Not only did he direct, but for the first time he also took credit as producer—further evidence that the project mattered to him. By the end of June 1942, he had a finished film: on the available evidence, one with a mixture of slapstick and melodrama even more unsettling than that of *Sullivan's Travels*, and with a chronology more elaborately scrambled than *The Power and the Glory*, or for that matter *Citizen Kane*.

Keeping up a pace that was as breathless as his films, Sturges started writing *The Miracle of Morgan's Creek* almost immediately, in early July 1942. *The Palm Beach Story* was ready for release later in the year, and for *Triumph Over Pain* he had nothing more to do except go through previews, after which would come the negotiations with his producers about editing—a normal procedure, he might have thought. Everything seemed in order, except for the objections of the Paramount executives to the film's title—they'd thought up an alternative he disliked, *Great Without Glory*—and an unusually mixed response from the preview audience.

And then there were the skirmishes over a long foreword that Sturges was determined to include, despite the executives' concern that it sounded the wrong note for a country at war. Maybe their resistance ought to have alerted Sturges that his new picture was in trouble.

As *Triumph Over Pain* began, a "clear, pleasant voice" was to have said, over an image of the neglected gravestone of W. T. G. Morton:

> One of the most charming characteristics of Homo Sapiens, the wise guy on your right, is the consistency with which he has stoned, crucified, burned at the stake, and otherwise rid himself of those who consecrated their lives to his further comfort and

well-being so that all his strength and cunning might be preserved for the erection of ever larger monuments, memorial shafts, triumphal arches, pyramids and obelisks to the eternal glory of generals on horseback, tyrants, usurpers, dictators, politicians and other heroes who led him, usually from the rear, to dismemberment and death.

We bring you the story of the Boston dentist who gave you ether. Before whom in all time surgery was agony. Since whom Science has control of pain. It is almost needless to tell you that this man, whose contribution to human welfare is unparalleled in the history of the world, was himself ridiculed, burned in effigy, ruined and eventually driven to despair and death by the beneficiaries of his revelation.[2]

It's tricky to round on the audience. If you do it, you usually want to strike when you're well along in the piece, after you've drawn the people in, rather than put them off preemptively; and it's best accomplished in a quick thrust, not by dumping the contents of a thesaurus over their heads. The impatience of this foreword to *Triumph Over Pain*, the too-muchness of its rhetoric—above all its sneering rancor, emphasized rather than mitigated by the pleasantness required of the speaker—suggest a fervor unsuitable for a Hollywood filmmaker. A writer-director who was focused on the subject at hand with no unseemly personal investment might have dramatized the incalculable benefits of Morton's work, juxtaposed them with the dereliction of the man's burial place and reputation, and let the irony speak for itself. But the foreword goes far beyond Morton. It seeks justice for all secular martyrs—perhaps including Sturges himself, who believed that he too had alleviated human suffering, through his comedies, and now seemed to nurse a grievance.

Although the foreword gives no hint about the nature of that grievance, it betrays a personal identification with Morton that may help explain Sturges's tenacity. He kept arguing for his foreword and title throughout the later months of 1942, while shooting *The Miracle of Morgan's Creek*. Perhaps he should have compromised sooner. At some point late in the year, on the orders of Paramount's head of production, Buddy DeSylva, with whom Sturges already had clashed too often, the studio recut *Triumph Over Pain*.

Henderson has looked closely at the sequence of events and believes the reediting must have taken place between the beginning of September and the end of 1942. I agree, on the assumption that DeSylva used the troubling August previews as an excuse to exert control. I also suspect that the disappointing critical and commercial response to *The Palm Beach Story* upon its New York release on December 10 strengthened DeSylva's hand. Sturges was too preoccupied just then to defend *Triumph Over Pain*; his work on *The Miracle of Morgan's Creek* kept him busy full-time until December 28. DeSylva, meanwhile, knew exactly what he wanted to do with *Triumph Over Pain*, having solicited a detailed memo from Paramount's editing department in June, almost as soon as production was done, to make the story unfold more conventionally. I would guess that DeSylva handed Sturges the fait accompli of a reedited *Triumph Over Pain* toward the end of December. Sturges's conditional surrender followed in February and March 1943, when he wrote a new, much less aggressive foreword. By late April 1943 the picture, now retitled *The Great Moment*, was ready for release.

But it wasn't released. Neither was *The Miracle of Morgan's Creek*. Paramount held them both back while Sturges finished shooting *Hail the Conquering Hero*. Mixed responses to the previews of the latter film, in late 1943, prompted DeSylva to subject it to a fate similar to that of *Triumph Over Pain*. With three films blocked and his contract about to expire, Sturges exercised his right to leave the studio.

He was not yet done with Paramount, though, or with *Triumph Over Pain/The Great Moment*. When Paramount at last released *The Miracle of Morgan's Creek*, in January 1944, it immediately vindicated Sturges, becoming his greatest box-office hit. The next month brought further vindication: Paramount previewed DeSylva's reedited *Hail the Conquering Hero* to a dismal response. When Sturges offered to return to Paramount to fix the picture, without salary, the studio could only say yes.

But when Sturges subsequently appealed to DeSylva's boss, Y. Frank Freeman, to let him do the same for *Triumph Over Pain*, the answer was a flat no. Paramount dropped its muddled *The Great Moment* into London theaters in July 1944 and in August started to roll out the movie in the United States. Sturges had come to the end of his five-year campaign to present the story of W. T. G. Morton—and all other reviled benefactors of humankind—as he'd envisioned it, and was now effectively on his own: a writer-director without a studio.

He was not the only one.

In April 1942, when Sturges went into production on *Triumph Over Pain*, his funhouse double Orson Welles was on leave from RKO, shooting the intended four-part nonfiction feature *It's All True* on location in Brazil. Though the project might seem to have been twice blessed—it was begun as part of the U.S. war effort under the auspices of the Co-Ordinator of Inter-American Affairs, Nelson Rockefeller, who also happened to be a major shareholder in RKO—the studio's executives felt Welles was off on a frolic of his own, burdening them with an expensive boondoggle they'd never sell to U.S. audiences. (It was in many ways the most politically radical film Welles would ever undertake.) The RKO executives were also upset at Welles for having left for Brazil before he'd finished editing *The Magnificent Ambersons* (though Rockefeller's office had ordered him to do just that) and were unimpressed by his efforts to supervise the work from Rio. Welles knew that if he wanted to protect *Ambersons*, he would have to drop *It's All True* and return to Los Angeles; but he had an official commitment to the film he was now shooting and had begun to feel emotional and political attachments to it as well. He went on as if he might somehow save *Ambersons* at long distance.[3]

A change in studio ownership and wretched previews—some Wellesians believe RKO rigged them to yield a bad result—put an end to his hopes.[4] Around the same time in summer 1942 as Buddy DeSylva was commissioning a plan to reedit *Triumph Over Pain*, RKO cut *The Magnificent Ambersons* into something the executives thought was suitable. The picture went into release in August 1942 with a running time of eighty-eight minutes—down from the 131 of Welles's original cut—and with a happy ending slapped on. George Schaefer, the studio president who had brought Welles to RKO, was pushed out. Driving home the message of this front office revolution, Schaefer's successor, Charles Koerner, introduced a new corporate motto for RKO: "Showmanship in Place of Genius."

To put the matter in *The Magnificent Ambersons*'s terms, Welles had received his comeuppance, three times full and overflowing. It's tempting to ask what he'd done to deserve such treatment, other than give RKO two of the greatest films of all time, and why his downfall came just then, at a moment so close to Sturges's. The real question, though, might be why Hollywood had wanted Welles in the first place.

The answer, which of course says something about Sturges's career as well, has to do with the economic structure of Hollywood in the 1930s and the labor struggles that were endemic in the industry.

By the mid-1930s, the major studios were hungry for artists who could give them prestige. As Thomas Schatz explains in *The Genius of the System*, the industry found it was making its highest profits in the first-run market. To compete for that revenue, the studios needed to channel resources into pictures that would burnish their reputations and appeal to a relatively sophisticated urban audience, while investing less in fare that would fill out the bottom of a bill at small-town and rural theaters. Schatz cites the demise of the Warner Bros. B-movie unit—phased out of existence by 1940—as evidence of the market pressure during these years for high-quality productions.[5]

At the same time, the studios were also undergoing an internal reorganization that favored artistic expression. The model of centralized production that Irving Thalberg had perfected in the 1920s gave way by the mid-1930s to a system in which unit producers and producing directors enjoyed increased power over creative decisions. In part, this shift reflected the victory of the craft guilds and unions in winning collective bargaining rights after years of bitter, sometimes bloody confrontations with studio management. Department by department, the people who labored in movie factories gained a say in their wages and working conditions. The top talent—members of the actors', directors', and writers' guilds—even achieved a measure of influence over their assignments. It was only to be expected that producers, too, would enjoy more freedom, especially as front-office executives called on them to supply higher-quality pictures.

You can see how these tendencies played out in the career of William LeBaron, the Paramount producer who had agreed to let Sturges direct. Far from conforming to the stereotype of the Hollywood vulgarian, LeBaron was a college-educated Midwesterner who got his start as a songwriter, Broadway librettist, and magazine editor. The late 1920s found him heading production at RKO, where he oversaw lavishly designed blockbusters such as *The Case of Sergeant Grischa*, *Cimarron*, and *Rio Rita*. These were the sort of pictures that the studios would want a decade later—but with the onset of the Depression, LeBaron's timing was off. Having lost money for RKO, he moved to Paramount, a studio that especially favored the unit-producer model; and there, while making films with the likes of Mae West and W. C. Fields, he worked his way back up to bigger productions: *The General Died at Dawn*, *Union Pacific*, *Beau Geste*, and *If I Were King* (screenplay by Preston Sturges).

LeBaron's character and experience, and the context of Paramount in the late 1930s, suggest why he was willing to take a chance on Sturges, a man who was as yet untested as a director but who clearly knew a lot about comedy and was highly motivated to work on schedule and within budget. LeBaron perceived that Sturges might give Paramount not just a marketable picture but an award-winner, and he understood how much that would benefit the studio.

RKO's George Schaefer, by contrast, had no hands-on experience of making movies—he was a veteran of the sales and distribution side of the business—but the policies he set when he became president were in keeping with the same trends that Paramount experienced. As Richard Jewell notes in *RKO Radio Pictures: A Titan Is Born*, Schaefer began his tenure in 1939 by drawing up a production plan that emphasized big pictures and severely curtailed mid-size or "borderline" productions. Declaring that he would search for "important" properties and make deals with independent producers, Schaefer began a series of high-toned literary adaptations (*Ivanhoe*, *Little Men*, *Tom Brown's School Days*) and brought independents such as Samuel Goldwyn and Gabriel Pascal into RKO. (The latter controlled the film rights to Shaw's plays.) Schaefer's move to sign Welles was not an anomaly but rather one more rational element of a plan to buy prestige.

But by the middle of 1942, conditions had changed again, in ways that were unfavorable to Welles and Sturges. The industrial ramp-up toward America's entry into World War II had given the economy a dose of military Keynesianism, putting money into people's pockets, and by extension into theater admissions. Schatz reports that the combined profits of the eight biggest studios increased from $19.4 million in 1940 to $35 million in 1941, and then reached $50 million in 1942.[6] To oversimplify, the studios now enjoyed the wartime collaboration of the federal government and an all-but-captive home-front audience clamoring for distraction.

They were also starting to see that they might not need to keep high-priced talent under contract. One development of the guilds' victories in the 1930s and the greater frequency of independent production was that top-rank actors, directors, and writers sought more opportunities to work as free agents. The studios were perfectly happy to go along, paying them as needed and letting them go otherwise. As Schatz notes, a change in the tax code encouraged such autonomy. Individuals who were able to incorporate themselves could hold on to a much greater share of their income by receiving it as company profits, rather than salary. Although nobody foresaw it at the time, this was the start of the self-dismantling of the studio system. By the end of the decade, the studios would be moving production offshore, selling off real estate holdings, and curtailing their contracted workforce in one of the corporate world's early exercises in outsourcing and globalization.

That was where the economic logic would lead. But to pull the story back to 1942: the studios at that time still wanted to produce big pictures with prestigious artists such as Welles and Sturges. If Welles and Sturges seemed too headstrong, though, the studios were now in an excellent financial and managerial position to let them go. It didn't matter how the resident geniuses had reached this point—that one of them was a staunch Popular Front supporter who had always preferred to run his own operation, while the other detested unions and had flourished artistically only after assimilating himself into a studio. Both had become expendable.

The protagonist of *Triumph Over Pain* is emphatically not a genius; but he, too, becomes an expendable man after great achievement, not so much because of mistreatment by individual specimens of *Homo sapiens* as through an indifference that seems built into society. Like Sturges, the Morton of the film falls victim to the logic of a social and economic order; and like Sturges, he exhibits a certain talent for self-torture.

It's still possible, with a little effort, to trace the outlines of this theme. DeSylva did most of his considerable damage by reshuffling and oversimplifying the first of the three main sections of *Triumph Over Pain*. The other two remain intact in large part, though altered in effect, in Paramount's *The Great Moment*. By watching *The Great Moment*, which is available on disc, and comparing it to the screenplay of *Triumph Over Pain*, you can get a sense of what the picture might have been: one of Sturges's most formally daring works, which offers ample rewards for your curiosity while trying your patience with some of his worst tendencies.

Triumph Over Pain begins with act 3 of Morton's story: the long years of suffering after his downfall. (*The Great Moment* begins here as well, though with a difference. DeSylva spliced in all sorts of cheerier interpolations, which fail to lighten the mood but succeed brilliantly in baffling the viewer.) After this section, both *Triumph Over Pain* and *The Great Moment* proceed to act 1—episodes of Morton's youth and his pursuit of a method for painless dentistry—and then culminate in act 2: scenes of Morton's ambition to extend the method into the field of general surgery, leading to the climactic self-sacrifice.

In fairness to DeSylva (the first and last time I will write those words), what we can discern of act 1 of *Triumph Over Pain* is almost unbearable. After a few introductory throat-clearings, Sturges's intended cut begins in a retrospective and funerary mood, reminiscent of the framing device of *The Power and the Glory*. There, a middle-aged fellow had sat down with his wife to recount and justify the career of his recently deceased best friend, the film's flawed hero. Here, the middle-aged fellow is Morton's loyal friend Eben Frost (William Demarest, looking as if he'd wandered absently into his nineteenth-century costume and couldn't find the way out). Sitting down with Morton's widow Lizzie (Betty Field), Eben listens, and listens, as she laments her husband's flawed career and early death.

In its surviving fragments, this opening plays like an elocution lesson spoken by a plaster figure. Lizzie carries on and on with her voice rising and falling hypnotically, her eyes staring into the middle distance as if focused on the ghost of her husband (or perhaps an assistant director who might remind Sturges that it's time for lunch). Meanwhile Demarest, having been given nothing to do, abandons himself to uncharacteristic immobility. This is Sturges in his tragic mode. He is serious; he is instructive; he is lugubrious.

Slog past this monologue into the scenes of youth, where Lizzie is the daughter of a boarding house proprietor and Morton is her impecunious suitor, and you're still not in the clear. Whatever respect Sturges was willing to afford Lizzie, he has expended it in the opening solemnities. For the rest of the picture, she will be the opposite of a venturesome Sturges heroine: a mere adjunct to her husband and a burdensome one at that, decorative, spoiled, flighty, and complaining. Worse still: she owns a black lap dog she calls Nig. It hardly matters whether Sturges meant this detail to amuse or to demonstrate Lizzie's shallowness as a Southern belle. Many contemporary viewers will choose this as the not-great moment to stop watching.

But for the patient souls who remain willing to keep toggling between watching *The Great Moment* and reading *Triumph Over Pain*, what awaits is an astonishingly complex, moving, and credible story about two intertwined processes of discovery—one scientific, the other moral—and the marriage that they almost ruin.

Sturges's concern with the emotional side of this discovery, as much as his flouting of narrative convention, moved Paramount to recut the film. DeSylva was willing for Sturges to show how Morton stumbled forward, step after unsteady step, to learn the use of ether; but caring only for that practical side, he would not allow Sturges to spoil the plot (as he imagined would happen) by having Morton talk in an early flashback about the culmination of his scientific work in the first surgical application of anesthesia. DeSylva didn't see that, to Sturges, a conversation about the surgery at the start of the film gave away nothing essential but was mere foreshadowing. The movie was to reach its true climax just *before* the operation, in a moment of moral illumination and self-sacrifice.

Sturges's plan was to begin with the gloom of Lizzie and Eben's postmortem reflections and then jump back in time to the celebration after his historic operation. At that point, all is giddiness, satisfaction, and marital concord, with Lizzie asking Morton to forgive her for not having understood his long hours of obsessive work. Then, as husband and wife prepare for bed, Morton cautiously confesses that to complete his achievement—to gain permission from Massachusetts General Hospital for his method to be used—he'd been required to reveal the chemical composition of his anesthetic, which until then had been the trade secret of his lucrative practice in dentistry.

Suddenly, according to the screenplay, Lizzie is "on the verge of hysteria." She wants to know if Morton has been "such a fool" as to give away "the most valuable secret in the world." He replies, miserably, that there had been no other way: "They were going to take her leg off without it."

"Whose leg?" she demands. To which Morton replies, ending the scene, "I don't know . . . some servant girl!"[7]

With this astonishing exchange, the screenplay leaps far beyond the limits of a cut-and-dried chronicle into the realm of drama. To keep a socially insignificant stranger from unnecessary suffering, this man has abruptly risked the basis of his fortune and put his marriage in danger, and the audience does not yet know why.

Viewers of *The Great Moment* still get to see Joel McCrea, as Morton, come to this momentous choice in the final scene, as Sturges had intended. But the Paramount release does not alert you that this decision will be the central issue in the film, nor does it permit you to experience the dramatic irony in full, knowing in advance, with certainty, what Morton can't foresee: that the most noble deed he will ever perform will be his undoing. *The Great Moment* begins simplistically, mechanistically, as the story of a frustrated man trying to collect a reward from the federal government and enforce a patent. *Triumph Over Pain* begins as the story of a man who is proud and yet a little puzzled about having committed a sudden, extraordinary act of kindness, optimistic and yet a little worried about being able to claim the honor and profit that should be his due.

The Great Moment eliminates one other strand of the exposition of *Triumph Over Pain*, with equally damaging results. In narrating the troubles Morton faced after he revealed the secret of ether, Sturges's screenplay consistently shows individuals and groups volunteering financial and moral support. The trustees of Massachusetts General Hospital provide a thousand dollars and a testimonial. A French academy sends a large medal inscribed "to the benefactor of Mankind." Even the banker who holds the mortgage on Morton's rural house steps forward to help. Instead of foreclosing, as he could do immediately, and putting the young family out of its home, he suggests that Morton stay on the property and pay off his debt by farming. By including these instances of generosity, recognition, and gratitude, *Triumph Over Pain* enhances the audience's belief in the importance of Morton's achievement while making the man's struggle seem that much more poignant. Morton comes into focus as a decent, determined, but naïve and relatively uneducated man, who never anticipated being in a situation of such magnitude and is too small to handle it. By contrast, *The Great Moment* shows only the rebuffs, attacks, and humiliations that Morton suffers, and to which he seems to react almost mindlessly.

Paramount's version makes him a helpless and all-but-isolated victim of political chicanery, journalistic abuse, and mob hysteria—as if to confirm the very allegations against *Homo sapiens* that the studio had banned from Sturges's foreword. In

Sturges's version, though, we aren't necessarily such a bad species, one by one. It's the institutions established by *Homo sapiens*, and their hierarchies, that are likely to crush a person.

In acting out this drama, Joel McCrea is much like the ether that Morton uses in his work. He comes before the camera in "highly rectified" form, with the stolidity, obstinacy, and slight dimwittedness of his John L. Sullivan and Tom Jeffers purified into a pleasingly unheroic persona. While remaining the very picture of a Hollywood leading man, McCrea exposes the vulnerabilities that run through Morton's character even at his most single-minded.

As the young Morton, standing with Lizzie on a moonlit porch and hesitating to declare his feelings, McCrea worries with downward glances in a way that suggests something deeper than insecurity about her romantic interest. (He is, after all, still Joel McCrea—though with all the ruffles dripping from his shirt, he seems a bit ridiculous, as if he were being consumed by mushrooms from Outer Space.) Morton has just abandoned medical school because of its cost, and McCrea's tentativeness conveys a sense of the man's shame at his poverty. When Lizzie responds warmly to Morton, McCrea lends an almost pathetic eagerness to his immediate instinct, which is to promise to make good money in his new trade of dentistry.

In the first few scenes in Morton's dental office—exercises in greater and lesser degrees of slapstick—McCrea uses his size, bad temper, and harshest voice to cow others into submission. That is, he tries to. His failure to make anyone do as he orders seems like evidence of a secret wobbliness beneath the bluster. The patients might not want to challenge Morton by walking out right under his furious gaze, but as soon as he looks away, they're ready to slink.

Before the advent of ether: the threat of dental care.
Courtesy The Museum of Modern Art

Perhaps they've caught onto the softness in Morton, which McCrea reveals in his ensuing conversation with Lizzie. His problem isn't just that the screaming of the patients gets on his nerves—though McCrea seems rattled enough as he makes that charge. The worst of it is that "you'd have to be deaf or a demon or something, who *liked* to see people suffer." Here is the beginning of the search for anesthesia (a word he doesn't even know and will never quite learn to pronounce). His scientific curiosity seems to spring from Morton's sympathy with the people in his chair, as expressed by the way McCrea gnaws at his thumb throughout this tirade. Morton has complained that the patients bite him; now he's taken their place and is biting himself.

A keen awareness of the suffering of others, uncertainty about his status in the world, a lingering sense of humiliation about his level of education and income, a longing to prove himself to his wife: McCrea manages to play all these traits while keeping Morton's hot-headed determination on the surface, as the outward but not motivating element in his character. All these qualities contribute to the next stage of Morton's moral and scientific development, as he consults with his old medical school professor Dr. Charles Jackson (Julius Tannen) and gradually translates prideful obstinacy into something more admirable: an ability to stand firm in the face of authority.

Having now reached the point where Dr. Jackson begins to figure in the movie, both in the plot and in Morton's emotional life, this might be a good time to pause over a peculiar feature of *Triumph Over Pain/The Great Moment*: the way in which Sturges diverges in this film from the ordinary use of his stock company. This time, he brings out darker notes in his actors.

Tannen, for example, had entered the Sturges company as *Christmas in July*'s Mr. Zimmerman, the kindly but excitable old gent with the thick Yiddish accent. Sturges was to use Tannen repeatedly as this stock figure, most often as an immigrant merchant or tradesman who has gone too far in taking an American name (Rafferty in *The Miracle of Morgan's Creek*) or whose Lower East Side manner isn't quite up to the Frenchified image of his store (*The Palm Beach Story*). The deferential public defender that Tannen plays in *Sullivan's Travels* and the pince-nezed divorce attorney who declares everything "highly irregular" in *The Lady Eve* are essentially the same Jewish type, one generation removed from Castle Garden.

But in *Triumph Over Pain/The Great Moment*, Tannen plays Harvard Medical School's "sarcastic old blow-hard" Jackson: an officious drunk who speaks in an overbearing Boston bray, laughs in Morton's face, and berates his former student as a congenital dullard who ought to have stayed where people of his class belong, behind a plow, rather than clutter a medical school. It's a deliberately grating and thoroughly rounded characterization—the biggest that Tannen would ever undertake for Sturges. As Diane Jacobs reports, Sturges praised Tannen to others for the exceptional fineness of his acting.[8] This was no doubt the performance he had in mind.

It also seems significant that of all the actors available to Sturges, Tannen was the one he chose for this role. He's so convincing that a viewer might imagine Jackson as the unpleasant reality hidden beneath Tannen's more genial persona. Scratch a Zimmerman or Rafferty, and you find intellectual arrogance, snobbism, mockery, and avarice. I would of course be dismayed if I thought Sturges was imputing these faults to Jews in general; but I don't think that's what's going on. Rather, I think he's implicitly grappling with a fault of his own—his reliance on stereotypes—by digging beneath the surface.

This excavation proceeds up and down the cast list of *Triumph Over Pain/The Great Moment*. Esther Howard, once the flirtatious "fortune teller" of *The Great McGinty* and the genteel but oversexed widow of *Sullivan's Travels*, is now laid bare as a pathetic streetwalker, whose john beat her and broke one of her teeth. In the role of Horace Wells, Morton's one-time friend and new rival, Louis Jean Heydt exposes the nasty underlayer of pride, reckless ambition, and entitlement beneath the role he'd played as the sappy, self-pitying Johnny of *The Great McGinty*. Porter Hall, who had seemed like such a clever, self-possessed executive in *Sullivan's Travels*, now shows himself to be a mediocre, indecisive time-server as President Franklin Pierce. Most troubling of all is the change in the perennial sidekick, William Demarest. He still shadows the leading man and takes care of his needs; but his street smarts and pugnacity have been rubbed away, revealing a base of dumb, servile masochism. As Eben Frost, the fiddler who assists Morton in his experiments, Demarest willingly reduces himself to the function of a pincushion, allowing himself to be pricked over and over while lying in an etherized stupor.

If you think about *Triumph Over Pain/The Great Moment* in isolation, you can take these performances at face value as strong, memorable portrayals of the characters at hand. But if you recall the importance of existing types to Sturges, and his practice of writing roles with specific actors in mind, and if you then think about these casting decisions within the rest of his work, a program comes into view. Sturges is systematically undermining whatever might be charming, worthy of affection, or simply forgivable in the characters with which he usually populates his movies. In so doing, he gives the boastful name of *Homo sapiens* its rudest, most deflating translation. Who could be more of a "wise guy" than Dr. Charles Jackson?

The spirit of Sturges's original foreword lives on in these pairings of characters with actors. But if that were the whole of the experience—if Sturges were doing no more than giving vent to the spirit of Thersites—then *Triumph Over Pain/The Great Moment* would not be so affecting, nor would the problem that it lays out be so complex.

The difficulty isn't simply the conflict between good people and bad, but also the tension between good people and their institutions. Sturges assumes the necessity of courts of law, military procurement offices, medical societies, and the like and admits that the rules by which they function may do "much more good than harm" (as one of the film's most admirable characters says). And yet these institutions show a brutal disregard for the individual. Worse: the hierarchies they keep in place can provide a refuge for the base, the stupid, and the self-interested, while obstructing the efforts of Morton and others of good will.

As I've noted, Morton has his friends and champions, notably Dr. John Collins Warren of Massachusetts General Hospital (played by the forever down-to-earth Harry Carey), whose benevolent open-mindedness and humble manner make him the counterweight to Dr. Jackson. But Warren can do only so much, given the standards he's bound to respect, while Morton, with his professional and intellectual limitations, can only blunder ahead, sometimes as if in a willing quest for self-harm.

If *Triumph Over Pain/The Great Moment* had a money shot, this would be it:

Morton has been carting home bottles of ether late at night and experimenting in the parlor, with comic results. He inadvertently lays himself out on the carpet like a drunk, chases the dog on all fours, smashes knickknacks, and dopes the goldfish, all of which periodically rouses Lizzie from her bed to scold him. But now when she comes downstairs with her candle and Southern belle flightiness, alarmed by a strange smell, the tone changes. Finding her husband slumped at his desk, unconscious from the first experiment he's conducted on himself, she screams in terror. The shriek awakens Morton just enough that he lifts his eyelids groggily and slurs a few words of pride and pleasure that he "never felt it." Then the camera pans down through the nocturnal gloom to show what Lizzie has seen: his left hand, impaled clean through on a letter spike.

Especially after the comic build-up, the sight is sufficiently gruesome to make even today's audiences shiver. In 1942 (and '43, and '44), when blood seldom flowed on-screen no matter how many people were shot or stabbed, the shock must have been extraordinary—all the more so given the inescapable connotation of crucifixion. In a single image, Sturges makes palpable Morton's identification with his patients' suffering (he's no longer merely biting his thumb), claims an heroic level of strength and determination for the character, and foreshadows the capacity for self-sacrifice that will be essential to the film's climax. All this, as well as confirming the touching vulnerability of his protagonist, who as a researcher is not just isolated but also poorly equipped, inadequately informed, and clumsy.

The events that follow the Night of the Letter Spike continue to combine slapstick (Morton's first encounter with Eben Frost and original misadventure with dental anesthesia), mounting excitement (the runaway success of Morton's practice, once he gets the ether right), and horror (the observation of an

Marital harmony, achieved through love, good business prospects, and a bottle of ether. Courtesy The Museum of Modern Art

amputation performed in Dr. Warren's surgical theater). The momentum of rising action carries the film without interruption past the boundary of the second act into the third, which begins in mid-scene with Eben Frost still anesthetized in the chair:

MORTON: If I could make this sleep last a little longer.... Lizzie, *I tell you I can do it.*
LIZZIE: You mean fill teeth in some—
MORTON (interrupting): Nothing to do with teeth.

You don't know which of Morton's traits has contributed most to this leap of insight: scientific curiosity, a tradesman's ambition, the desire to prove himself to the Jacksons of the world, or the long-ago promise of middle-class comfort he made on the moonlit porch. (It's crucial that the sometimes-impatient recipient of that promise just happens to be in the office to witness his first successful use of ether, and to hear but not understand his brainstorm.) What's important is that all the motivations are now advancing as one, with Sturges's characteristic rapidity driving them onward. The brooding rhythms of act 1 have fallen away. Nothing like them will recur until the very end, when Morton will have to make his decision.

The setting at that climax is a shadowy, low-ceilinged hallway in Massachusetts General Hospital. There's something vaguely ecclesiastical about the architecture, with the broad ribs of its vaults receding into the depths of the picture. When Morton and his sidekick Frost have been in this space before, they've always violated its dignity: sneaking through it into forbidden areas, or running full-tilt across the tiles because they've arrived late, or even collapsing onto the floor because Frost has fainted at the sight of an operation. But as Morton now walks slowly toward the camera, it's clear that he's a changed man: no longer the rude mechanical who attacked dental patients with his collar askew and a large mallet sticking out of his coat pocket, but a silent, solitary figure who has acquired gravitas.

According to the screenplay, he's mulling over a problem that "is too great for him." The dilemma foreshadowed in act 1 of the screenplay is now upon him—whether to reveal that his proprietary drug is just common ether, or to guard the secret and allow surgical patients to go on suffering—and he can't make up his mind. Enveloped in a physical atmosphere that seems as meditative as his mood, Morton steps into a shaft of light and looks to his left, toward the sounds of an off-screen murmuring. In a

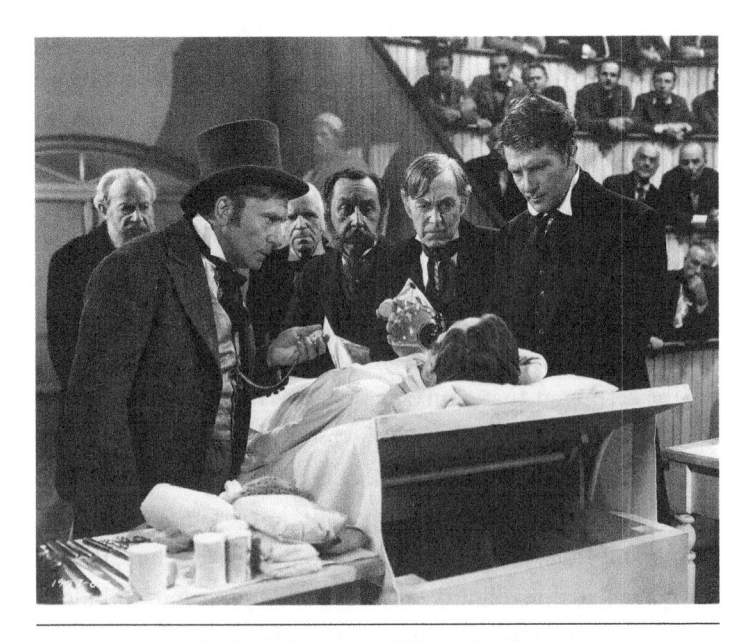

Eben Frost, Dr. John Warren, and W. T. G. Morton observe the first general surgery performed under anesthesia. Courtesy The Museum of Modern Art

side corridor that might just as well be an apse, a priest kneels by the gurney of the nameless servant girl whose leg is about to be lopped off.

Sturges had never before attempted a scene in a register of such pathos and hushed, quasi-religious solemnity. The closest equivalents would be the backwoods church service in *Sullivan's Travels*—but that's brightly lit and full of vigor—and Lizzie's retrospective monologue in the first act of *Triumph Over Pain/ The Great Moment*, in which she might be called saintly, if you think of sanctitude as stilted. Here, though, there's no sense that you're watching plaster figures in a niche, despite the all-too-obvious choice of "Ave Maria" for the soundtrack music. Some viewers find it cloying; but a young Catholic girl is at prayer, and Sturges has made you aware that real flesh and blood are at risk.

He also has facts at his command to help ward off sentimentality. He knows the full name of the young woman on the gurney, Alice Mohan (though he doesn't use it in the dialogue). He knows, as did his audience, that corridors and windows in older hospitals often do have a look of the cloister, as a vestige of their historic roots in the church and an assertion that medicine is a high vocation. Above all, he knows that Morton in fact surrendered his trade secret—a piece of information the audience would have had as well, if his cut of the film had been preserved. The audience, wanting to see the realization of its foreknowledge from act 1, would have imaginatively urged Morton to act. Even without this extra impetus, though, Morton's demonstrated sympathy for the suffering of others pushes him forward. So, too, does his lingering respect for the institution of medicine, as represented by the architecture that surrounds him and as embodied by Dr. Warren, who waits in the surgical theater.

As Orson Welles said of the bullfighting story that he'd intended to incorporate into his South American picture—a yarn about a bull so brave that it's pardoned in the ring and allowed to live—"all of this is nonsense except that it's true."[9] But as Welles also knew, truth in the movies is only as persuasive as the director who wields it. At the conclusion of *Triumph Over Pain/The Great Moment*, despite the "Ave Maria," Sturges is compelling.

He positions Morton and Alice in the center—Alice's gurney lying parallel to the picture frame, Morton standing behind her as he faces the camera—with heavy wooden doors running across the back, blocking the view and confining the figures to a shallow foreground. You'd hardly even notice that the panels are doors rather than a wall, except that a narrow, arched transom at the top allows a glimpse of faces beyond: men sitting in tiers in the surgical theater. As soon as Morton lifts his head and announces his decision—no one will ever again have to suffer—the doors swing back as if on their own, the space of the shot opens to an unexpected depth, and Morton turns away from the camera, to walk toward an ecstatic Dr. Warren.

That's all. As director, Sturges deletes almost a page of unnecessary screenplay dialogue so that the full impact of the climax can come from a single image: the theatrical revelation of a new vista—the future, you'd think—combined with the bittersweet sight of a departing Morton, momentarily in glory but stepping toward the vanishing point of twenty years of emotional pain. The brevity, the compression, are stunning; the sense of asymmetry, vertiginous. (You are in the middle of a story, the rest of which has just dropped into an abyss.) The absence of any summarizing talk, any closing text or moral, cuts off sentiment as sharply as a scalpel.

Whatever rancors and frustrations Sturges may have poured into his portrait of Morton, however much he warped the film's foreword into a diatribe, he ended with an abruptness that's possible only for someone who has taken the selfless long view. This is how history is made: by people who grope and fumble and sometimes achieve great things to their own detriment. Step back and see, because that's how you stop being a wise guy and attain some understanding.

For his pains in reaching this understanding, Sturges would lose his career at Paramount. But he would still have two films to go at the studio. They would be two of his best; and now that he'd broached the theme of heroism, he would continue it in both.

7

PSYCHOLOGY

The Miracle of Morgan's Creek

Perhaps the miracle of *Morgan's Creek* is that the film was made at all.

The Hays Office, the Office of War Information, and Buddy DeSylva all objected to the very idea of the movie—and behind these authorities loomed self-appointed censors such as the Catholic League of Decency, preemptively fuming like volcanic deities whom the officials had to propitiate. Everyone understood that it might be permissible to tell the story of a young woman who gets pregnant without benefit of a marriage certificate, or for that matter an identifiable husband, so long as the film was a melodrama or a cautionary tale. But it would be distasteful for Sturges to treat the young woman as a sympathetic figure, more inept than blameworthy, whose predicament becomes something to laugh about. It would be disloyal of him during wartime to make the instrument of her pregnancy a combat-bound U.S. soldier, who blithely disappears like an unholy ghost. And it would be blasphemous to rescue the young woman as Sturges meant to do by having her deliver the fruit of this sin on Christmas, not once but six times, in an excess of fecundity that makes her almost as famous as the Virgin Mary, and much harder working.

The project was impossible. Yet despite the Hays Office's seven-page, single-spaced letter detailing everything that Sturges was not allowed to do, the memos from on high ordering him to show that GIs were *not* drunken skirt-chasers (even though the plot plausibly said they were), and the many evidences of DeSylva's kindly oversight ("these scenes must be rewritten and approved as I never liked them anyway"),[1] *The Miracle of Morgan's Creek* finally burst into theaters in January 1944, having been held back for a full year after completion, looking very much like the movie Sturges had intended to set loose.

The opening, frantic beyond even the standard of *Sullivan's Travels* and *The Palm Beach Story*, plays as if the energy that Paramount and the censors were struggling to contain had just broken free. Vic Potel and Julius Tannen, got up to resemble a small-town newspaper editor and a music-store proprietor, begin the show on a decorous note by racing full-speed at the camera, shouting incoherently and waving their arms. The faraway target of their excitement—Brian Donlevy, brought back for a guest appearance as Governor McGinty—picks up the telephone to speak with them and promptly sets his pants on fire. He dumps a glass of water into his lap—it's the quickest solution—while Tannen, on the other end of the line, keeps throwing his hands into the air as he kibitzes in his ripest Yiddish mode, until Potel has to reach over and restrain him. Meanwhile, more and more people crowd into the cross-cut settings, packing the frame with curiosity and uselessness. Reprising his role as the Boss, Akim Tamiroff strolls in, hears that the hubbub is about a place called Morgan's Creek, and automatically proposes that it must need a dam; but the suggestion has already come too late and is much too little. Nothing is going to hold back this movie's flood of animal high spirits, or the splinters of social convention it bears along.

Or maybe the opening merely reflects how hectic the production turned out to be.

Sturges spent mid-October 1942 repeatedly reworking a partial script in an attempt to accommodate everyone's objections. He began shooting, as scheduled, on October 21—just in time to receive the full set of demands from the Hays Office. As a result, as Brian Henderson writes, he "started shooting without even a first version of a finished script. This was the only time in his career that he did so."[2]

Such quasi-improvisatory methods were frowned upon in the studios but not unknown. Leo McCarey, for example, had made up much of *The Awful Truth* on set (as James Harvey learned when he interviewed Irene Dunne for his book *Romantic Comedy in Hollywood*).[3] But McCarey had got his start as a gagman in silent comedy. Sturges was a much different kind of artist, who now had to go home to the typewriter each night and try to get a step ahead of his own production. He was seven weeks into the shoot before he completed the script, on December 10. By then, he'd already put himself and his cast and crew through an experience that was uproarious at times, with the actors unable to get through their scenes without laughing, and at others nearly intolerable. James Curtis reports that Sturges was so overbearing toward Betty Hutton, who played the lead role of Trudy, and Diana Lynn, who played her kid sister Emmy, that they repeatedly broke down weeping.[4] Diane Jacobs quotes Eddie Bracken, who played the accidentally heroic Norval, as saying he eventually felt the need to threaten violence. Although he was cast (as usual) as a put-upon, rubber-limbed shnook, Bracken had been a champion amateur boxer. After one too many directorial explosions that he deemed unnecessary, he looked Sturges in the eye, smiled, and explained his objection with his right hand cocked.[5]

All this was hard enough. But in making *The Miracle of Morgan's Creek* this way, Sturges caused yet another difficulty: he challenged the premise of this book. However carefully he planned the theme and plot and worked out the characters' natures—his preparation, as Henderson documents, was exhaustive—and however dictatorially he behaved on set, it's clear that happenstance, off-the-cuff invention, and his cast's proclivities all shaped the outcome. Under these conditions, did he really live up to my claim and make a work that coheres as an argument?

In this case, maybe he didn't need to. You might say that he'd done a great enough service by revolting against the stultifying, transparent hypocrisy of Hollywood filmmaking, which is as much as to say the enforced moralism of American culture itself. The long lines at the box office for this runaway hit suggested that the public felt the rebellion was overdue, and that Sturges had gotten away with it by making one of the funniest movies of all time. But for all his cussedness, he was not one to tear things down for the sheer glee of destruction. *The Miracle of Morgan's Creek* is not *L'Age d'or*. It seems reasonable to ask what he left standing, or perhaps even built up, in place of the falsehoods he'd dynamited.

His working notes, which Henderson reviews, give the first inkling of an answer.

As Sturges struggled to define the story, he reminded himself that "The classic form for this type of comedy is to plunge the heroine into trouble and keep her in ever-increasing trouble until she triumphs over all by the very degree of her trouble."[6] Soon, identifying a character type who would prompt such a narrative, he wrote that the film would concern "a well-meaning but clumsy and impulsive kid in a small town: the type who tore the seat out of her dress at the high school graduation exercises" and "can't remember names, including the name of a departing soldier whom she marries impulsively, or the town in which it happened. All in all, Trudy Kockenlocker is quite a girl, but being innocent, she is also the elect of God and accordingly protected." The next step was to invent Norval's character, making him into a second hapless, trouble-prone innocent, but one who would suffer everything for Trudy's sake and ultimately achieve an unmerited triumph beyond even hers.

With Trudy and Norval coming into focus, the presence of McGinty and the Boss in the frame story became more than a brief, self-referential joke. Their movie was about the danger to a crook of doing so much as one honest thing. Trudy and Norval live in a movie about the opposite danger: the devilish complications that two people put themselves into when they feel moved to lie and cheat without having the ingrained skill. They're like the Yankee bank employee in *The Great McGinty* who ruined his life through "one crazy moment" of dishonesty—except they're not mopes like him, and their "crazy moment" is deliciously prolonged, and at the end they're still naïfs, who happen to benefit from an outstandingly corrupt pair of *dei ex machina*.

Even at first glance, an intuition about innocence, and perhaps election, begins to peek through Sturges's wised-up travesty of the Nativity. Although his cynicism was never more active than here, he tempers it with the notion that even the greediest earthly powers may do some good. (You might say that McGinty and the Boss function as Magi, delivering gifts to the wondrous offspring. The third Magus, I suppose, is the press.) But this is only as much as you can get from the frame story.

Over the course of the full four-act structure, *The Miracle of Morgan's Creek* turns out to be a story about the blessings of emotional breakdown—a series of breakdowns, in fact, in which one character after another, having been made grotesque by the conventions of small-town life, at last finds them insupportable. Not that Sturges knew anything about small-town America. His experience of it seems to have been limited to passing through a few little places on the train, when he'd relocated from New York to Los Angeles with his lover and superbly canny secretary Bianca Gilchrist. But Sturges knew the conventions of portraying small towns in the movies—he'd deployed them himself, mostly in films written for other directors—and he knew the dynamics of human personality, which was enough. His Morgan's Creek resembles a movie small town in its appearance (borrowed from materials left behind from other pictures) and in its cast (Georgia Caine, for example, as the very image of a motherly landlady), while resembling a real small town principally in the way it compresses the residents. They're continually aware of one another, continually on show, with the result (in Sturges's view) that their hearts, too, become compressed and warped.

True to its allusions to the Nativity, the film is a redemption narrative, in which a handful of people are freed from the deformations that have been worked into them by living in a tightly packed version of America. The salvation that Sturges offered American cinema as a whole through *The Miracle of Morgan's Creek* he extended internally as well, to his characters.

Given that it's about a community, *The Miracle of Morgan's Creek* is less the story of a woman and a man than the tale of two of each.

The sisters seem almost inseparable, with fourteen-year-old Emmy continually conspiring with Trudy, staying by her side even for consultations with the doctor and lawyer, and at the end standing in for her semiconscious sister as the temporary keeper of her brood. For his part, Norval is tightly linked with William Demarest as Constable Kockenlocker—"tightly" as in grabbed by the shirt, throttled, threatened at the point of several guns, and eventually invited, even begged, to inflict assaults of his own. Norval touches Trudy lightly several times throughout the film; he even kisses her once; but the member of the family with whom he's most intimately, physically caught up turns out to be the raging father.

When characters pair off like this, you begin to wonder what draws them together beyond circumstances invented for the sake of a plot. What deficiencies do they overcome in one another? What unspoken, perhaps unequal emotional exchange do they carry out? These aren't questions you'd ask about McGinty and the Boss, whose mutual reliance is so practical a matter, apart from the desire of each to prove he's the tougher. Betty in *Christmas in July* and The Girl in *Sullivan's Travels* hardly have enough substance to lend any to Jimmy or Sullivan, who aren't the type to give back, anyway. As for John D. Hackensacker III and the Wienie King, Gerry does seem to feel some affection for each, of the kind you'd have for a toaster that's served you well. *The Miracle of Morgan's Creek*, though, takes us into different territory. I would be embarrassed to become deep-dish, as Sturges would have said, and call its motives psychological, except that the film announces the possibility as soon as the story begins.

The camera looks down on the central intersection of Morgan's Creek—apparently the only intersection busy enough to require a traffic cop—where Kockenlocker stands in the middle, keeping order (as he sees it) by shouting insults and issuing threats. The lowering of the camera from on high is a condescension of sorts, as if the film were proposing Kockenlocker as a suitable case for observation. He certainly seems disturbed, as he yells at GIs who have done nothing worse than ask for directions, or information about young women they might invite to a dance. The peace officer is at the point of provoking violence when a sergeant in the military police—played by Sturges's unchallengeable bruiser Frank Moran—comes by to settle things down. "This is Mr. Kockenlocker," he informs the soldiers ("with exaggerated courtesy," as the screenplay specifies), "a sergeant in the other war"—a point that explains why Kockenlocker feels free to call the young GIs "rookies" but does nothing to resolve the mystery of his uncontrollable animosity. Maybe Kockenlocker is one of those doughboys who never entirely came home from the trenches. While that thought hangs in the air, the MP calmly sends the soldiers away and instructs a temporarily mollified Kockenlocker on the modern method of exerting control, which does not involve immediate recourse to the truncheon. It's all done with kindness, the MP and his partner explain. "It's more psychological."

That word returns, strangely twisted, in a later scene that Sturges interpolated to assuage the military censors. He shows the GIs looking improbably clear-eyed and inspection-ready after the long, debauched night of partying that has left Trudy, without her knowing it yet, in an embarrassing situation. The soldiers are departing cheerfully for their next post, with every man accounted for and nobody in the brig. The MP reports the successful tally to his officer and then ends the scene on a note of satisfaction, saying to himself, "Psychology."

Why does the MP bungle a word he'd handled perfectly well in the first scene? I suppose it's because even then, the sound of it was too highfalutin in his gravelly mouth. By letting it roll on for too long now, with a hint of misplaced pride, he's confirming to the audience that the principles of this discipline are a mystery to him, and the name itself a pretension. And more: by making "psycholology" an object of faint ridicule, the MP wards off any suspicion that Sturges himself might have been interested in the stuff.

I can find no hard evidence that he was. His memoirs refer to psychiatrists just once, to disclaim his having any of their scientific knowledge. Nor did he seek their expertise for himself. The record of his activities at the peak of his career suggests a man determined to keep all his moments occupied, so there'd be no cubbyhole in which a vagrant introspective thought might hide. Still, his memoirs are full of keen observations about how the mind works. To give one example of many: there is the episode in which his first wife, Estelle, called at his mother's house, three years after the divorce, and Sturges (who happened to be there to let her in) failed to understand who she was, until she finally put down the coffee he'd served and identified herself. "Because I didn't love her anymore," Sturges concludes, "I didn't recognize in this rather ordinary-looking woman the Estelle that the eyes of love had imprinted on my memory. *She* hadn't changed; my perception of her had changed."[7]

If this is less than Freud, it's more than idle speculation. In fact, Sturges credits this insight with later enabling him to imagine how Charles Pike could be persuaded that he'd never before set eyes on the Lady Eve. I will take this as solid enough proof that Sturges liked to discover bits and pieces of psychology, in his unsystematic way, and put them to use in his work. By the time he came to make *The Miracle of Morgan's Creek*, other people in his business were equally willing to plumb the mind, and much more ready to talk about it.

The great age of psychoanalysis in movie scenarios was just beginning in the early 1940s, but people in Hollywood had been fascinated with the subject for a while. Samuel Goldwyn, a man who was clever enough to know the advantages of pretending to be a boob, was the first producer to pursue the new science, traveling to Vienna in 1924, accompanied by suitable press agents, to offer Sigmund Freud $100,000 for a screen story. It didn't matter that Freud would not receive Goldwyn, let alone his check. The public now knew that if you wanted a spicy movie made by someone who wasn't afraid to spend, you should see a Goldwyn picture.

In the 1930s, when many of the intellectuals and artists fleeing fascism settled in Los Angeles, a local culture of psychoanalysis took root. Naturally it was the most worldly people in the film business—the people with whom Sturges got along best—who liked to discuss these arresting new ideas, or who sought treatment. By the early 1940s, David O. Selznick and much of his family, Hollywood's royalty, were lying on a couch and talking to Dr. May Romm, and they didn't care who knew it.[8]

Psycholology was in the air. Sturges, as usual, did not want to let on that he was thinking about anything fancy. But given the environment and his own turn of mind, it would have been surprising if he hadn't gotten a little under the skin of his characters and given one of them—Norval Jones, say—a psychosomatic ailment.

"The spots." Scarcely has Norval edged his way into the movie—shuffling into the music store where Trudy works, so he can try to wheedle a date—than he's talking about the unexplained symptoms that keep him out of uniform. At first, it seems as if jealousy and wounded pride prompt the tale. A full squad of GIs has pushed to the counter to see Trudy, and Norval has observed, from the back, how she beams and poses for them. When they file out at last—maintaining such a boisterous camaraderie that they don't realize they're stepping on his feet—he suffers an even worse pang, listening to Trudy's vague, sing-song excuse that duty, and duty alone, compels her to attend a farewell dance for these soldiers, rather than go to the movies with him. He knows better than to believe her. And so, to prove he's as much of a man as any of them, Norval sputters into an account of his recurring misadventures at the Army physical: the mounting worry that he won't pass, the racing of his heart, and finally, swimming before his eyes, "the spots."

Leaning forward on the counter, almost touching his hand in sympathy, Trudy says "the spots" with him. She's evidently heard the story a hundred times. She can lip-sync to it as well as she'd mimed to a phonograph record only moments earlier, when she was entertaining the soldiers.

From this, you learn that Norval isn't merely a high-strung man given to fits of nervous half-blindness. He's the kind who talks about his symptoms all the time and does so while denying that there might be an underlying cause. (A couple of scenes later, sitting on the front-porch steps of his boardinghouse and repeating the same story to his landlady, Norval insists that "I'm as cool as ice" at the Army physical. Then the telephone rings, and with a shriek he splays his feet into the air and pancakes onto the steps.) I wouldn't go so far as to categorize Norval as an hysteric in the late-nineteenth-century sense, when the word was applied only to women; but in conventional mid-twentieth-century terms, he does have what would have been called an unmanly tendency to convert anxiety into physical signs of distress—thrashing, flailing, stammering, high-pitched whinnying—and an equally unmanly habit of brooding over his disorder.

When watching other films, viewers might feel no need to look beyond these behavioral traits; someone like Norval would be adequately understood as one more of Sturges's fleshed-out comic types. But the defining feature of *The Miracle of Morgan's Creek* is its combination of pure farce—spiraling plot complications, acrobatic pratfalls—with characterizations that are deeper than they need to be, if the goal were just to incite laughter.

As evidence, consider the backstory that Sturges invents for Norval. It's not so much of a history as to delay the proceedings for more than a beat, but enough so you understand that Norval was not born as an hysteric but came into his frazzledness gradually, and for a reason. It seems he grew up as an orphan—a fact that Norval doesn't care to mention but that Trudy callously points out. During her first long talk with him, when arguing that some of the departing soldiers have no families and therefore need volunteers, pretty ones, to see them off, she asks, "How about the orphans? Who says goodbye to them? *You* ought to know about *them*." To which Norval replies, with a little more bitterness than might be expected from this overly polite man, "The superintendent probably goes down from the asylum—for old times' sake."

With this stunningly efficient revelation, Sturges both informs you that Norval grew up in an asylum and invites you to think about a childhood without affection. If the closest thing that Norval can imagine to a loving farewell is a kiss from the superintendent—and clearly he can't imagine it—then the obsessiveness of his love for Trudy begins to be more than a prompt for laughter or pity. It becomes comprehensible. You understand that sexual desire for the prettiest girl of his childhood is too little to account for Norval's willingness to make any sacrifice for Trudy, to endure any humiliation. Throughout their schooldays, she must have extended the same solemn, cooing sympathy that she gives in the music store when listening yet again to his complaint about the spots. Back in school, too, it would have been a formulaic comfort—but who else would have offered it? For Norval, Trudy seems to have been his sole connection to the supposedly normal world from which he was excluded, a world of warm, familial relationships.

This is where the psychology of *The Miracle of Morgan's Creek* becomes truly strange—because out of all the women on whom Norval might have fixated, he's chosen one who is herself a semiorphan, having lost her mother at an early age. What's more, she's a woman who scarcely knows what a warm, affectionate household might be. She's grown up under the tutelage of Constable Kockenlocker.

What if Trudy in herself wasn't everything Norval had wanted? What if he'd chosen her so he could also have Kockenlocker?

Vistas of perversity unfold in the mind of the staggered moviegoer. At first it seems impossible; after all, Norval will do anything to avoid Kockenlocker, at least when returning a noticeably dizzy Trudy from the movie date she'd supposedly spent with him, and it's eight in the morning. But consider Norval's very first exchange with Kockenlocker, when picking up Trudy for the date that he doesn't yet know will be fake. Addressing the entire family, Norval says, "Hello, Trudy, hello, Emmy. Good evening, Mr. Kockenlocker, well, I'm certainly glad you're going to the picture with me." To which Kockenlocker replies, "Who, me?"

It's just an offhand bit of wordplay, but unsettling as well—because for a moment, a puzzled Kockenlocker seems to think that Norval *does* mean to take him to the movies. Then, compounding the confusion, Trudy responds to the pleasantry by saying, "I'm very glad to go with you, Norval," and sounds almost as if she's stepping forward to take her father's place.

This strange misdirection, of emotional drives as much as of words, reaches a crisis in the later scene where Norval comes back to the house with Trudy—by now, he knows everything and is trying to help her out of her jam—and Kockenlocker, sitting on his front porch and cleaning his guns, demands a man-to-man talk. There's been gossip about his daughter and Norval—Morgan's Creek is the sort of town where everybody knows everyone else's business—and Kockenlocker thinks he'd better cut it short by forcing an engagement, before Trudy gets into exactly the trouble he doesn't realize she's already in. That Norval is manifestly incapable of getting her into such trouble does not seem to enter Kockenlocker's mind. Waving one gun after another in the general direction of a stammering, mirthlessly cackling Norval, he insists on knowing not if but when they'll marry.

"She won't have me," Norval manages to blurt, after what appears to be a chain of petit mal seizures. "I just asked her."

To which Kockenlocker shoots back, "You didn't ask her right," and blows energetically through the barrel of the gun. The act is not quite as explicit as the direction Sturges gives in the screenplay—in which Kockenlocker "rams a brush through the barrel of his six-shooter"—but it's enough to punctuate a discussion of the "right" way for a man to handle a woman.

"Ya gotta be more *forceful* in these matters," Kockenlocker snarls, with William Demarest's gruffest voice and most level-eyed scowl, the one that makes him look in profile like a goat nerving itself up to dine on a tin can. "Dames like to be bossed." Trying to wriggle out of the conversation, Norval excuses himself with, "All I can do is ask." And Kockenlocker replies, immediately, "We accept. You're in," and shakes his hand.

So now, without even having gotten that movie date, Kockenlocker has agreed to marry Norval. I realize, of course, that Kockenlocker thinks he's done no such thing. The "we" simply comes from a man who believes, wrongly, that he's in charge of

Kockenlocker, blowing Norval a kiss through the barrel of a gun

his daughters, or ought to be. The plural also reminds the audience of a truth obscured by the propagandists of romantic love but perpetually rediscovered after every honeymoon, that you think you're marrying a person but are really getting a family. All the same, it's unmistakable that Kockenlocker is imposing on Norval a shotgun (or six-shooter) wedding for reasons that satisfy his own needs while taking no account of Trudy's. And Kockenlocker intends to be a full participant in these nuptials. "You gonna go in and ask her," he finally shouts, "or do you want me to do it for you?" First he spoke for the bride, accepting Norval's proposal; now he's going to speak for Norval and ask for (or seize) the bride.

At this point, with Kockenlocker symbolically sandwiched between the putative lovers, his pistol fires. This, too, is very *Interpretation of Dreams*—as is the way that Norval, dazed by the ballistic ejaculation, walks away dreamily, to enter the Kockenlocker house by piercing the membrane of its screen door.

It's always difficult to define an artist's intentions, and some critics think it's a mistake to try; but there's no need to determine whether Sturges at this point really meant to make use of Freud, given that this consummation scene takes place in the most dirty-minded comedy any studio filmmaker had yet attempted. Judged solely on the basis of what you see, the only open question is whether Kockenlocker has shocked Norval into finally penetrating *something* (the house, the marriageable daughter), or whether Norval himself has just been penetrated in spirit. He's certainly been "bossed," which dames allegedly like, and confronted at close quarters with a long, hard, explosive object. Maybe the rip in the screen door is an externalized image of the inner experience that has left him dazed and limp.

As often happens in the plots of movies about psychoanalysis (see *Spellbound*, for example), this tumble with Kockenlocker unblocks Norval, opening him to a sudden, liberating insight—"almost an inspi-inspi-inspiration." Right at the movie's halfway mark (Sturges's management of time, as always, is impeccable), as Norval escapes into the backyard with Trudy, he gets the idea that he believes will solve all their problems. What he's really about to do, of course, is set off the disasters that will mount giddily throughout the second half; but for the next nine or ten minutes, he will be active, forceful, confident, even commanding—everything that is ordinarily so foreign to him, and yet, oddly, so consistent with the image that Kockenlocker seems to cherish of himself.

Maybe this is what Norval had wanted from Kockenlocker all along: not a paternal model (that would be too bland for Sturges) but a version of the asylum superintendent who takes a more hands-on approach, giving Norval, if not love, then focused attention of a dangerous kind that makes the heart beat faster, culminating in a hot, sweaty shove into manhood. The evidence? Now that Norval has had his screen-door moment, he's fully alive for the first time and feels he can merit the woman of his dreams—though Trudy, being Kockenlocker's daughter, puts a few twists of her own into the conventions of manhood.

To return to the early scene in the music store, which introduces the future couple: You hear evidence of Trudy's presence before you see her. The action begins with an establishing shot, as a few soldiers enter the store to the strains of a *basso profundo* nautical dirge, "The Bell in the Bay" (composed by Preston Sturges). Cut to the apparent source of the singing: Trudy, shown behind the counter in medium close-up. Looking very feminine with her blossoming blonde curls and hair ribbon, she is nevertheless pounding the air with a fist, in the middleweight contender style of *lieder* performance, while rounding her lips into an aperture large enough to match the sounds of booming, mournful heroism. Cut to a close-up of a record spinning on a turntable, then back to Trudy, who continues to maintain an appropriately solemn expression, apart from being almost cross-eyed with the strain of mock-bellowing. As the tempo relents for a plunge to the final note, Trudy begins to sink behind the counter, and the soldiers on the other side bend their knees in sympathy. Look at their faces. Some of the GIs are still grinning, a little, but most now seem entranced, as you might expect of men whose bodies yield physically, as a group, to whatever emotional power this woman wields.

We might call it "charm," which in everyday usage implies an allure that's light, superficial, perhaps domestic. The Circean possibilities of the word usually go unnoticed—and they certainly wouldn't spring to mind now, with Betty Hutton bouncing in

Trudy, channeling her basso profundo power

delight at her own joke (now that she's taken off the record) and telling the soldiers, with her widest smile and twangiest vowels, that they'd better leave or else buy something "before Mr. Rafferty gets after me." The employer's authority is reasserted and the spell broken, quickly enough that you've already forgotten how complex it was. By the trick of contrasting herself to a gloomy male voice, Trudy has heightened the soldiers' impression of her youth, high spirits, and femininity. She's made herself into exactly what the GIs are looking for—but in the same gesture she's diminished their ability to claim the prize as a warrior traditionally would, since she's made masculine gravity into something ridiculous. No wonder the men bow as a group to her will, for the moment at least. She's a cornfed Midwestern sorceress—but one who will soon overestimate her strength.

With the impotently blustering Kockenlocker as her father—a petty tyrant who makes life unpleasant for his dependents but can't master them—Trudy has reason to believe in the efficacy of her wiles. But she can't get around Kockenlocker by herself. She needs the collaboration of Emmy, who is younger but in most cases functions as the wiser one. Emmy gives Trudy the comfort and understanding that might have come from a mother, combined with a shrewd, ironic distance of which the older sister is incapable. In return, Trudy provides Emmy with vicarious excitement, living out the adventures that the fourteen year old can't yet enjoy, but will no doubt undertake much more deftly when her turn comes.

Emmy is a girl who can affect a "refined" manner of speech, batting her eyes in mock innocence, and then drop without transition into deflationary slang. One minute she's playing the Wagner wedding march on the parlor piano and telling a wrought-up Kockenlocker, with sugary condescension, that of course she thinks about marriage. What else would she think about? The next minute, she's rolling out some barrelhouse blues ("What kind of music is that?" Kockenlocker demands) and helpfully suggesting to Trudy and Norval that when their movie is over, they might like to try the little boogie-woogie joint down the road. What does she know about that joint? "Oh, nothing," Emmy tells her father. "I just heard *you* were there—digging quite a trench."

She's figured him out, along with all of Morgan's Creek. "You can't tell how a town's going to take things," Emmy later says to Trudy, while insisting that she secure some legal pretext, however false, to explain her pregnancy, "a town that can produce shnoooks like Papa, all suspicious and suspecting the worst in everything." Emmy is equally ruthless in choosing the instrument of salvation. "There are very few dopes like Norval, honey," she assures Trudy. And more: in a turn of phrase that would have been harsh enough for Jean in *The Lady Eve*, Emmy says Norval was *made* to be the chump in a fraudulent marriage, "like the ox was made to eat and the grape was made to drink."

Sturges doesn't portray Emmy as entirely superior. He's too much a student of human complexity for that, and (though not concerned with realism) too aware that audiences invest emotion only in characters they find plausible. When facing a stressful situation, Emmy is still enough of a little girl that she wants to retreat to her father's lap, to his discomfort and surprise though not displeasure. But for the most part, she serves as a kind of alien intelligence embedded within Morgan's Creek: a representative of the point of view of those moviegoers who find the townspeople woefully, hilariously backward. As a quasi-outside observer, she's a bit like McGinty and the Boss, though without their urge to squeeze financial gain out of a ripe situation. As an insider with a more sophisticated mind than most, she's like the town lawyer, Mr. Johnson (Al Bridge, in his finest role), though she lacks a middle-aged man's willingness to work with things as they are. With the disillusioned wit of a grown-up and the impulses of a young girl, Emmy chafes at the constraints of Morgan's Creek and schemes against them. So, too, does her sister—except that Emmy is better at it. She brings a higher cynicism to her role as Trudy's instigator and accomplice, and so in a way operates as if she were an agent for the audience, advancing the plot on their behalf.

The one thing clever, conniving little Emmy doesn't have is charm—not the instinctive kind that seems to flow from her sister. When Trudy is released onto the dance floor in the church basement, she inspires one soldier after another to cut in for a chance at this taffeta-gowned armful. It wouldn't be wrong to say they're passing her around, especially considering the night's outcome; but from the way Trudy handles herself it looks more as if she's the one taking each man for a spin. When the partygoers gather at the punch bowl, where the lemonade is probably spiked, Trudy stands near the center of the group. When some of the GIs and their dates drive in a clump from the church to the country club, the country club to the roadhouse, Trudy is in command behind the wheel. After all, it's her car—or, rather, the car she talked Norval into lending her, after she'd walked out on their purported date and ordered him to sit through a triple feature on his own.

The innate force that pours through Trudy—whether in arguments, blatant lies, or false tears—is more than enough to overwhelm Norval. It would probably be enough to overmaster the soldiers, too, if they were tapping into her one at a time. But when they have her surrounded, Trudy no longer directs her vital current but is herself carried away by it, as can happen to people who put too much faith in their own gifts and are too apt to manage them by instinct. On the level of plot, a series of external influences conspires to undo Trudy: the spiked lemonade in the church basement, the Champagne at the country club, the knock on the head from a reflector ball at the roadhouse. But on the level of character dynamics, which makes the plot ring true, it seems as if Trudy winds up in trouble because Emmy wasn't with her. The sister who could have steered her through the party was too young to go.

It remains to be seen whether an argument might be embedded in these thorny relationships, waiting to be teased out; but already it's evident that this story has no moral. The only counsel *The Miracle of Morgan's Creek* offers is prudential, delivered by drawling, nasal, sarcastic, jowls-shaking Al Bridge, with his head that looks like an enlarged, irritated peanut. The pregnant Trudy has gone to consult Bridge—that is, the local attorney, Mr. Johnson—under the transparent pretense of seeking help for a friend, only to hear that this phantom third party "ought to be ashamed of herself." But that's not because the nameless friend has sinned:

> I mean because of her carelessness. The responsibility of recording a marriage has always been up to the woman. If it weren't for them marriage would have disappeared long since. No man is going to jeopardize his present or poison his future with a lot of little brats hollering around the house unless he is forced to. It is up to the woman to knock him down and hog-tie him and drag him in front of two witnesses immediately if not sooner.

Although this tirade has a ventriloquistic tone, as if spoken through an authorial mouthpiece, it conveys a truth consistent with the world the movie has established and not inconsistent with our own. Mr. Johnson correctly understands that whatever a town full of suspicious shnooks may choose to do—indulge in malicious gossip, fret over newspaper editorials, listen to hellfire sermons (such as the one Sturges deleted on the censors' orders), or prettify the fundamental reality with an overlay of Wagner—young women do in fact get pregnant, and the men they gratify sometimes abandon them, leaving behind only a vague memory that their name might have been Ratzkiwatzki. *The Miracle of Morgan's Creek* accepts the idea that such an inconvenience can befall even a decent young woman like Trudy. The movie does not accept the notion that disgrace must attach to such a person, as if by natural law. On the contrary: the movie shows that the project of imposing blame on women and exercising hypocrisy requires psychological effort, and a lot of it. The strain is everywhere. You see it in the chronic, self-defeating anger of Kockenlocker, the gun-toting enforcer of masculine standards, who is forever aiming kicks at people's backsides and forever winding up flat on his own. You see it in the flailing hysteria of Norval, who can't live up to a masculine standard—Kockenlocker's, the Army's, anybody's—and seems to want someone to force him into it. You see it in Trudy's undiscriminating urge to let loose her high spirits, no matter who she has to trample to do it, or how the adventure will leave her stepped on. And you see it in Emmy, the arch little reality principle of this four-person complex, who pays for her good sense and self-control with the pain of contempt (for her father and Norval) and with the anxiety that comes from letting Trudy do the misbehaving for her.

It takes the film's first half hour for Sturges to sketch out these discontents of civilization in Morgan's Creek. But once Trudy and Emmy have formulated a heartless scheme to sucker Norval into marriage—a scheme that would allow sexual hypocrisy not only to continue but to worsen—the destructive emotional status quo begins to crack. It doesn't do so all at once and for every character; but one by one, these people reach a limit.

Trudy is the first to break. After inviting Norval to dinner at the Kockenlocker house, the better to soften him up, she takes him onto the moonlit porch, intending to sucker him into a proposal of marriage. As she carries on with a prepared speech about her domestic yearnings and essential submissiveness—womanly platitudes, which her plan of entrapment contradicts—notice how she idly twists and turns a leaf she's plucked from a climbing vine. The gesture is identical to the tic she'd exhibited

A film of emotional breakdowns: Trudy and Norval,
reduced to hypoarticulation

in the music store, when Norval had asked for a date and she'd demurred while torturing a scrap of paper. This is how Trudy relieves her nervousness when lying, and how she expresses her ability to wrap Norval around her fingers. For a long moment she seems to be succeeding brilliantly, too, staring toward the camera with only the occasional sidelong glance to check on how well she's winding him up, while Norval, in profile, grows so excited that he all but levitates, before tumbling off the porch.

She's landed him, literally. But she's not prepared for the outpouring that comes next, with their positions reversed: Trudy in profile, growing more and more unsettled as she listens, while Norval faces the camera, still unsure of whether he's allowed to pour out his feelings while looking into her eyes and so speaking his heart to the audience. His confession is one of abject, unmanly longing, including a memory of how he "took all kinds of subjects I didn't give a hoot about" in high school just so he could be in a classroom with her: "The cooking wasn't so bad, but the *sewing*." This is a lot for a man to say to a young woman who pretends to sing in basso profundo—a young woman who had walked to that fake movie date with Norval holding on to her arm, instead of the other way around. Now Norval is babbling ecstatically about how his entire life has been devoted to subservience to her, and Trudy can't take it. She begins to sob—not for purposes of manipulation, as on the movie date, but in the first genuine sign she's shown him of conventional feminine emotion. You might say her essential kindness has emerged, except that it's never yet been evident—so maybe it would be more accurate to say she's finally seen the cost of maintaining a false front against the town's moralism, and she can't bring herself to pay it. Trudy realizes that to save herself through her current plan, she'd need to adopt her father's bullying version of masculinity on a permanent basis and spend the rest of her life dominating this helpless man, in effect keeping him in a version of the constrained femininity against which she has revolted. She can't do it, to Norval or to herself.

What follows this breakdown is the second long tracking shot of Trudy and Norval walking through the center of town. He's no longer dangling from her arm; they go hand in hand. It's too soon immediately after the porch scene for Trudy to feel anything positive toward him, but in her desperation she treats Norval for the first time as a fellow human. He deserves to know why she began sobbing when he proposed marriage, why she now feels it's impossible to accept him, and also (incidentally) why he, too, might soon become an object of suspicion and blame, to the town in general and the furious Kockenlocker in particular.

She is about to broach a subject so adult that the censors would scarcely allow it to be named—which is why it's telling that before she speaks, she swears Norval to secrecy in the most juvenile way possible. "Cross your heart and hope to die, and boil in oil and stew in lye," she makes him repeat, as if they were still the schoolchildren Norval had recalled for her only moments earlier. He solemnly takes the playground oath. She then explains the problem in a series of hints that Norval is repeatedly slow to understand, and to which he reacts with escalating spasms of spots-seeing. Stammering that this is "the terriblest thing" he's ever heard, he reverts to (or rather maintains) the childish level of language that Trudy has established, and so underscores the theme that Sturges had sketched in his preliminary notes: the persistent innocence of these two, even in the midst of their adventure in out-of-wedlock, no-name pregnancy.

In the screenplay, Sturges had imagined that Trudy and Norval would drive around town during this conversation—much as he'd thought they would drive to their bogus movie date—but when it came time to film *The Miracle of Morgan's Creek*, he decided to make them walk, while having the camera trail them in long traveling shots through the backlot set. The change had the obvious, immediate benefit of freeing Bracken to perform sustained marvels of physical comedy, slipping moment to moment and on the move from electrified, bolt-upright outrage to fluttering bafflement to a molten, sickened helplessness, then back with a jolt to having every muscle tensed. But there was a second great advantage to these repeated promenades through the Morgan's Creek that Sturges's production designer had cobbled together, repurposing facades from earlier Paramount movies. These little tours embed Trudy and Norval's youthful simplicity in the ongoing life of a town full of busybodies, snoops, and scolds.

Emmy is right. When Norval is later delivered back to Morgan's Creek after his botched wedding, having been arrested by four different police forces, Kockenlocker orders the curious townspeople to get off his property and leave the matter to the officials—to which the neighbors respond by pushing right into the house after him, in a muttering horde. They're still crowding the place when Kockenlocker leads Norval away to the town jail for safekeeping. Cries of "Shame on you, Norval Jones!" rise from the parlor interlopers. Kockenlocker's distress at this public exposure has the ring of truth. "You're just a kid," he tells Emmy about the scandal, after the house clears. "You can duck down the alleys. Me, I gotta stand out in the middle of the street and take it, from every rat in town."

By this point Kockenlocker, too, is on the way toward shattering his emotional status quo. He does not reach the crisis, though, until he's made a final assertion of paternal absolutism.

The episode begins in the shadows. (What other point of origin could there be for a man psychosocially conditioned to cover up so much of life?) After Norval has been shut in a cell and the multiple arresting officers have gone into the night, one legally constituted authority lingers—the back-country justice of the peace *cum* motel proprietor—whispering to Kockenlocker from a dark cranny. First the JP returns the two-dollar fee that Trudy and Norval had paid. Then he produces their marriage certificate, which seems to be the main piece of incriminating evidence, and tears it up before Kockenlocker's eyes. "I might ask *you* a favor some day," the justice of the peace says, with a man-to-man leer. "I might call on *you* some day." Kockenlocker is so moved by this brotherly chicanery that he says, three times, "That's mighty white of you."

Almost all moviegoers today hear that phrase as Kockenlocker's most damning self-indictment. How many would have thought it revolting in 1942, I don't know. It's possible that Sturges believed the majority would think nothing of the awful words; perhaps he ground them in so many times only to maintain the expected level of speech for Kockenlocker, and not to expose his bigotry. But the screenplay suggests another interpretation. As the justice of the peace exits, according to the script, "Kockenlocker looks after him and shakes his head . . . his faith in man restored." This entire exchange, "mighty white" included, is evidently what passes for uplift in Kockenlocker's mind. It's all a testimony to his moral deformation.

Which Kockenlocker then proceeds to demonstrate with pride to Trudy and Emmy, striding into the parlor to lecture them about his wisdom and to boast of having disposed of the marriage certificate.

"I could be wrong, too, y'know," he says, pacing away from his daughters to give himself extra room for declamation. But he doesn't sound like someone who believes he could be wrong. He barks at Trudy and Emmy, and having given himself a runway comes charging back to throw down the two dollars in disgust. Then he shows his daughters the shreds of the marriage certificate, which he claims he "got the guy to tear up . . . just a little politics."

Politics: in Kockenlocker's Aristotelian system, the art by which men accommodate one another's interests. Even when Trudy, with all hope lost, confesses her pregnancy, her father's first thought isn't of her but of a man. As the news sinks in, Kockenlocker crosses the parlor once more, weakly this time, as if wanting to escape what he's heard but no longer having the strength to move away at full speed. He stops, glances back at his daughters, looks down in silence, and looks back a second time. He has never gone so long without talking. When he finally recovers the power of speech, it isn't to inquire about his daughter's well-being or offer her reassurance but to ask about Norval: Had he known everything when he agreed to marry Trudy? The answer, when it comes, is enough to restore Kockenlocker's vitality, so that he charges at Trudy again with a list of the crimes—*her* crimes, it seems, in her father's eyes—for which Norval, as the man, will now be responsible in the *polis*.

"Papa, that really isn't being helpful," Trudy tells him, when his accusations boil over into a death threat to Emmy.

"Well, what do you want me to do, learn to knit?" he shouts, still in full sarcastic, masculine rage. And exercising an option to which men have had recourse for millennia, as Mr. Johnson had reminded Trudy, Kockenlocker simply abandons the women. "I'm going out for a walk," he says, and leaves them to their worries.

Despite the slalom of emotions that Demarest has run so effortlessly in this scene, including that pivot where he was poised in unaccustomed silent thought, you don't see him undergo a transformation, as you do, for example, when Jean wakes from her nightmare in *The Lady Eve*. But after the cut, when Kockenlocker steps back into the frame to visit Norval in jail, it's clear that something has changed in him while he was off-screen. He speaks softly now and sits side by side with Norval on the bunk. He confesses weakness: "I didn't understand." And for the first time, he takes Trudy's feelings into account and even speaks on her behalf: "All she's worried about is *you*." What's cracked in Kockenlocker?

The answer emerges as Kockenlocker tries to aid Norval, at great risk to himself, only to find that his new surrogate son won't cooperate. Despite the shift in his emotions, Kockenlocker in the first part of this scene still holds on to the illusion that he can manage problems and hide inconvenient truths by using the town's prevailing nod-and-wink methods—in this case, a series of hints that a way to escape is open, with each suggestion made more broadly than the last, only to be refused with ever-mounting gormlessness. In the past, Kockenlocker has talked at Norval more than he's listened to him, and so he's flummoxed by the novelty he now discovers: a man so instinctively honest that he wrote his own name rather than "Ratzkiwatzki" on the marriage certificate (after all that practice), a man for whom truth comes to the lips so automatically that he spoiled every one of Mr. Johnson's attempts to lie him out of trouble. Yes, Norval had tried to help Trudy by donning the disguise of a surplus World War I uniform, but the seat of the pants had torn off, twice, as if in sympathy with his continual urge to lay himself bare. Now, despite his peril, Norval can't conceive of performing an underhanded act, no matter how insistently he's invited to. And why should he? Norval at last has everything he'd ever wanted—Trudy's love, and Kockenlocker's paternal oversight—and seems to feel that if he stays in jail, these boons will be permanently locked in with him.

As for Kockenlocker, his exasperation both conforms to the pattern we've seen and exceeds it, since he has now been forced to recognize the inadequacy of his powers of scheming. His daughters, who must have learned their conspiratorial ways from him, have revealed how little he knew about the affairs under his own roof, and how much better they were at concealing unpleasant facts—though not good enough, as it happens. Kockenlocker knows he's been bested by mere women, one of whom has in effect gone over to the other side by allying herself with the pathologically candid Norval. Everything that Kockenlocker has prided himself on and used to justify his rage—his suspicious nature, his low cunning, his controlling strength—has failed his daughters and left him exposed to scandal, and it is currently being shredded like tissue paper by a young man who may seem like an idiot but has done more than her own father for Trudy.

Kockenlocker is irate at the situation—as usual—but for the first time he turns some of his anger inward. When he hints to Norval about various escape scenarios, he mimes the process, in effect performing acts of mayhem on himself. And when Trudy and Emmy show up lugging jailbreak equipment—they haven't been idle in his absence—Kockenlocker for the first time yields to someone else's ideas. "See if *you* can do anything with him," he tells Trudy, and then falls in with the plan to encourage Norval to search for Ratzkiwatzki—even though it will implicate Kockenlocker in one of the very few felonies not yet on the indictment, bank robbery.

From here through the end of the movie, Kockenlocker is a much-chastened man. He does not change so deeply that he'll refrain from throwing a punch—but after the third act concludes with his volunteering to be bludgeoned, the fourth discovers him living a quiet rural life with his daughters, and sufficiently humbled to make good on an earlier boast. Toward the start of the film, he had told Trudy and Emmy that he needed to be both father and mother to them. That was mostly his way of asserting authority twice. Now, in exile and with Christmas approaching, he finds enough of the traditionally maternal in himself to give his daughters comfort.

Let's say that act 1 was the story of how Trudy sneaked out to the dance, having taken grievous advantage of Norval, and realized the next morning that she was one of those poor dopes she vaguely recalled who got married with a curtain ring on one finger and a false name on the certificate. In act 2, trying to lie herself out of trouble, she entrapped Norval and suffered an emotional breakdown for it, after which he had his own crisis, brought on by a shattering front-porch meeting with Kockenlocker. The third act, which incorporated Kockenlocker's change of heart, took the couple through Norval's disastrous plan and its aftermath and ended with the bank robbery. Each act lasted about twenty-six minutes.

Act 4 is marked as distinct, beginning after the passage of some months and with a change of season. It's a little shorter than the others—twenty minutes—but is so overstuffed with incident, and veers so wildly through moods, settings, and chronology, that it might qualify as the strangest mishmash of Sturges's career. The contents include

- the frightening citizen's arrest of Norval Jones at gunpoint
- an inspiring speech by Kockenlocker, reminding Trudy that Jesus was born in a stable
- an interruption by a wandering cow
- a Christmas visit from the heavily Jewish, turkey-toting Mr. Rafferty, who has sheltered and nourished the not-so-holy family
- a violent town meeting, conducted on the top floor of a fire station, which ends with Kockenlocker sliding down the pole and popping Norval's tormentor Tuerck on the nose
- a tense, prolonged scene of waiting in the corridor of the maternity ward, until Trudy surprises everyone and rescues her family by giving birth, and giving birth, and giving birth
- the ensuing round-the-world hullabaloo, presented in rapid flash-forward, with comic inserts of Mussolini and Hitler
- and the liberation of Norval Jones: sprung from jail, valorized without a word of explanation, reunited with an exhausted

Trudy, made sentimental by the sight of a nursery on Christmas day, and at last left in a state of renewed, half-blinded hysteria.

Maybe it was this absurdly busy fourth act, with its lurches, dips, and careening turns, that prompted James Agee to write that watching *The Miracle of Morgan's Creek* was like taking a nun on a roller coaster. But without denying the fun to be had, Agee also felt the conclusion was too facile—that Sturges had cheated his artistic instincts by imposing a clever solution on the plot's complications, rather than digging a dramatic resolution out of the movie's themes.[9]

The solution is certainly clever; but I'm not sure it's simple. If you've paid attention to Norval's psychology, you recognize an irony bordering on horror in the trick that fate has played on him. A compulsively honest man, Norval is now trapped for life in a gargantuan lie, which is officially enforced and believed by millions. A rootless man who has ached for a family, Norval will now live in a stupefyingly large one, which isn't his.

The irony is no less stinging for Trudy, as she lies limp in bed. The charmer who had wanted to dance away from domesticity and whirl through an entire church basement full of soldiers now has six children to drain her vitality and must meet the public's expectation that she'll be the best of housewives. No doubt she'll be dutiful toward Norval, in keeping with the emotional shift she's undergone; but will she be satisfied with him? As Diane Jacobs writes, "She doesn't give this ungainly clunk the time of day when her mind's on romance."[10]

Kockenlocker is more fortunate. He's been recalled to Morgan's Creek, elevated to chief of police, and given a spiffy new uniform, so presumably he'll be back at work on the day after

Christmas, bullying everyone again and taking special pleasure in tormenting Tuerck the banker.

As so often happens in Sturges's films, the characters wind up back where they started. (Even McGinty and the Boss have returned, apparently exonerated after their flight to Latin America.) It does seem a waste, after all the psychological changes these people have gone through. Kockenlocker needn't have bothered to learn softness and humility, because he's not going to use them. Norval, having developed a backbone and won a somewhat curdled version of what he'd wanted, is nevertheless reduced again to blubbering helplessness. Trudy has come to appreciate kindness and generosity in a man, but she is now trapped at home even more inescapably than when her father wouldn't let her go to the dance.

Move up from individual to group psychology, and the implications of this eternal return become even more dire. The crowd that has assembled for Norval, to cheer for a magnificent act of virility he hasn't committed, seems to ignore Trudy. She's been the sole agent of change in act 4—first insisting against the advice of Kockenlocker and Rafferty that she go to Morgan's Creek to try to free Norval, and then making the truly heroic effort of giving birth six times—and yet the applause is all for her husband ("retroactive," as the Boss and McGinty would say). It's as if the society that is Morgan's Creek writ large thinks of her as a mere vessel, to be filled with male seed and then emptied of six new boys, in a too-literal interpretation of her introductory joke about being puffed full of a bass voice. Ask why the citizenry neglects her, and you might imagine a wartime population feeling anxious about the loss of manhood—of men. The newspaper headlines that flash across the screen imply as much: people are excited because nature has answered the call for more males who can be put into uniform. Granted, Trudy's babies are hardly prepared for the front; but since the order of things seems never to alter, it's only a matter of time before one war or another is ready for them.

In the meantime, in grand self-delusion, the crowd can allay its anxiety about manhood by applauding Norval's and so lapse into an hysteria of its own. The folly infecting everyone becomes visible at the end, when Norval at last finds out how many babies he's got and comes sliding and crashing back to Trudy's bedside, frantically signaling "no" with his head, lips, and hands. Sturges superimposes "the spots" on the film's final image so they now cover the screen, as if not just Norval's vision is clouded but the world's.

Of course, none of these disturbing undercurrents (except the spots) plays across the movie's surface. The mood, after Norval has been yanked from jail, is best summarized by the jubilation of the crowd that engulfs him and by the hilarity of Bracken's final virtuoso traveling shot, in which he walks toward the camera while casting baffled glances from side to side, trying to smile at people, beginning to salute before thinking better of it, and in the midst of his forward progress half-sinking with buckled knees, as if the loops of gold braid, white gloves, and sword that have been slapped onto him are too heavy to support. The shnook has never looked spiffier, more triumphant, or less sure of himself; and as he's swept onward by waves of undeserved acclamation, you're borne along on a full flood of laughter.

It's not just a happy ending but a delirious one. Trudy, when still ignorant of what she's done to cause such a stir, smiles warmly at Norval from her bed, assures him (in an echo of Marcel Pagnol's *Fanny*) that he will indeed be a true father, and murmurs before dropping back to sleep that she's very happy. You can see she's speaking from the heart by the way her fingers toy with his lapel, as they had toyed earlier with a scrap of paper

Norval, with greatness thrust upon him

and a torn leaf, in a gesture that has now been transmuted into tenderness. Norval, too, has attained happiness—or he'll get there after the shock wears off. A closing title assures us of that, borrowing from no less deep-dish a source than Shakespeare.

But happiest of all is Emmy. Looking more like a young lady than before—she's had her hair done and is wearing a smart new plaid dress—she has cast off the childishness that had suited her so poorly, and with it her burden of contempt. Standing by Trudy's bedside, she kisses Norval on the cheek, not impulsively but with deliberation, earning a startled sidelong glance from the former dope, ox, and clump of grapes. Then, in keeping with the responsibilities she's always shouldered, Emmy takes it on herself to conduct Norval to the nursery and break the news to him. The way she does it suggests that she, alone among the characters, has experienced a permanent change.

Sturges films the moment of revelation from within the nursery, so you see Emmy and Norval from the crib side of the observation window and watch them converse without hearing the dialogue, as if in a dumbshow. Bracken is eloquent in miming Norval's soft-hearted cooing and misguided curiosity; and Lynn expertly prolongs the suspense with her hesitations and grimaces, as Emmy holds out for as long as she can against the inevitable explosion.

She doesn't delay to preserve herself. She does it out of concern for Norval. This alien intelligence among the principal characters, who alone didn't go through a breakdown (and then revert to type), ends the film by extending pity and forbearance toward one of the saps. Of course, being what they are, the others aren't likely to recognize the presence of a sane, mature mind among them—especially since Emmy will forever be a kid in their eyes—and Sturges isn't going to draw their attention to this wonder. But an alert moviegoer might notice Emmy's discretion and feel that for at least one person in this town, a modest escape might be possible from things-as-they-are.

Which concludes the argument Sturges has made with such miraculous coherence in *Morgan's Creek*.

8

THAT'S ALL YOU KNOW HOW TO HURT

Hail the Conquering Hero

As if accommodating himself to Buddy DeSylva's thrift in repurposing characters and recycling gags—as if launching into his own equivalent of the Crosby-Hope *Road* movies—Sturges hurried in mid-1943 from *The Miracle of Morgan's Creek* to *Hail the Conquering Hero*. A preliminary and ultimately misleading inspection of the new film's contents might have suggested an alternative title: *Son of Morgan's Creek*.

A backlot facsimile of a small town, left over from the previous film and now renamed Oakridge; a detachment of military men; a blustering William Demarest; and Eddie Bracken, pushed unsuitably into the mold of a triumphant he-man: such were the ready-to-hand materials out of which Sturges assembled his next comedy. When *Morgan's Creek* and its successor eventually reached the theaters, after Paramount's long delay in releasing them, audiences could even perceive a continuity of theme. At the end of *Morgan's Creek*, Bracken achieves greatness without having done much more than see spots. As soon as the plot of *Hail the Conquering Hero* gets properly started, Bracken again finds himself acclaimed on fictitious grounds, this time for a military career that no one knows was aborted almost before

The town of Oakridge: assembled, and intending to stay that way

it began. Chronic hay fever—he'd sneezed too much for the Marines.

The unearned, almost unprompted enthusiasm of a crowd figures in both films, though much more prominently in *Hail the Conquering Hero*, which after its initial setup plays as a nonstop public commotion, which seems to happen almost in real time. Over the course of a long day and the next morning, a homecoming celebration for Bracken, supposedly returned from combat with a chestful of medals, flows into an awkwardly multidirectional parade, a church convocation, a torchlit political rally, and a town-hall meeting, with one character after another improving these events with his oratorical skills and four brass bands vying to out-blare one another.

With this hullabaloo—the busiest, most thickly peopled of Sturges's career—comes a cynicism about public opinion expressed more loudly than ever. "You didn't know a good man when you saw one," Bracken cries out to the people of Oakridge at the climax, speaking in the character of Woodrow Truesmith, the purported war hero and unwilling mayoral candidate, "so you always elected a phony instead. . . . Until a still bigger phony came along. Then you naturally wanted *him*."

Beside issuing this rebuke to the democratic masses, the film also pokes fun at the civic monuments on which Sturges had focused his scorn in the abandoned foreword to *Triumph Over Pain*. Upon returning to Oakridge, trailing clouds of borrowed glory, Woodrow is asked to lay a wreath at the memorial statue of General Zabriski and then is told that the town intends to erect a monument to *him*, too. One would be as false as the other. As Woodrow explains to Demarest, in the character of the visiting Marine sergeant who has put him into all this trouble, nobody knows who Zabriski was. "The town bought him from an iron works that was going out of business. He just happened to be a bargain."

Yet despite these similarities, *Hail the Conquering Hero* is not at all a sequel to *The Miracle of Morgan's Creek*. It's more like a variation on a theme, in which the familiar notes of the previous film function as a bass line upon which Sturges modulates into a remote key and troubled harmonies. There is plenty of boisterous fun in this new movie, but there are also overtones of bereavement, loss, and miscommunication. (The townspeople don't really know what Woodrow's accompanying Marines have been through, and the Marines can't speak of it except in tales of derring-do.) Above all, the film dwells on a civilian's sense of unworthiness in the face of military sacrifice, and on his accompanying, understandable dislike of feeling unworthy.

Such complexities are not new for Sturges. He had tried for a similar mixture of tone and emotion in the first film in his heroism trilogy, *Triumph Over Pain*, but (so far as we can know) hadn't been so adept and persuasive in achieving it. In *Hail the Conquering Hero* he carries off the effect brilliantly.

He manages the trick, in large measure, through the introduction of a figure who is even more troubled than Woodrow and slowly grows into his counterpart.

The private known as Bugsy, played by Freddie Steele, separates himself a little from his buddies from the moment the film's sextet of Marines materializes out of a nocturnal fog, on leave for several days in San Francisco and flat broke after an ill-advised craps game. Bugsy is the one who shrewdly held back fifteen cents from the communal gambling stake and so, with enough money for one beer, can lead the way into a dockside saloon, where the Marines discover Woodrow sitting glumly at the end of the bar. Soon, Bugsy detaches himself from the group for a second time to make a call from a pay phone and sets the plot in motion.

At this very early moment, before the gears engage, Sturges already has contrived for Woodrow to explain to the Marines most of what you'll need to know about his background. (The son of a highly decorated Marine hero who was killed in action in World War I—right in front of William Demarest, by a strange coincidence—Woodrow had groomed himself from childhood for a military career and is now too embarrassed at having received a medical discharge to let anyone back home know of his failure. He's spent the past year working at a shipyard without telling his mother, who presumably thinks he's in combat.) At the same time, as if in passing, Sturges has the Marines tell Woodrow an equal amount about Bugsy, and about him alone.

They understand how strange it must seem that this dark-haired man with the Greek profile and unchanging expression is so offended when he learns that Woodrow has left his mother in doubt. "That's a terrible thing to do to your mother," Bugsy keeps saying, in his oddly flat voice. "You oughta be ashamed of yourself."

"He never had any mother," Demarest's sergeant explains apologetically about Bugsy. "He's from a home."

"He's a little bit screwy, too," the corporal adds. To which the sergeant replies, quickly and protectively, "He's all right. He got a little shot up, that's all."

But the nickname, Bugsy, contradicts Sarge, as does the man's almost affectless manner and his decision, made without consulting anyone, to call Woodrow's mother and say that her boy will come home on tomorrow's train, honorably discharged. "Are you nuts or something?" Woodrow will ask much later in the film; to which Bugsy will reply, after a short pause and with flabbergasting candor, "Maybe."

Six Marines carry Woodrow back to Oakridge, ostensibly against his will (but why doesn't he protest more firmly?), and encourage the town to think he has prevailed in combat. Of the six, Bugsy is the one who cozies up closest to Mrs. Truesmith. He volunteers to her that she can "put me on your flag. I sure ain't got anybody else." He sits on her left in church with Woodrow on her right, as if the two men were sons flanking her. And when Woodrow eventually invents an excuse to skip town, out of disgust and fear at having to keep up his imposture, Bugsy alone reacts violently to this fresh insult to Mrs. Truesmith, turning himself for a while into the one antagonist Woodrow faces in the movie. (Woodrow's political rival, Mayor Noble, doesn't count, since Woodrow resists running against him. His rival in love, Noble's son, doesn't count, either, since Woodrow spends much of the film hoping his former girlfriend Libby will forget about him and marry someone nonfelonious.) Affronted at Woodrow's filial callousness, Bugsy absents himself from the other Marines and goes alone into the street, so he can stare at his opposite number like a guilty conscience. Then he marks the film's climax, when the unwilling impostor confesses all before a town-hall meeting, by abandoning his disapproval and once more standing with Woodrow.

Bugsy starts the movie on its course, and he alone among the Marines gets the privilege of ending it. The film's final lines, spoken as the Marines chug away on the train, are exchanged between Woodrow and Bugsy.

> WOODROW: I knew the Marines could do almost anything, but I never knew they could do anything like *this*.
> BUGSY (*smiling*): You got no idea.

To which Woodrow whispers back, as if sharing a secret, "*Semper fidelis*," and so seals the brotherly pact.

Only Sarge, by virtue of his rank, his decision to seize control of the trip to Oakridge, and his incarnation in William Demarest, has a closer and more continual relationship with Woodrow. Had that been Woodrow's sole pairing with any of the Marines, the plot of *Hail the Conquering Hero* would have rumbled along just as well, from the unanticipated welcome ceremony (which prevents Woodrow from slipping home quietly) through the complications with Libby and the mayoral candidacy to the climactic confession and happy ending. Nothing would be missing from the story; but almost everything would be missing from the emotional substance. The urgency of Woodrow's predicament doesn't come simply from an expectation of arrest (although that looms throughout) or from the likelihood that the crowd will turn on him in rage once his fraud has been exposed. What drives the movie is the ongoing comparison between Woodrow and Bugsy: the combat veteran Woodrow had aspired to be, the maybe-crazy victim of shell shock he might have become.

Need I point out that Hollywood features produced during World War II generally did not make a big deal of posttraumatic stress disorder? The subject was so unwelcome in the midst of the war effort, and even after victory, that when John Huston made a documentary for the Signal Corps about the psychological toll of combat, *Let There Be Light* (1946), the military suppressed all copies of the film, permitting it to be released only in the 1980s. It's fair to say that Bugsy is as exceptional a figure in the American cinema of the era as is the preacher in *Sullivan's Travels*.

Even more exceptional for a character who is so crucial to the film: he's played by an actor who was untrained and all but nonprofessional.

A retired prizefighter who had held the world middleweight title from 1936 through 1938, Freddie Steele entered the film business in a boxing picture titled *The Pittsburgh Kid* (1941), in which he made a cameo appearance as himself. Over the next couple of years he found work as an extra in a dozen other movies, always uncredited, always treated (in the industry's term of art) as "background." You can find him amid the press of GIs in *The Miracle of Morgan's Creek*, where I believe he's the soldier who picks Betty Hutton off the floor after she's been rammed headfirst into the mirrored ball. According to a Paramount publicity handout that Diane Jacobs cites in her biography, Sturges recognized Steele among the extras on *Morgan's Creek*, took him to lunch, and eventually promised to write a part for him.[1] Maybe there's some truth to the story. Sturges attended the fights every Tuesday and Friday night without fail and sometimes brought boxers back to the restaurant he'd established, The Players, where the clientele was as motley as his stock company, and the only requirement for a free drink, or an uncollected tab, was that the proprietor find the customer amusing. Steele was exactly the sort of man Sturges enjoyed collecting.

But what kind of speaking role could Freddie Steele play? I suspect Sturges figured it out when he was in the earliest stages of drafting *Hail the Conquering Hero*. This insight set the tone for the entire picture; and it very likely was inspired by the war news that Sturges had tried for so long to ignore.

I've mentioned Sturges's studied indifference to the war. In 1939 and 1940, the years of the production and release of *The Great McGinty* and *Christmas in July*, he would not have been alone among Americans in thinking of the conflict in Europe as a distant, phony war from which the United States ought to refrain. (Republican isolationists held this view, but so too did some on the left, such as Pete Seeger and the Almanac Singers, who released their antidraft, anti–Lend Lease, anti-Roosevelt album *Songs for John Doe* in May 1941, only to yank it out of circulation a month later when Hitler broke his nonaggression pact with Stalin. Evidently the war *was* real.) Sturges gave the fighting only a passing nod in *The Lady Eve*, an allusion in *Sullivan's Travels* (through the figure of the young Whippet tank driver), and no acknowledgment at all in *The Palm Beach Story*, which went into production just before Pearl Harbor. There was, of course, no occasion to mention the war in *Triumph Over Pain*, although William Demarest did lead an hallucinatory charge against the Mexican army while under the influence of ether.

This record of neglect is not unusual. Though it would be hard to exaggerate the commitment of film industry personnel and organizations to the war effort, it's easy to overestimate how many war-related features came out during the conflict. The proportion of these subjects varied sharply from studio to studio. In 1943, for example, anybody working at Warner Bros. might as well have been employed by the Army Signal Corps; twelve of the studio's fourteen top-grossing movies were about the war, including an Eddie Cantor backstage musical. But Fox had only five war pictures out of its sixteen top films that year, MGM had four out of sixteen, and Universal had just one, *Corvette K-225* (featuring Ella Raines), with the rest of its top dozen being devoted to fare such as Abbott and Costello in *Hit the Ice* and Maria Montez in *Arabian Nights*.

Paramount's commitment to wartime subjects was right in the middle. So what changed in Sturges between July 1942, when he began writing *The Miracle of Morgan's Creek*, and May 1943, when he started work on *Hail the Conquering Hero*? What happened to his imaginative world, that instead of thinking about soldiers having a hot time before going off to war he considered how they might feel coming home?

What happened was Guadalcanal: the campaign from which the Marines in *Hail the Conquering Hero* have returned. The Battle of Midway, fought over a few days in June 1942, had been America's first victory in the war, but it was a defensive action, which halted the advance of Japanese forces. Guadalcanal was the first American offensive, and it dragged on brutally, from August 1942 until February 1943, when a defeated Japanese command withdrew.

At the outset, few people on the home front had any inkling of how long, difficult, and crucial the engagement might become. As Sturges moved toward production on *The Miracle of Morgan's Creek*, he might have been excused for thinking that nothing much had happened on this small island in the Solomons except for the capture of a Japanese landing field by a detachment of Marines. But by early October 1942, newspapers were reporting that the action on Guadalcanal was likely to develop into a decisive battle. Journalists and camera crews embedded themselves with the troops, producing a torrent of on-site accounts throughout November and into the new year. Nobody was unaware of the fighting and its import. On February 10, 1943, the *New York Times* wrote that "Every American heart must have thrilled yesterday at the news that the battle of Guadalcanal was over and that the victory is ours." Every American heart also knew the cost: more than seven thousand Allied troops dead, most of them U.S. Marines, and more than seventy-seven hundred wounded.

Sturges understood he was not the right person to attempt a movie about combat.* But in the early months of 1943, he could not have avoided the subject that was in front of his eyes: the feelings of civilians about the men who were fighting the war. Whether from a showman's intuition about reaching an audience or an artist's conviction that he had to confront his own situation, Sturges evidently began to think that the public's attitude toward American troops might be a little more complex than mere submission to "the spell cast by jingling spurs."

Those were the words of a clergyman, Dr. Upperman, in a scene cut from *The Miracle of Morgan's Creek*, in which the pastor warned his flock against martial intoxication. "That was my moral," Sturges wrote in his memoirs. "I am sorry that it was left out."[2] Of his motivation for making *Hail the Conquering Hero*, though, he wrote nothing—which is an interesting omission, considering it was the last film he directed at Paramount, and the one he would later judge to have "less wrong with it" than any of the others. (So he told Andrew Sarris in an interview

---

* When he got around to conceiving of *Hail the Conquering Hero*, he toyed with the idea of beginning with newsreel footage of the Marines on Guadalcanal. Fortunately, he reconsidered.

conducted in 1957.)[3] Perhaps, in keeping with his characteristic reluctance to acknowledge deeper meanings in his films, Sturges felt free to mock the outward expressions of hero worship but could not bring himself to discuss the underlying sorrows and fears. Those feelings are absent from the memoirs; but they are inescapable in *Hail the Conquering Hero*, no matter how many oratorical flourishes the film's marching bands mistake for cues to start playing, and no matter how many flagrant lies the Marines feed to an adoring crowd.

On the evidence of the film he came to make, it seems probable that between February and May 1943—the end of the Guadalcanal campaign, and the first drafts of *Hail the Conquering Hero*—Sturges thought more seriously than before about the war effort and the home front. If so, a colorful newspaper account published at just that moment would have added to the material he was pondering.

Barney Ross, a prizefighter who had been the world lightweight, light welterweight, and welterweight champion in 1933–34, had enlisted in the Marines not long after the United States entered the war, and though in his early thirties he had asked for combat duty. The Marines deployed him to Guadalcanal, where (according to reports in December 1942) he defended himself and three wounded comrades while under a nightlong assault, single-handedly killing all the attackers, and at dawn carried the one surviving Marine to safety on his back. On February 25, 1943, the papers reported that Ross had been decorated and shipped back to the United States, where upon landing in San Diego he knelt and kissed the ground before giving a voluble press conference.

Well, prizefighters are show people, too. Sturges might have read these articles and wondered how greatly Ross and the Marine Corps might have embellished the account of his exploits. But whatever doubts Sturges might have had, he was an ardent boxing fan with ties to Ross's hometown of Chicago and must have known about these reports.

Jump three months ahead from Ross's homecoming to May 29, 1943, when Sturges composed the first story draft for *Hail the Conquering Hero*. Actually, it's two drafts. As Brian Henderson notes in his introduction to the published screenplay, Sturges sketched out the beginning of the story, about an encounter between a civilian and a decorated war hero, and then broke off and wrote, "HOLD EVERYTHING! IS IT POSSIBLE I HAVE BEEN SMITTEN BY AN IDEA??????????" Sturges then began again, shifting the viewpoint from one character to the other. But there's a puzzle. As Henderson observes, "The differences between these two story sketches do not seem great enough to merit Sturges's eureka. . . . [T]he circumstances and the likely consequences of the two meetings seem quite similar."[4]

But what if—this is pure speculation—what if the inspiration that struck Sturges had nothing to do with the plot and did not demand to be worked into a story draft? What if it was an idea for casting? I think it's possible that as Sturges began writing, he recalled Barney Ross's homecoming and in so doing also remembered another boxer, Freddie Steele. The notion that made him want to "hold everything" might have been that he could make good on his promise to Steele by writing him into this new movie as a returning Marine, like Ross. And perhaps, with that idea, came the flash that Steele's inadequacy as an actor could be turned to his advantage. Steele would play a man suffering from shell shock.

In another few years, Sturges's good friend William Wyler would win acclaim by choosing a nonprofessional, the wounded veteran

Harold Russell, to play the major role of a returning amputee in *The Best Years of Our Lives*. Sturges's casting of Freddie Steele as a psychologically injured Marine was not as great a coup, but it anticipated the impact of Wyler's decision, working a strong reality effect into *Hail the Conquering Hero*.

If the gap in emotional stability between Bugsy and the other characters rings true, it's largely because Steele suffers from a performance gap with his fellow actors. He sounds so different from them. Some members of the cast—Georgia Caine as Mrs. Truesmith, Ella Raines as Libby, Raymond Walburn as Mayor Noble—speak with the resonant tones and clipped, neutral enunciation that used to mark stage actors. Others—Demarest, of course, as well as Al Bridge as the political boss of Oakridge and Jimmy Conlin as Judge Dennis—color their characters' pronunciations with variations of class or region, while forcing the voice up the nose, squeezing it at the top of the throat, or making it carom off the palate with a clack like billiard balls. But whether kept conventionally pleasant or manipulated for expressive purposes, these sounds are all intentional. The actors mean to inhabit their words—whereas Steele, though as fully present in body as you might expect of a champion athlete, doesn't know how to project himself into his voice. To put it in terms of his real profession, his line readings are like punches thrown without leverage.

Given the character Steele is playing, this vocal awkwardness comes across as authenticity. Consider the scene in which Woodrow falls out of bed in the middle of the night, and Bugsy, who has been guarding his door, comes to help him off the floor. "I must have had a nightmare, I guess," Woodrow says, sheepishly, to which Bugsy replies, "You're lucky." The statement puzzles Woodrow; and so Bugsy explains, very simply, "You're lucky you don't have them all the time—like some guys." An actor might have added subtle emphases within the line, calculated the pause, perhaps dropped the pitch at a crucial point—put in any number of little tricks that would inject emotion into the remark and so contradict its intention, which is to convey a guileless stoicism. When Steele says the line, without inflection, the words sound as they should—casual, matter-of-fact—and so suggest a pain that seems more terrible for the way Bugsy accepts it. He doesn't even admit that the bad luck he's mentioned is his own. He's just talking about "some guys."

But I've cheated a little by jumping ahead. Just as it took about a month of writing before Sturges built Bugsy into a major character, so too does it take a while until the audience gets a sense of the gravity of Bugsy's condition and the grace with which he bears it. At the beginning, he just seems as the corporal describes him—a little screwy—which in a comedy is a fine thing to be. Like countless funny, marginal figures in the movies who add incidental idiosyncrasy to the background, Bugsy emits repetitive verbal tics and is obliviously rude. He does set off the plot; but Sturges almost immediately has Sarge take command, so Bugsy can continue to seem like a minor source of amusement, charmingly odd and nothing more. Then, by increments, Sturges builds up his presence and deepens his pathos, until Bugsy becomes the moral counterweight to Woodrow.

Sturges follows such a pattern everywhere in *Hail the Conquering Hero*, moving on all fronts from silliness to substance. Empty words take on weight throughout the course of the film; clichés gain the force of truth. Although the plot is built on lies—Woodrow's lies to his mother and Libby, the Marines' lies to Woodrow's mother and the town of Oakridge, Libby's lies to her department store mannequin of a fiancé—the governing principle is a progressive deepening of feeling.

A buffet shot in the Oakridge church: Georgia Caine as
Mrs. Truesmith, flanked by Woodrow and her would-be son Bugsy,
with Sarge filling out the pew

There's something genuine to be discovered even in the cult of motherhood.

Hail the Conquering Hero begins in full *McGinty* mode, with a tap dancer flashing her legs to stimulate the carnal hungers and thirst for booze of a saloon jammed with men. They're mostly working stiffs and military personnel on leave, by the look of them, though the place puts on just enough airs to have a manager seat the patrons, if they want a view of the floor show. This dockside dive features another high-class element as well: the young women who provide its entertainment are not limited to shaking their appeal on the upbeat. Next on the bill after the tap dancer is a chanteuse with upswept blonde hair, a strapless gown, and long gloves, played by the big-band singer Julie Gibson: a conventionally glamorous type, who nevertheless had enough sense of the ridiculous to have taken skirt roles with the Three Stooges. Lips moist and head held high, she glides among the tables accompanied by four singing waiters and a violinist, giving everyone a close look at her charms. Meanwhile she warbles about a completely incompatible feminine ideal, in the slow, lilting "Home to the Arms of Mother" (words and music by Preston Sturges).

A grey-haired old dear, waiting hopefully in the gloaming by her little cottage: the fantasy exerts such power over the predominantly roughneck audience that some men literally cry into their beers. Woodrow doesn't. Alone at the end of the bar, hunched over his own stein, he sounds the first of what will be many aggrieved notes, as he complains to the bartender about being made to listen to such mawkish stuff. ("Why don't they sing something gay?" he asks; to which the bartender replies, in effect, that for a guy in Woodrow's mood, it wouldn't help.) In fact, all Woodrow needs for a laugh would be to take a good look at Gibson (who in that get-up would do better to sing "How High the Moon," or "Moonlight in Vermont," or "What a Little Moonlight Can Do"—any of those lunar numbers), notice the "jaunty little hitch of poignance" she packs into "mother" (to quote James Harvey), and catalogue the other ineptitudes on show, such as an adjustment in mid-performance to the color of the stage light on her deadpan face. To the film's audience, this all makes for a superb travesty of sentimental guff. To Woodrow, it's a form of torture. Why he seethes, the film has not yet revealed; but it seems that the thought of motherly love must touch him more deeply than he'd like, and so might not be a pure sham.

Is there also something more than sham in military heroism? The opening scene poses that question, too, as Sarge and his men try to con the bar's manager into giving them a livelier night than Bugsy's spare change can buy. In a gruesome pantomime, Sarge pulls an Elks Club tooth out of his mouth, identifies it as having been yanked from the corpse of "General Yamatoho," and offers to sell this historic souvenir at a distress price. But the manager is ready for him. He counters by removing a length of fabric from a pocket and proposing to sell Sarge "the flag they buried him in.... I could make it very reasonable. I have it in several sizes." He goes on pulling items out of his coat: "MacArthur's suspenders, the first bullet to land in Pearl Harbor . . . and last but not least we have a button from Hitler's coat, although that one I don't personally believe."

The travails of a global conflict, reduced to counterfeit bric-à-brac. Like Woodrow, the manager isn't buying any phony ideals; and like Woodrow, he already seems to have bought plenty. If he's so cynical about these fakes, how did he acquire such a store of them? Maybe he, too, wants to intuit something genuine behind the fraud.

The mood so far has been light, and lightly jeering. So it continues, as the Marines unexpectedly receive a round of free beers and sandwiches and go looking for the benefactor who sent them, Woodrow. They banter and accept more drinks on his tab, joking about how his one month in the service hadn't been enough to put corns on his feet, consoling him about his chronic hay fever, and telling him a yarn about an allergy-stricken girlfriend who sneezed into her noodle soup. It's all easy cross talk, in which the Marines neither sneer at Woodrow for being a civilian nor try to impress him with the battles they've fought. (All Bugsy bothers to say about Guadalcanal is that "it's a great place to be *from*.") And then, in the first instance of the film's not merely alluding to more solemn feelings but touching on them, the emotional register unexpectedly darkens.

Reminiscing about his history of admiration for the Marines, Woodrow begins to recite by memory the list of their engagements from the War of Independence onward: "New Providence, Fort Nassau, the second Battle of Trenton, the *Bonhomme Richard* and the *Serapis*, 'I have not yet begun to fight.'" As he speaks, the camera dollies in to a tight close-up of Bracken, whose mouth is set in almost bitter determination, whose eyes gaze blindly ahead, until he concludes, to an echo of "Taps" on the soundtrack, "They bled and died."

At which point, Sturges needs to find a way for *Hail the Conquering Hero* to resume being a comedy.

He manages it in stages. First, he has Bugsy rescue the mood by breaking in with a cranky, seemingly irrelevant to-do about Woodrow's mother—a quick distraction from this brooding over the casualties of war. But a consciousness of violent death can't be cast off so readily; and so Sturges takes the next step by having Sarge discover his connection to Woodrow's late father. "I saw him fall," Sarge says, with a mournfulness that's mitigated by the unlikeliness of this chance meeting with Woodrow, and by the revelation that the heroic father's Great War nickname was Hinky Dinky. An inadvertent insult later—"He was a fine lookin' fella. He didn't look anything like you at all"— and the movie is once again rolling along jocularly, with Bugsy about to hatch his crackbrained scheme to get Woodrow home to the arms of mother.

Things are once again normal, for a Sturges movie: busy, rushed, improbable, uproarious. They'll stay that way, and then some, through the raucous homecoming. But the audience has been put on notice: at any moment, the mood might become serious again. And just as the unexpected ceremony at the railroad station will be a marvel of perpetual motion, with all sixteen principal characters colliding in an intricately cross-cut pandemonium, and the screen so crowded with extras and marching bands that you don't see the town itself, only churning waves of faces and bodies, so too will the high spirits and satirical laughter now flow without pause through darker thoughts. The recitation of the Marines' battles was the film's first discrete change of tone, and the last. From here on, everything will unfurl in a single snap.

Of course, something substantial must be risked in every effective comedy, even those starring Julie Gibson's past collaborators.* But in *Hail the Conquering Hero*, Sturges is almost relentless in toting up the dire magnitude of the stakes, even as he keeps the laughs coming.

The film has scarcely caught its breath from the reception scene when it enters the home of Mrs. Truesmith—the fantasy mother from the song, you'd think, now called up in the flesh—and makes you reflect not on the perfection of her image but on the realities of a lifetime of widowhood. The occasion is a visit from Schultz the grocer, who comes bearing gifts to help feed Woodrow and the Marines. He's played by Torben Meyer, the actor Sturges often relied on to deliver moments of sincerity, as the regretful ship's purser in *The Lady Eve* or the prostitute-rescuing doctor in *Triumph Over Pain*; and when Mrs. Truesmith tries to thank him, he again uses his mild German accent to strike a solemn note. "I'm very happy for you," he says quietly about Woodrow's return, as he goes out the kitchen door. "One in the family is enough to lose."

---

* To quote Lore Segal's novel *Her First American*, "The Three Stooges disseminate a deep truth: Calamity is the mother of calamity."

That's a light touch of sympathy in passing. The full weight of grief bears down a minute or two later, when Mrs. Truesmith asks the Marines to come into the parlor so she can show them her husband, Sergeant Truesmith, as a framed photo on the wall. But it's more than a photo. This is a shrine, with the full-size image of the dead man's face and shoulders bedecked in medals and insignias to the point of grotesquerie. Woodrow isn't present for the memorial rite—he's upstairs, changing into a suit from the uniform he'd been thrown into—but as the six Marines stand in line with his mother and salute, you feel how the dead hand of Hinky Dinky Truesmith has suffocated him. "Did you know your father got the Congressional Medal of Honor?" Sarge had asked in the bar scene, to which Woodrow had replied, "I grew up with it. They hung it on me." Well, there it is, dangling on its sash. You can imagine how it must have dragged on a young boy's neck.

Not that Sturges gives you time to dwell on the thought. In an instant Mrs. Truesmith and the full squad are heading out the door toward a new plot complication, with Woodrow and Sarge bickering in their wake and the streets once again filling with citizens out for the next excitement. (People in *Hail the Conquering Hero* almost always move in a pack. The Marines roam like a twelve-legged beast. The public will march or rally at any excuse.) But while Woodrow is being led toward further embarrassment, and the crowd is working up its delusions, two contrary attitudes toward war have begun to clash in the viewer's mind, the heroic and the antiheroic. The first attitude, as suggested by Schultz, is that people on the home front may justifiably honor warriors, who do in fact bleed and die and leave behind survivors who deserve kindness. The second, as suggested by the shrine, is that people on the home front are mad to adulate

Martial oratory: William Demarest as Sarge rouses the crowd

warriors, and diminish themselves, through the collective folly of militarism.

The tension between these two attitudes soon takes over the foreground. Eager to serve the death cult of Hinky Dinky, Sarge delivers testimonial speeches to Woodrow, which overflow with bloodthirsty, onomatopoetic blather about the hay-fever warrior. ("*Zing*, he got another one! *Zang*, another one hits the deck!") In contrast, the terse, deeply wounded Bugsy stands as a living rebuke to such shoot-'em-up fantasies. (He, too, contributes a tall tale at Sarge's direction—but one with a horrible underlying reality that Bugsy is ordered to deny.) As for Woodrow, he tries hard not to participate in this festival of fabulation; but the more he insists that he hasn't earned any medals and doesn't deserve any praise, the more the crowd imagines he's being bravely self-deprecating. All on their own, they turn his truth into a militaristic lie.

Because the movie so frankly respects the veterans of Guadalcanal (whose experiences, if related factually, would overwhelm the civilians), and because it defers movingly toward the widows and orphans of war, it's possible to underestimate how far Sturges pulls his theme toward the antiheroic pole. And, of course, the harshness of his satire on militarism was *meant* to be underestimated. (Compared to *The Miracle of Morgan's Creek*, *Hail the Conquering Hero* seems to have received few objections from censors.) Even so, the contempt for "jingling spurs" that Sturges had wanted to register in *Morgan's Creek* comes out at full voice, especially in the scene deep into the movie where Woodrow, fed up, lets out a string of sarcasms: "I'm a great hero. People *run* when they see me coming. I kill Nips with a wave of the hand. I *blow* them down. I shoot them from all angles, backwards, forwards, while looking in mirrors. I swim into the water and drown them like rats."

Bracken gives this speech the angriest, most bitter delivery of a notably angry, bitter performance. (I particularly commend the vigor of his two-handed pantomime of throttling an enemy under water.) Woodrow is repulsed by the crowd's longing for death-dealing supermen; and I suspect he's also disgusted at how the crowd characterizes the people whom a superman kills as "Nips" and "rats." Of course, such talk is common in all armed conflicts; Sturges might have included some of it just to answer the demands of verisimilitude. But by the time Woodrow makes this speech, other characters in *Hail the Conquering Hero* have resorted to these slurs more often than necessary and with too much pleasure—as does Sarge, for instance, in his tales about slaying "brown brothers." Without imputing unprovable intentions to Sturges, or expecting him to have been as outspoken as a superman while working at Paramount, I think the filmmaker who was capable of the church scene in *Sullivan's Travels* was also capable of objecting to the dehumanization that is as necessary to warfare as courage and endurance.

Moral ugliness and moral strength are both found on the home front—and presumably on the front lines, too, though Sturges makes no pretense of addressing that subject. He is concerned primarily with the civilians, who send young people off to war and later receive some of them back, in one piece or not. Here, too, Sturges develops a tension, between responsibility on the one hand and self-respect on the other.

Judge Dennis, as leader of the town's reform party, speaks about the first quality when he and his colleagues draft Woodrow to run for mayor: "There is something rotten in this town.... The motto of this town is 'Business as usual,' but a lot of us feel war time ain't a usual time and that business as usual is dishonest. That's why we need an honest man for mayor, an honest man who will wake us up and tell us the truth about something he knows all about."

That the reform party sees this honest candidate in Woodrow, who is currently the biggest liar in Oakridge, does not invalidate the judge's position. Civilians must make sacrifices in wartime. The fallacy lies in thinking that only a combat veteran can effectively tell them to do so. Before civilians can feel worthy, they need to grovel.

Not surprisingly, this contradiction has caught the attention of the reform party's perennially unsuccessful candidate, Doc Bissell (Harry Hayden). When Woodrow tries to escape town by inventing yet another lie, this one about being recalled to active duty, Bissell objects that the Marines are unnecessarily depriving Oakridge of a public servant. "That is one of the weaknesses of the military viewpoint," he intones, with a pedagogical rectitude guaranteed to drive away voters. "It does not always recognize the importance of civilians in war time."

Woodrow himself does not recognize that importance. Because he has not served in uniform, he feels he's nothing. *Hail the Conquering Hero* is designed to teach the people of Oakridge, and Woodrow, that he is a valuable person even though he hasn't killed anybody. Six Marines, all survivors of Guadalcanal, go far out of their way to help impart that lesson.

Libby teaches it, too.

She is a victim and a perpetrator of lies: a victim because Woodrow, intending to free her from his worthlessness, had sent a letter claiming he'd fallen in love with another woman; a perpetrator because she conceals the ring she accepted from the tallest, richest, most handsome and well-spoken young man in Oakridge—surely she can't let a hero glimpse the ring the minute he gets home—and throughout most of the day fails to inform Woodrow of her engagement. She protests that it's not her fault. Every time she starts to speak, a band strikes up or a political rally breaks out, which is maddeningly true. Still, Libby shows clear signs of wanting to abandon the stiff but otherwise eminently marriageable Forrest in favor of Woodrow. The movie's machinery must prevent her from doing so until Woodrow has confessed to his lies, so she can know she's choosing between two civilians, rather than between a civilian and a military man.

Since her field of action is limited to a marital decision, and her happiness in making it matters less than the movie's theme, I'd say Libby falls short of Sturges's best female characters. She's rescued, though, by her crankiness. Libby seems better suited to Woodrow than to Forrest—even though the latter is played by the lanky, chisel-featured former rodeo rider Bill

Edwards—because of a shared irritability. Forrest is spoiled but polite. Libby, like Woodrow, is always snapping at people.

She snaps at Forrest as soon as she comes on-screen, at the ceremony at the railway station, where her utterances begin, more or less, with, "Oh, shut up." Forrest has pointed out that if Woodrow had been held back another year from his homecoming, she might have greeted him with a baby in her arms. "That's what marriage is for, isn't it?" he asks, very reasonably. Libby grouses that he's probably right, if you think of marriage "like a breeding farm."

Her peevishness continues, and with it her marked criticism of conventional marriage, as she walks through town with Forrest later that afternoon. When he proposes that she probably wouldn't want to go on working as his father's secretary after the marriage, she shoots back, "What was I going to do, stay home and weave?" To his suggestion that she might take care of her children—what with the servant problem—she coldly answers, "Thank you for warning me." Soon her conversation descends to outright insults. Reminded that Forrest's father will be her children's grandfather, Libby asks, "What are you trying to do, depress me? If I thought they'd look anything like him—"

"Well, *I* don't look anything like him," Forrest says, mildly.

With restrained savagery, Libby replies, "I've noticed that. I pin my hopes on it."

So she's not a Jean Harrington or Gerry Jeffers, but she's not a pushover, either. Adding to her force is the presence of Ella Raines in the role. As Sturges had done before with Veronica Lake, he cast against type. Raines, too, would command attention during a dawning career for a sultry image, strengthened in her case by the downward cast of her mouth, which gave her a wised-up, discontented look, and by the contrast between her dark hair and light-colored cat's eyes. Buddy DeSylva thought she didn't look anything like a movie small-town girl, and he was right. Even worse, from the studio's perspective: Raines had never before played a part as big as Libby, had no proven record in comedy, and had to be brought over from Universal. But Sturges thought he was onto something and insisted on having her for a role summarized in the screenplay in a single sentence: "Libby is a pretty girl."[5] With Raines's inherent tartness, Libby became more than that.

Raines also became, against her will, the point of contention that made Sturges's break with Paramount irreparable. After DeSylva watched the rushes of her first scenes, he ordered Sturges to fire her immediately, scrap what he'd shot, and start over with a Paramount actress. Even though Raines herself later admitted that her first days on set were bad, Sturges refused to dismiss her, in an incident he later recalled in his memoirs with regret: "The awful day about Ella Raines will be with me always."[6]

Sturges's stated reason for keeping Raines, and very likely throwing away his impending contract renewal with Paramount, was that he couldn't bear to ruin the reputation of a young actress at the start of her career. His pride must have played a part, too; he had to prove he could beat DeSylva, at least temporarily. A modern observer looking back also might wonder if Sturges had a more personal reason for wanting Raines in the picture. His marriage to Louise Sargent had broken down, and he was openly conducting an affair with Jeannie La Vell, whom he'd plucked out of the Paramount secretarial pool. There would have been nothing unusual about a powerful director's also gratifying himself by exerting his seigneurial rights with a starlet he'd just cast. But Sturges seems not to have conformed to this stereotype, and the biographies produce no evidence of an affair with Ella Raines. Apparently, he believed in her; and in the end, she gave him a pretty girl who could grumble as acidly as Woodrow.

Libby gets the honor in the final scene of confirming Woodrow's worthiness, despite his being a civilian. Her love for him even validates the tendency of Oakridge to fall into mass hysteria. "Politics is a very peculiar thing, Woodrow," Doc Bissell says, as he explains that Woodrow still looks likely to be elected mayor. "If they want you, they want you. . . . They find their own reasons. Just like when a girl wants a man." It's an uncharacteristically optimistic construction for Sturges to put on the electorate. With Libby's concurrence, it sticks.

And that's a problem for viewers who think Sturges could not possibly believe what he's saying. The cynic who created *The Great McGinty* and has reveled throughout this picture in the idiocy of the crowd, the satirist who showed up the world's amorous fools by inventing some of the smartest, strongest-willed, most cheerfully dishonest heroines in screen history, now reverses himself at the last moment in *Hail the Conquering Hero*, placing his faith in the wisdom of the Oakridge crowd while making the sharp-tongued Libby subject herself to Woodrow, with a murmur and a coy upward glance. As Manny Farber wrote, "Sturges evades the whole issue revoltingly and runs off to a happy ending."[7]

But I suppose that depends on which issue you're talking about.

Is it Woodrow's cowardice? I don't mean his reluctance to fight—if anything, he's too eager for battle—but the denial of his own wishes. You can easily imagine that Woodrow has left it to the Marines to act out his fantasies for him, taking on the work of reuniting him with his mother and parading him around town. It's all *their* excursion; he's just the unwilling passenger, or so he tells himself. For this self-deception, as much as for the deceit he practices on the town, Woodrow arguably deserves punishment. But just because Sturges does not let the hammer fall does not mean he evades the implications built into the picture. In the plot, Woodrow goes free. In the audience's judgment, he may be held to account.

Or is the issue the credulity and bloodthirstiness of the public? Again, I don't see how Sturges evades a problem that by now he's dramatized for ninety-five minutes straight. In the scene of the town-hall meeting, he's even had Woodrow tell his fellow citizens to their faces that they're fools. Is Sturges at the finale supposed to make people, in aggregate, *stop* behaving like dolts? Isn't it more consistent, more honest, to let the mob be the mob, right to the end?

Or is the issue the notion that civilian life must always rest on a foundation of state violence?

There I might agree that Sturges dodges the question he's raised, in a resolution that comes as close as he ever did to Capracorn. Even so, just as the thought of violent death isn't shrugged off in the opening scene in the bar, neither do the movie's darker shadows vanish at the end just because the plot's been wrapped up. Whatever the marriage of Woodrow and Libby will be like—and good luck to this union, with its partners' glum yet waspish temperaments—the prospect of a wedding cannot make up for the public's willful ignorance of the suffering of flesh-and-blood men, compared with the nobility of statues acquired on the cheap from a foundry.

The final image of *Hail the Conquering Hero* does not show the citizens' joyous farewell to the Marines, or even Woodrow's whispered affirmation of the Marines' motto, *Semper fidelis*. The film ends on a shot of the unpopulated parlor of the Truesmith house, with the dead father looking out from the wall. Where's the evasion? Every day for the rest of his life, Woodrow will continue to face the dread, and the impossibly heavy burden, that have warped his character.

And, of course, Libby does not have the final say on whether Woodrow deserves to live with respect among his town's capricious, gullible people. The ultimate approval must come from a madman. Bugsy is all smiles as he stands at the back of the caboose, waving goodbye to Woodrow and accepting his acknowledgment of the Marines' superiority. (Can they do almost anything? "You got no idea.") But Woodrow has come to know from Bugsy the exact nature of that superiority, and it shames him.

When Woodrow had invented his excuse to skip town and Bugsy had erupted, the immediate target of his fury was a fellow Marine, Juke, who had helped with the scheme. Sturges shows Bugsy launching himself at the man, with all the power of Freddie Steele bursting out of the corner, and then cuts to a shot that reveals the damage to Juke's face. Woodrow interprets this attack, correctly, as an insult; *he's* the man Bugsy should have assaulted, but he's evidently considered too inconsequential to hit. Woodrow is so incensed by the slight that he takes a cheap shot at Bugsy—whom the other Marines are restraining—and punches him in the mouth. In the sudden, terrible silence that follows, the others free his arms, and Bugsy spits blood.

Then he snarls, "Go find a woman to fight with, that's all you know how to hurt." And he stalks off, leaving Woodrow unpunished.

"That's all you know how to hurt." No matter how loudly the people cheer in the last scene, neither Woodrow nor the audience

Freddie Steele as Bugsy: "That's all you know how to hurt"

can forget what Bugsy has taught: that men are measured by the degree of pain they can inflict. It's a terrible thought to infiltrate into the final celebration of *Hail the Conquering Hero*. But if you imagine it's faded from the picture, all I can say is, you got no idea.

9

YOU AROUSE THE ARTIST IN ME

The Sin of Harold Diddlebock

So far in this zigzag through Sturges's films, I have dodged the clutches of psychobiography. Now that I've reached *The Sin of Harold Diddlebock*, though, I find I'm like the movie's football-playing protagonist: in the grasp.

As grips go, it's imprecise. To surrender by stating the obvious—that Preston Sturges, like his character Harold Diddlebock, was a man undergoing a mid-life crisis—would be to fail on scale alone, like reducing Milton's Satan to a wounded narcissist. The antihero of *Paradise Lost* acts in a theater that encompasses heaven, Earth, hell, and all of history. Diddlebock, though merely human, nevertheless mounts an impressively grand rebellion of his own, involving thirty-seven lions, fourteen tigers, nine jaguars, seven beautiful young women (all named Miss Otis), half the bankers on Wall Street, most of the downtown Manhattan police force, and an alcoholic potion capable of blowing up 14.2 percent of the week. Previous Sturges characters had gone to considerable lengths to escape the horrors of stasis—always a looming danger in his films—but none before Diddlebock had required such a monumental self-rescue.

I have to admit, though, that Diddlebock rebels for a mundane purpose: he wants to rejuvenate himself. Who is "that old crackpot with the spectacles," he demands at a moment of crisis, glimpsing himself myopically in a barroom mirror. "That old *tramp?* How long have I been looking like this? . . . *This*, is a *calamity*, that must be *remedied*, immediately!" By the time Sturges dreamed up the character who would say those words, he too was in need of remedy.

He was forty-five years old when he quit Paramount at the end of 1943. Corpulent and boozy, with sagging jowls, a white streak through his hair, and a five-pack-a-day cigarette habit, he was bored with marriage to Louise Sargent—their conversation had long since declined to the purely logistical—and was apt to talk about "living in contemplation of death."[1]

And yet, intimations of mortality aside, he had much to cheer him as 1944 began, especially the runaway success of *The Miracle of Morgan's Creek* and the Schadenfreude of returning briefly to Paramount to rescue *Hail the Conquering Hero*. Beyond that, he had the excitement of becoming one of Hollywood's new elite of producer-directors, like John Ford with his Argosy Pictures and Orson Welles with Mercury Productions. In pursuit of independence, Sturges established a company with a man he mistakenly imagined to be his match in dynamism, inventiveness, and disdain for penny-pinching: Howard Hughes. While contract negotiations over the nascent California Pictures dragged on, occupying much of the year (as Jacobs and Curtis relate), Sturges went about blithely issuing statements about his ambitions. When the partnership with Hughes was at last settled in August 1944, in time for Sturges's forty-sixth birthday, he seemingly had command at last of a production outfit of his own into which to pour his energy.

Even so, he showed signs of feeling his age. His fascination with the past, which had helped animate *The Great McGinty* and *Triumph Over Pain* and had crept into the argot of *The Lady Eve* and *Sullivan's Travels*, now seemed to preoccupy him more than ever, just when he ought to have been thinking up novelties for California Pictures.

In July 1944, even before he signed his devil's bargain with Hughes, Sturges decided that one of the first things he wanted to do at his company was revive the career of D. W. Griffith. He would bring back the master of silent film to direct a movie version of the play *9 Pine Street*—itself an historical curiosity, as a retelling of the Lizzie Borden story—with Lillian Gish in the lead. She had starred in the Broadway production, which Sturges might have seen in 1933, if he'd been quick. It had survived for all of twenty-eight performances. Whatever thoughts of bygone days had moved Sturges to dredge up this creaky project, Griffith put an end to them. According to Jacobs, the great man showed up an hour late for his initial meeting with Sturges, reeling from drink, and demanded to know why anyone would think he wanted to direct another film.

Still thinking about the past, Sturges decided to make a film based on a favorite book of his early years, Joseph Hergesheimer's novel *The Three Black Pennies*, published in 1917. Hergesheimer had been a highly regarded author—in the late teens and twenties. By the time Sturges approached him to ask about the rights, his florid prose was out of fashion, and he hadn't published a novel in ten years. A film of *The Three Black Pennies* would have been another reclamation project, perhaps with its own silent-era allure, since the movie version of Hergesheimer's story "Tol'able David" had been a hit for director Henry King in 1921. This time, though, as Jacobs notes, Sturges himself drifted away. Perhaps he realized that a picture based on this historical saga of a steel-working family in Pennsylvania might be compared to a very recent Oscar winner, John Ford's *How Green Was My Valley*, and would have to work hard to be as good.

Sturges's mind slipped backward in another direction as well: toward the France where he'd spent so much of his childhood and youth, and to which he continued to feel a bond through friends such as Jean Renoir and René Clair. During the brief California Pictures period, according to Curtis, Sturges considered casting Spencer Tracy in a version of Louis Verneuil's stage comedy *La Banque Nemo* (1931), which Marguerite Viel had filmed in 1934. Sturges also made an initial effort to adapt Frédéric Mauzens's comic novel *Le coffre-fort vivant* (*The Human Strong Box*, 1917), which Verneuil had helped transform in 1938 into a lavish operetta at the Théâtre du Châtelet. Only a few years before the establishment of California Pictures, Sturges had described himself to reporters as a no-nonsense, business-minded American who felt amused contempt for the European artiness to which his mother had subjected him.[2] Now he was draping himself in frou-frou in full view of the press.

He never got far enough with the Verneuil projects to learn how they would have fared at the box office; but he did manage to put a third old-fashioned Gallic fancy into production. He decided that California Pictures should make a period drama— not a wildly improbable notion, perhaps, except that the source he chose was Prosper Mérimée's novella *Colomba* (1840), set in rustic post-Napoleonic Corsica. To his great credit, Sturges initially gave the film to the exiled Max Ophuls to direct; but the assignment didn't stick. After the passage of several years, multiple changes in the creative team, and much editing by Hughes, *Colomba* was tortured into the flop *Vendetta* (1950).

But Sturges had one more backward-looking idea in store, and by autumn 1944 he was on his way toward realizing it.

In this scheme, the neglected artist he would bring back was America's most popular slapstick comedian of the 1920s,

Harold Lloyd—a performer who hadn't enjoyed a hit since the talkies began, had effectively retired from filmmaking in 1938, and initially demurred when he was approached. Lloyd had to be wooed; and then he walked away in a huff when Hughes (making a move that Sturges ought to have recognized as ominous) offered him a paltry fee. Sturges had to talk Hughes into raising the offer, meanwhile persuading Lloyd that in the end the project would be worth his trouble.

Indeed, Sturges's idea for the film was one of his most ingenious, and in execution would be one of his most daring as well—almost as suicidally risky as the stunts that Lloyd had famously performed two decades earlier. Lloyd would reprise his role in *The Freshman*—the part of a college boy who wins a big football game through the triumph of irrepressible enthusiasm over complete lack of athletic ability—but he would take this character from youth to middle age in a single, sudden leap. The first sequence of *The Sin of Harold Diddlebock*, set in 1923, would simply consist of the last reel of *The Freshman*, altered only by the insertion of a few shots that introduce a new character, Mr. Waggleberry.* Sturges would then jump to the future of the young, indomitably peppy Harold. Twenty-two years later, in 1945, he would be Waggleberry's gray-faced, shuffling bookkeeper.

This breathtaking concept would require a contemporary audience to sit still for—no, laugh at—about six and a half minutes of antique comedy, after which it would reward their patience with the image of a defeated Harold Lloyd, cloaked for work in a wretched, torn jacket and unable to rise from his stool

---

* The introductory title of *The Sin of Harold Diddlebock* dates *The Freshman* to 1923, claiming this was when its football game was photographed. The year of release was 1925.

without a painful, two-fisted stretch of the lumbar muscles. Forget about "living in contemplation of death." This was to be a contemplation of living death: endlessly lingering failure and decline, with no hope of release until Diddlebock is fired from the only job he's ever held.

On one level—the level that the star would have preferred to contemplate—the darker side of this premise was simply an excuse to revive the public's delight in a beloved comedian. As soon as *Diddlebock* had settled the cobwebs on its hero, it would brush them off again and return him to his glorious exploits. With Sturges as the gag writer, these would go beyond even the human-fly escapade that had left Lloyd dangling from the hands of a skyscraper clock in *Safety Last!*

But on another level, the premise of *Diddlebock* turned Harold Lloyd into a one-man memento mori. To Sturges's

"Poor Mr. Diddlebock" confesses his love to the most recent Miss Otis. Courtesy The Museum of Modern Art

contemporaries, even those who were too young to have seen *The Freshman* in 1925, its football scene would have seemed like a shared memory of innocence and optimism in the bygone years before the Depression. By carrying the source of this nostalgia into the present, Sturges would not so much reawaken happy memories as debunk them, mocking whatever residual belief the audience still might harbor in America's myth of unlimited opportunity. Every man is the architect of his own fortune! Prosperity is just around the corner! There is no greater satisfaction than starting at the bottom and working your way to the top! As a young college graduate newly hired by Mr. Waggleberry, Diddlebock tacks up a solid wall of such platitudes to decorate his cranny. The cut to 1945 would make the neglected, middle-aged, soon-to-be-out-of-work Diddlebock a living refutation of these pieties.

There's room to doubt whether the audience needed any such refutation in 1947, when *Diddlebock* was released. The strain of American cinema that had seized the public's imagination by then, film noir, was very far from tales of pluck and luck—as distant in its way as the French poetic realism of the late 1930s had been from the boulevard comedies that Sturges belatedly thought he might import. But then, with *Diddlebock*, Sturges had no intention of mounting a thoroughgoing attack on Horatio Alger, as he'd done in *The Great McGinty*. His new film would expose the fraudulence of the cult of business success, but only to reaffirm the wisdom of betting big on a closely related American ideal, the pursuit of happiness.

The stakes were high for both the drooping Diddlebock and his creator. Sturges was almost the same age as the character he'd imagined. (The film specifies Diddlebock's year of birth as 1901.) Like Diddlebock, he'd lost his job. (Never mind that Sturges had chosen to leave Paramount. As far as he was concerned, a cabal of mediocre, hypocritical gasbags had pushed him out.) He, too, was short of funds. (Again, this was his own doing; but he nevertheless felt the grind month after month, just as if he'd been an impecunious office clerk.) Worst of all, he had no love in his life. His marriage was stale. His affair with Jeannie La Velle had become an office romance, heavy on the office.

The reason I can't avoid a biographical-psychological interpretation of *The Sin of Harold Diddlebock* is because the remedies Sturges offers his character—remedies common among middle-aged men—are identical to those he adopted for himself:

- *Strong drink*: Diddlebock, a lifelong teetotaler, comes back to life thanks to his first experience of alcohol. The ten-minute-long episode in which a bartender devises an elaborate cocktail for the novice, and Diddlebock under its influence changes into a sort of chatty, caterwauling, inebriated Mr. Hyde, is easily the best part of the movie, and one of the funniest scenes Sturges ever created. For Sturges himself, unfortunately, the liberating effects of daily tippling came with a cost not reckoned in the movie.
- *Financial profligacy:* As soon as Diddlebock regains his spunk, he grandly declares that money is "nothing but a symbol that costs practically nothing to print. There is no shortage of it at any time." Sturges managed the budget for *The Sin of Harold Diddlebock* in exactly this spirit.
- *A new lover*: When sent packing from his job, Diddlebock takes a moment to say goodbye to an officemate, Miss Otis, who is the most recent in a line of sisters with whom he has been infatuated. He confesses his feelings to her, but only so he can sadly, finally, abjure any hope of love. At the end, though, he discovers that he's won her, thanks to his new extravagance with cash and alcohol. Miss Otis is played by

Frances Ramsden, a woman twenty two years younger than Sturges, whom he'd decided to screen test on first sight, having met her casually in 1942, and whom he quickly recruited for his new film, and his bed, upon encountering her again in 1945. She was a commercial model from New York with no acting experience. He told her she didn't need any.[3]

I can't say that the decision to cast Frances Ramsden harmed *Diddlebock*, except by confining the main female character to a few scenes in which she is given minimal dialogue, so as not to place undue demands on the performer. As John L. Sullivan remarked to the police in *Sullivan's Travels*, "There's always a girl in the picture"—but in the case of Miss Otis, the least substantial female lead Sturges ever created, the girl is nothing more than a fantasy that gets magically fulfilled in the final scene.

With Ramsden by his side every day, the re-energized Sturges had more and more trouble getting to that last scene. It wasn't her fault. Part of the problem was that Sturges and Harold Lloyd had different ideas about how the scenes should be played—and Lloyd had written a clause into his contract specifying that Sturges would film alternate takes on demand, doing them as Lloyd preferred, so they could see who was right. The duplication of effort took its toll, as did the necessity of cajoling Lloyd into performing his own stunts, including those involving a full-grown lion named Jackie.

But much of the delay in filming *Diddlebock*, and the attendant cost overruns, resulted from Sturges's determination to have fun in Ramsden's company during production, now that he was free from the time-and-money scolds at Paramount. He maintained a carnival atmosphere on set. He stopped work to entertain visitors and would order lunch for everyone from The Players. If asked about the long stretches of down time, according to

Curtis, he would reply, "It's my money."[4] (Actually, it was Hughes's. Sturges's was tied up in his restaurant.) And according to his biographer Donald Spoto, he thought nothing of interrupting work so he could take off on a horseback ride with Ramsden, leaving the cast and crew idle.[5]

The picture went into production on September 12, 1945, with a budget of about a million dollars—the largest yet entrusted to Sturges—and was to wrap on November 24. Sturges finished shooting two full months late, having overspent by $600,000. He might as well have been his own hero, frolicking with the beautiful Miss Otis while proclaiming that money is a mere symbol, of which there is never any shortage.

But when making a biographical-psychological interpretation, it's a mistake to assume that one character, and one alone, acts out its creator's drives, anxieties, and fantasies. A second figure in *Diddlebock* may also stand in for Sturges, or express an aspect of him. I would argue that the bartender played by Edgar Kennedy, who invents the Diddlebock cocktail and so sets the protagonist on his erratic course, plays an authorial role.

Like Sturges, the bartender is hyperarticulate, and tellingly is not mocked for his fancy talk. On the contrary: his slightly off-kilter eloquence suggests he's a person of talent and imagination who has been deprived of adequate challenges. What's more, he describes himself, twice, with a word that no one has previously used in a Sturges film: *artist*. When informed that Diddlebock has never before tasted alcohol, the bartender turns toward the camera, as if sharing his thoughts with the audience rather than the other characters, and says dreamily, "You arouse the artist in me." (Note the precision, almost the delicacy, with which Kennedy pronounces the t's. He sounds like a man used to finer things.) When asked, a bit too late, if he has concocted an overly large batch of Diddlebocks, the bartender replies, in words that Sturges might have spoken to Hughes, "The artist does not weigh his clay."

Here's the important biographical-psychological detail that escapes the midlife-crisis reading of *Diddlebock*: when Sturges quit Paramount, he also cut himself loose from the studio ethos, in which only a pretentious fop would have claimed to be more than a maker of entertainments. Sturges was at last ready to say, out loud, that he was an artist.

But his new protagonist was *not* an artist—a flaw in conception that undermines *The Sin of Harold Diddlebock*.

At first glance, you wouldn't expect such a fault, given the care that Sturges took, as usual, in developing the character and preparing the plot's turning points. By the time Sturges gets to the bar scene, he has suggested to the audience again and again that Diddlebock is a man who for too long has repressed his urges— for sex, for luxury, for fun—and now is ready to blow.

Starting with the scene set in 1923, when Diddlebock takes a job fresh out of college, Sturges portrays the character as someone hopelessly addicted to the most deadening counsels of prudence. At this early moment, Lloyd still plays Diddlebock as a grinning, chest-puffing optimist. (He carries off the impersonation of youth remarkably well, too.) Meanwhile, though, Sturges is busy showing how Diddlebock pours his self-defeating faith into old maxims and adages, which he declaims while drawing himself up and shaking his left index finger. He looks as if he's giving someone, perhaps himself, a good scolding.

"He who loseth honor loseth everything!" Diddlebock declares in this scene to his new boss, E. J. Waggleberry (Raymond Walburn, once again playing the blustering, pop-eyed business owner, as he had in *Christmas in July* and *Hail the*

Conquering Hero). It's perfectly clear to the audience, though not to Diddlebock, that Waggleberry is a coddled-from-the-cradle blowhard who doesn't give a damn for any honor he can't find in his bridge hand. But as a born sucker, Diddlebock swallows the disappointment of being offered only a bookkeeping job and settles into his cranny, encouraging himself—what an encouragement—by decorating the wall with placards that advise, "One cottage in Canarsie is worth two castles in Spain. . . . An ounce of security is worth a pound of pipe dreams."

With these words of caution staring down at him, it's no wonder that after twenty-two years Diddlebock has not dared to budge from his stool. Once upon a time, as Waggleberry complains when summoning the hopeless fellow into his private office, Diddlebock had been "full of zing, full of zest, full of zowie." (Waggleberry runs an advertising agency and talks like his products.) But "the Earth has cooled considerably since you put on your first pair of sleeve-protectors out there," and Diddlebock must now be fired. "You have not only ceased to go forward," Waggleberry informs him, "you have gone backward. You not only stopped progressing, you have stopped thinking. You not only make the same mistakes year after year, you don't even change your apologies." Handing a slumped Diddlebock an appropriately inscribed Swiss watch (it chimes) and the meager contents of his company savings account, Waggleberry shows him the door.

Despite this dreadful reversal, Diddlebock is not yet ready to cut loose from being governed by platitudes. When approached on the street for a handout—the *schnorrer*, a horse-racing enthusiast named Wormy, is played by the diminutive Jimmy Conlin with a derby tilted back on his head and a toothpick making its unsavory way between his lips and fingers—Diddlebock once more points at the heavens and cries out a proverb. He even gets into an impromptu contest with Wormy, battling for supremacy in the recollection of old saws, and scores a win with Isaiah 28. But in the midst of this wisdom-slinging, Diddlebock betrays feelings that lofty sentiments and verbs ending in "-eth" can't contain.

Forking over some of his hard-earned savings—considerably more than Wormy had requested—Diddlebock explains his sudden extravagance by saying, "It's just that I've been [saving money] for 20 years, and I'm getting tired of it. It's what you call an impulse. It's like a man works all his life in a glass factory? Well, one day he feels like picking up a hammer." Lloyd delivers these lines with a mixture of biliousness and rage, his face soured as if from acid reflux, his left hand raised to smash an imaginary sheet of plate glass. He suggests that something violent is about to rise in Diddlebock—or perhaps something that might turn violent, if not permitted to break through.

With this groundwork laid, Sturges is now ready for the bar scene, where that key word, "impulse," comes up again. Denying that the divergence from habit he's about to permit himself is in any way significant, Diddlebock says the decision to try liquor is "just an impulse."

"Well, obey that impulse," Wormy says at once, and adds, sensing a further opportunity to mooch, "Why don't you have a cigar?"

But the artist-bartender is already mixing the potion that will blast through Diddlebock's inhibitions and free him to obey *every* impulse, including those that go well beyond a desire to treat his new friend to a smoke. Having drained his cup, Diddlebock abruptly grasps his lapels in mid-conversation, like an orator on the stump, lifts his face to the ceiling, and lets out the yowl of a moon-mad coyote. The bland puzzlement that follows—Diddlebock looks around, wondering if an animal is loose in the bar—suggests at first that his personality has been momentarily interrupted but will resume intact. But as a stream of grandiloquent opinions begins to pour out, along with more of the inarticulate but high-spirited howls that Diddlebock still can't identify as his own, it becomes clear that a long-suppressed inner man has taken charge and is growing louder by the minute. The dried-out old Diddlebock is now an abandoned husk, to be forgotten amid the new man's search for the fascinating beast that lurks nearby.

Diddlebock will find a real wild beast soon enough—in fact, he'll find an entire menagerie, and learn to identify with part of it, too—but for the moment all is delightful confusion in this ten-minute-long transformation scene. Maybe "conversion" would be a better word. While Diddlebock is being born

Diddlebock, surrounded by Sturges stock company members, experiences the metamorphosis brought on by the bartender's art. Courtesy The Museum of Modern Art

again—a process improved by Lloyd's initial persistence in owlish solemnity—the static, set-bound proceedings are enlivened by the intrusions of a cop and a neighboring barber (both wondering what the ruckus is about) and scattershots of some of Sturges's most absurd dialogue. When the bartender wants to express amazement, he exclaims, with near-Falstaffean excess, "Well, drown my kittens." Diddlebock, wanting to offer a toast but lacking experience, ventures a jaunty but off-target "Over your ears!" And Wormy, upon hearing a passing mention of posterity, wisely observes that "Posterity is just around the corner"—one of the few malapropisms to be uttered by a Sturges character, and also indisputably true.

The delirium rises to its climax as Diddlebock, in full stump-speaker mode and at the top of his crescendo, rails against the waning of the pioneer spirit: "They mined the earth and dug the rivers and tamed the wilderness, and brought forth peaceful homesteads in the shadow of the eagle and the echo of the thundering herd. And in the final analysis, where are they? I *ask* you. And I reply, 'Dead, my friends! Deader than a boiled mackerel!'"

To which Wormy might reply, "Carp diem."

Diddlebock, exhilarated to the point of stupor, is carried out of the bar after this—and you're carried with him toward the next scene, intoxicated by laughter and scarcely pausing to realize that this grand eruption, so elaborately engineered, was also completely unnecessary.

The Diddlebock you saw in the first six and a half minutes—the Diddlebock of 1923, who races onto the football field in such excitement that he lines up on the wrong side—would not need to be liberated by alcohol, for the simple reason that he would not have submitted in the first place to the tyranny of thrift and patient, dutiful labor.

When he's young, Diddlebock is arrogant enough to assume that his teammates (who ignore him) require arm-flailing pep talks, and that he should appoint himself to give them. When knocked dizzy, he retains enough enthusiasm to bounce back—though he then needs to be bounced around again, to get into position. Faced with a squad of onrushing tacklers, he is sufficiently composed, and dishonest, to trick them by unlacing the football and dangling it like a yo-yo. (He's also so ignorant that he stops short in the play, having been confused by a spectator's whistle.) He fails and fails and fails until he somehow finds himself in the open with the ball in his arms, at which point he runs and runs and runs, straight toward the most effectively moving camera you're going to see for the rest of *The Sin of Harold Diddlebock*.

It doesn't seem possible that this man would have taken a stool at E. J. Waggleberry's company and then sat there meekly for twenty-two years.

When you consider how much thought Sturges put into the inner lives of the residents of Morgan's Creek, you long for a justification of Diddlebock's decades-long hibernation. Not an explanation—movies work better when they don't spell things out—but some signs of internal consistency, which could prompt you to join imaginatively with the character's emotions. With Diddlebock, though, a sanctimonious obeisance to maxims of prudence is clearly imposed on the original character, not inherent in him.

Worse still, you're always staring at a chasm in his personality: the split between the period before he went to work for Waggleberry and the period after, the one before he tasted liquor and the one after. The break is so complete that after starting his transformative bender on a Tuesday, he loses Wednesday to a blackout and awakens on Thursday back where he'd started, as the old, defeated self, only perhaps even more bitter and querulous. The second half of the movie is the story of how Diddlebock realizes he must integrate his personality, harnessing his recently rediscovered recklessness to achieve a practical goal.

This is a very different project from Trudy's in *The Miracle of Morgan's Creek*. Her amnesia, though accidental, comes from indulging in the sort of thing she'd been doing all along. When she tries to cope with the resulting predicament—one that could not be more internal—she instinctively relies on the same wiles and resources that got her into the mess. By contrast, everything that drives Diddlebock is external. He loses Wednesday because two strangers entice him into breaking his lifelong habits; and the very large problem that remains after the blackout—a circus menagerie, which he has absent-mindedly acquired and must somehow feed—is so far outside his personal sphere that it resides in Queens.

To rescue himself, Diddlebock reaches beyond what we know of his adult personality, and does so twice. First, he declares to Wormy that he will go back to thinking about how to solve problems, as he used to do in college. (But this rings hollow. We didn't see him solve any problems in college. All he did was run frantically around a football field.) Second, he hits on a scheme in which he will once more wear the plaid-on-plaid suit and tall hat that he donned for his bender—an outfit that was conceived, as we've learned, for a vaudeville dog act—and hand out samples of the Diddlebock cocktail, not for the sheer fun of it (as before) but as a sales gimmick. He thinks he can unload his insupportable circus on one banker or another by peddling it as a public relations opportunity, with Jackie the lion by his side to demonstrate the potential to grab attention. The stunt is as desperately commercial as Jimmy's slogan-writing in *Christmas in July*, with the difference that Jimmy thinks up something risible while being self-serious, whereas Diddlebock forces his scheme onto the bankers (and the movie's audience) with back-slapping jocularity.

Despite the forced gaiety, there's still laughter to be had when Diddlebock springs his plan on an astonished financial district, parading in and out of banks in his vaudeville costume with Wormy sniveling along on his right hand and Jackie the lion on a leash in his left. Earlier that day, when Diddlebock had awakened as his same old self, he hadn't recognized the hideous suit and had been scared out of his seat—rightfully so—when introduced to Jackie by the circus's previous owner (Al Bridge at his most phlegmatic—which is saying something, considering he's petting an adult lion). Now, Diddlebock miraculously overcomes his fear of lions and distaste for optically disruptive clothing and carries on like a born showman, greeting passersby with a full-toothed grin and a tip of his hat. He looks as self-confident as the get-ahead maxims urged him to be all those years ago, while also conveying the air of a child up to some harmless, raucous mischief. Maybe he's able to perform this stunt because he's sampled the Diddlebock cocktails he's handing out, and they've enabled him to recapture his drunken self, this time without losing control. Or maybe he's reached back to his college days, with or without the assistance of booze, and recovered his long-lost foolhardiness. Either way, the mature Diddlebock, who is engaged in a calculated performance, has willed himself back into youth—as is suggested, perhaps, by his uncanny resemblance to the Man with the Yellow Hat in the children's book *Curious George* (published in the United States in 1941),

Diddlebock and Jackie the Lion explain the public's dislike of bankers.
Courtesy The Museum of Modern Art

with Jackie as the life-threatening substitute for a good little monkey.*

But when Diddlebock and friends intrude into the inner offices of banks, amid much panic, the juvenile insouciance drops away, and the scenes turn into an anomalous rejection of Sturges's long-cherished figure of the sensible, benevolent tycoon. A grinning, shouting Harold Lloyd declares to a succession of bankers, "You are loathed by everyone! You are abominated by everybody! You are reviled, despised, and detested by all

---

* In summer 1944, when Sturges began writing *The Sin of Harold Diddlebock*, his first child, Mon, was three years old. Sturges was often a distant father to Mon, but he was a father all the same. It's not inconceivable that he read *Curious George* to the boy.

normal people!" (As if to emphasize how thoroughly these attacks diverge from Sturges's earlier treatment of wealthy businessmen, the meanest of the bankers is played by Robert Dudley, the Wienie King.) I don't know what inspired Sturges to introduce these full-throated rebukes—maybe it was his experience of Howard Hughes's parsimony—but the pleasure of the telling-off spills from the screen.

Which is to say, Sturges had not lost his touch completely—not in the bar scene, not in the bustling events that immediately ensue, and not while cheerfully assailing bankers as a class. And yet, as Jackie gets away from Diddlebock, leading to the film's biggest set piece—an adventure along a skyscraper's edge, designed to recall and outdo *Safety Last!*—both the innocent laughter and the satirical laughter drain from the sequence, squeezed out by the thinness of Diddlebock's character and Sturges's lack of any clear idea about what to do with him.

Manny Farber complained that Sturges's satirical instincts were unprincipled and purposeless—that Sturges was spinelessly content to lambaste in all directions and take a stand for none. So far in this book, I have gone into perhaps wearying detail to explain why I disagree, having found coherence in these films on a level that can't be paraphrased in a political statement. When it comes to *The Sin of Harold Diddlebock*, though, I yield to the superior critic. First Sturges mocks Waggleberry, a bloated businessman who inherited his fortune, and who obtusely tells Diddlebock, while firing him, that the Depression was "hard on *all* of us." Then Sturges turns around and has Diddlebock decide that Waggleberry "may have been right to fire me." Harsh capitalist imperatives are good for the soul; job security (and the prospect of Social Security payments, no doubt) breeds mental laziness. Then Sturges turns around again, to have Diddlebock, Wormy, and Jackie the lion break in on a series of bankers and accuse them of rapacity, while implicitly threatening a *real* experience of the law of the jungle. The scene is fun, all right—but it doesn't come out of any steady sense of conviction in the character, or for that matter the filmmaker.

Worse still, the scene doesn't lead anywhere. The attenuated chase up a fire escape and onto a skyscraper's window ledge, with Diddlebock and Wormy in potentially suicidal pursuit of Jackie, does nothing except reproduce a Harold Lloyd stunt, minus the old panache. It's just another damned thing that happens, without consequences for the characters' ideas and emotions or for the plot. Had the police broken into Robert Dudley's office to arrest Diddlebock before Jackie jumped out the window, the last sequences of the movie could have been identical. The only difference, perhaps, would have been in your reactions. You wouldn't wonder how Wormy manages to see again after losing his eyeglasses in the chase, or why this bite-size sidekick hasn't wound up inside Jackie, who has not been fed for a day or two.

The excuse for these lapses—that movies are fantasies, and so are free to traffic in self-contradiction and improbability—cannot hold up in the context of Sturges's earlier achievements. There is coherence even in *The Palm Beach Story*, with its blatantly madcap tone and plot advanced by absurd circumstance. Like *The Sin of Harold Diddlebock*, *The Palm Beach Story* plays games with the star's persona, and with the audience's memories of a previous role. But once Claudette Colbert has been established as Gerry, with her peculiar set of dissatisfactions and talents, she does not diverge from the logic of the character, nor does the film relent, from beginning to end, in its teasing attack on the reign of monogamy and the myths of romantic love. The momentum of *The Palm Beach Story* comes from the integrity of its conception, even more than from the pace of its events. The sign that *The Sin of Harold Diddlebock* is a hodgepodge, even if the viewer doesn't catalogue its inconsistencies, is that the film so often lags.

Unlike *Hail the Conquering Hero*, which Henderson acutely describes as a breakthrough in continually unfolding action, *The Sin of Harold Diddlebock* falls back on being a series of set-pieces, most of them dialogue-heavy and shot from a primarily static viewpoint. You might argue that Sturges was mimicking the manner of Lloyd's silent comedies—but those were more visually varied in both image and performance. (Lloyd kept insisting to Sturges, throughout the production, that the scenes needed more business and less talk, and Sturges kept ignoring him.) Not surprisingly, the *shlep* factor reaches maximum intensity, and the shoddiness of construction becomes most glaring, in the two long scenes with Frances Ramsden as Miss Otis, Harold Diddlebock's love object.

Here, too, the movie opens a chasm. In the first scene, which comes immediately after Diddlebock has been fired, he confesses to Miss Otis in a lengthy monologue that he is hopelessly in love with her, as he loved the six Otis sisters who previously worked in Waggleberry's office. Lloyd manages to be both ridiculous and touching throughout this speech, and Ramsden lives up to the challenge of keeping a straight face while occasionally murmuring, without irony, "Poor Mr. Diddlebock." A viewer today might cringe when Diddlebock says it was inevitable he would fall for her, as he had for her sisters, and she replies, "Yes, they warned me." Suddenly he's no longer dear old Harold Lloyd engaged in a new comic role; he's that creep who's known to stalk women in the office and undress them with his eyes. But the moment passes, and Diddlebock says a sad, harmless, and generous farewell, violating Miss Otis's person only by venturing a light goodbye touch on Ramsden's magnificently lustrous hair, which all this time has been fascinating Sturges's camera.

The second long scene, this one slightly more of a dialogue, follows the successful conclusion of Diddlebock's scheme to unload the circus, explains the mysteries that have been left hanging (such as the events of that missing Wednesday), and brings the plot to its happy ending. It's another of Sturges's last-minute wrap-ups; but he usually plays them prestissimo, and this one is done largo, with ample talk and the actors locked into a medium-close two-shot. The mood is listless; and the big surprise (no spoiler alerts for films released in 1947) depends on an act of authorial deception. Diddlebock married Miss Otis on Wednesday and seems to have consummated the union with her—which certainly makes this scene a starkly distinct "after" to the office scene's "before." But even though she's still warm from his bed, Miss Otis has continued to address her new husband as "Mr. Diddlebock," for no reason except to keep the audience from guessing what happened. The movie ends with baseless behavior on her part, and badly fudged sleight of hand on Sturges's.

It ended badly in another way, too.

Sturges had declared his independence as an artist, a status that presumably would entitle him to spend and love as freely as does Harold Diddlebock when soused. But Diddlebock, as I've noted, is not an artist. He's a shifting, insubstantial figure who achieves financial and amorous success with very little foresight and no higher motive. The real artist is Edgar Kennedy's wizardly bartender—and Sturges, too late, would realize he'd been in a similar situation, grandiloquently mixing elements while shut in a cheap basement.

According to the biographers, Howard Hughes attended a preview of *The Sin of Harold Diddlebock* in late summer 1946, about half a year after the production wrapped, and neither laughed nor lingered. In late October, with the film still being edited, Hughes summarily called in Sturges's shares in California Pictures and dissolved the company. Sturges was on his own again.

About a year after Sturges had finished shooting *The Sin of Harold Diddlebock*, the film was at last released. As owner of the product, Hughes chose Miami for the premiere in February 1947, followed by screenings in San Francisco and Portland, Oregon. Hughes refused to open the film in Los Angeles or New York. In May, Jacobs reports, Hughes withdrew the picture from all theaters and set about editing it himself. He chipped away for several years, cutting nineteen minutes and for reasons only he understood adding a talking horse to the last scene, and then rereleased the picture in 1950 through his recently acquired RKO with the title *Mad Wednesday*. The reviews, for the most part, were kind. The movie flopped. By then, Sturges's Hollywood career was over.

But before he reached that moment in his long, painful slide into oblivion, Sturges joined with one more major producer who wanted him—Darryl F. Zanuck, at Twentieth Century-Fox—and made one last masterpiece. In that one, he came clean about the life of an artist.

10

EVERY EMOTION WAS EXAGGERATED

Unfaithfully Yours

Max Reinhardt, who knew something about show business, liked to say that if you spend all your time chasing audiences, you'll never see anything of them but their asses. Never was the cruel truth of this adage more apparent than in Hollywood on the cusp between 1946 and 1947, when Sturges went to work for Darryl Zanuck at Twentieth Century-Fox.

By ill luck, he did so just when the U.S. movie business went into free fall. In 1946, Hollywood enjoyed the most lucrative year in its history, with servicemen in the millions rejoining the throngs for whom moviegoing was a frequent habit. As Thomas Schatz reports, the combined profits of the eight major studios in 1946 reached a record $122 million. By the end of 1947, that total had plummeted 27 percent, to $89 million, and it continued to fall.[1] The ten films that earned the most at the domestic box office in 1947 combined to bring in $74.1 million, with none grossing less than $5 million. In 1948, the ten top films earned $40.35 million in aggregate, with none grossing more than $4.5 million.[2]

The industry's problems were manifold, even before the rise of television: federal antitrust actions (which would soon deprive the studios of their theater chains), the onset of blacklisting, protectionist measures in England that threatened important overseas revenue, and a shift of population to the suburbs, which began the slow starvation of the first-run movie palaces.

One perennial strategy for survival at such moments of uncertainty is to disregard Reinhardt's advice and rush to copy for next year whatever had made money the year before. There is safety in imitation—but people in Hollywood no longer knew what to imitate.

Look at the films that earned the highest domestic receipts in 1946 and 1947—I rely on *Variety*'s year-end summaries—and you see a mishmash. The most popular films were sudsy period romances (*Green Dolphin Street*, *Forever Amber*), a contemporary Technicolor melodrama (*Leave Her to Heaven*), musicals (*The Jolson Story*, *Blue Skies*, *Easy to Wed*), anything starring Bing Crosby (*The Bells of St. Mary's*, *Welcome Stranger*, *Road to Utopia*), overproduced Westerns (*Duel in the Sun*, *Unconquered*), domestic comedies (*The Egg and I*, *Life with Father*), Hitchcock movies (*Spellbound*, *Notorious*), a two-fisted man's picture (*Adventure*), an historical seafaring yarn (*Two Years Before the Mast*), and one nuanced, multilayered, unrepeatable drama that outgrossed them all (*The Best Years of Our Lives*). It wasn't unusual to find a range of categories in the top ten. The studios always strived to put out balanced slates, which covered all genres. But to judge from the wild irregularity of these most recent lists, the sense of balance was slipping, along with the studios' hold on a suddenly volatile public.

Keener and more adept than most, Zanuck forged ahead at Fox by churning profits with his most popular star, Betty Grable, while also pursuing critical acclaim with the occasional high-gloss picture, such as *Gentleman's Agreement*. By signing Sturges to a thirty-week contract in December 1946, he cleverly bought himself a filmmaker who could be expected to deliver both: pin-up revenue *and* prestige.

Not that Zanuck owned up to his plan immediately. As a condition of the contract, he bought an item from Sturges's trunk—a love-triangle story from 1933 titled *Matrix*, written with solemnity and a dash of homemade psychology—as a kind of signing bonus. Sturges had invested years of faith in this script and believed he would at long last get to make the picture. But even though studios were still producing melodramas, Zanuck agreed with the consensus that this one wasn't worth the trouble. He let Sturges keep up his hopes for two months or so, and then declared he wouldn't put money into *Matrix* and revealed what he really wanted: a star vehicle for Grable. Sturges was to elevate her reputation as a comic actress, as he'd done previously for Betty Hutton.

This was not at all the assignment Sturges had thought he'd get when he chose to sign with Zanuck, rather than the duller studio heads who had offered him contracts. Still, he made an effort and by August 1947 had written much of an initial screenplay. Then came word that amid its current financial straits, Fox could not afford to shoot the film in Technicolor. For the first time since her long string of hits had begun, golden-haired, azure-eyed, scarlet-lipped Betty Grable would appear in black and white.[3]

Now Sturges was stuck doing a piece of fluff that he thought was preordained to falter, if not flop. His solution was to bait and switch Zanuck, as Zanuck had done to him. He asked Zanuck to postpone the Grable project and put him to work first on the sort of movie that audiences and critics expected of him. He happened to have another property in the trunk—this one a startling comedy from 1933, titled *Symphony Story*—which he promised he could turn into a completed screenplay in just eight weeks. Zanuck bit—this was, after all, the other type of work he'd wanted from Sturges—and so committed the studio to a new prestige film, one as unlikely as any that would ever come out of Fox: *Unfaithfully Yours*.

Merely to synopsize the project is to demonstrate how little Sturges meant to chase after audiences. The setup, as I might explain it: "A world-famous orchestra conductor believes his beautiful, much younger wife is having an affair." So far, so good. But then: "Hilarity ensues when the conductor plays a Carnegie Hall concert featuring three pieces of varied emotional character, which set off contrasting fantasies that make his performances more thrilling."

Max Reinhardt might have approved. The idea would be marketable only to audiences who wanted to rise to the occasion; all others would have trouble even figuring out which category of movie they were being asked to watch. *Unfaithfully Yours* was to be a musical, but without singing and dancing. All the numbers would be classics of the orchestral repertoire (which during previews would drive an alarming percentage of viewers from their seats). The project would also be a contemporary melodrama—or, rather, a story containing melodramatic elements, which Sturges would mock—while at other times transforming itself into a thrilling film noir shot through with shadows, which looked ominous but portended only that the tortured hero would bang into something in the dark. *Unfaithfully Yours* would be a slapstick comedy (not a very popular genre in 1947) but would refrain from alerting the audience to that fact, piling up the great majority of its pratfalls into a single long debacle near the end. Initially, the film would seem like a ritzy comedy about life among the wealthy and sophisticated—but then would show its protagonist, in close-up, gleefully slashing his wife to death with a straight razor, which is something Hitchcock himself wouldn't dare for another dozen years.

The one genre into which the picture might have fit, had such a category been known at the time, was the confessional film, as Sturges's friends recognized at once. (Jacobs quotes a cable Sturges received after the premiere: "It is my opinion that you not only wrote, directed, and produced the picture but that you also played the lead.")[4] But who in that pre-auteurist era would have been content with a movie just because it seemed to lay bare its writer-director's soul? *Sullivan's Travels* was no precedent. Its protagonist may have seemed to speak for Preston Sturges at the end, but until the final scene Sullivan led a life of his own (as little as it revealed about him, other than a bad temper and a susceptibility to the common cold). *The Sin of Harold Diddlebock* went further. Under the guise of madcap comedy, it toyed with showing the excesses, irresponsibilities, and hangovers that may come with an artistic temperament. Yet it never identified its main character as an artist; and considering the troubles the movie had in mid-1947 as it staggered into release, that was probably just as well.

And yet, by November 1947, Zanuck had authorized Sturges to go into preproduction on the self-involved *Unfaithfully Yours* with a very substantial budget of almost two million dollars. In a business environment where no one other than Bing Crosby was assured of success, Zanuck bet heavily on an unclassifiable picture, in the belief that Sturges's wit and a swanky atmosphere would carry it through. Jacobs quotes Zanuck's memo to Sturges at the start of production in February 1948: "It is my opinion that this picture must reek with brilliance. By this I do not mean that everything should be lit up but that it should have a plush and rich feeling."[5]

In that, at least, Zanuck would not be disappointed. Rex Harrison—sleek, handsome, silver-tongued, and selective about his roles—agreed to play the conductor, an English baronet named Sir Alfred de Carter. When not traveling the world, Sir Alfred resides on the thirty-fourth floor of a hotel modeled on the Waldorf Towers, surrounded by his up-to-date paintings (a Rouault hangs prominently on one wall, a Dalí on another) and a tasteful scattering of African sculptures. His American wife Daphne, played by Linda Darnell, the actress *Life* magazine had once called "the most physically perfect girl in Hollywood," apparently lives without strain, except for the effort of digging up a clever bottle of Pol Roger '34 for her husband's snack and checking that her fur won't match her sister's at a concert.

Service personnel abound—a manager, a private secretary, a backstage valet—but the urban workforce is invisible, except for a pair of comic small businessmen granted complimentary tickets to Sir Alfred's performance. No grifters, opportunists, or disapproving strivers invade this world of luxury, as they did in *The Lady Eve*, *The Palm Beach Story*, and *Sullivan's Travels*. No working girl finds herself thrust blindly into it, as in *Easy Living*, and no scuffling bum breaks in to grab whatever he can, as in *The Great McGinty*. A few stray lines of dialogue allude to material want in England, and Sir Alfred frequently claims to embrace "vulgarity." But despite these passing acknowledgments of life outside the Waldorf Towers, the daily grind does not intrude on characters whose banter sometimes concerns Daphne's couture and sometimes the fingering for the first violins in the *Tannhäuser* overture.

Which is to say, no character on screen helps usher a mass audience imaginatively into the "plush and rich" setting of *Unfaithfully Yours*. Sturges planned to open the film only once to the point of view of his prospective ticket-buyers, in a scene of bumptious small-town comedy that showed how the future Daphne de Carter rose to her grand life from the soggy depths of Porthaul, Michigan; but he never figured out where to insert this incident and eventually cut it. To a remarkable degree, *Unfaithfully Yours* remains locked in a nonsatirical depiction of upper-class life, and (even more remarkably) in the mind of Sir Alfred.

When Sturges had decided to take up playwrighting, in 1928, he had learned about the craft by reading *A Study of the Drama* by James Brander Matthews, a professor at Columbia University who taught what might be called the audience reception theory of dramaturgy. As Sturges summarized it in his memoirs, "when one writes something for the public, aims it at the public, offers it to the public, and the public still doesn't want it, one has missed his aim."[6] Sturges had followed this advice, with greater or lesser command of the audience reactions he meant to set off, right up through *The Sin of Harold Diddlebock*. Now, instead of bringing himself to the audience where he found it, Sturges was counting on his artistry to take the audience where he wanted to go. Why not? Max Reinhardt had done it. So had Isadora Duncan—and Sturges's good friend William Wyler had just done it as well, with *The Best Years of Our Lives*.

Still, as *Unfaithfully Yours* began production in February 1948, more or less on a commercial dare for both Sturges and Zanuck, a disinterested observer might have wondered who this film was for.

The answer, it turned out, was later generations.

Visually, the most striking element of *Unfaithfully Yours* is the trick shot that on three occasions seems to come closer and closer to Sir Alfred as he conducts, bringing the viewer up to his face, then to a left eye that fills the screen, and then through the blackness of the pupil into the shadowy recesses of his mind. Each time, this illusion of pressing forward into Sir Alfred's head is followed by an opposite movement within the fantasy, as a distant door opens in the dark entrance hall of the hotel suite and Daphne steps toward the camera, with Sir Alfred following. Each time there's also a change in the to-and-fro. Think of it as a theme and variations: a different piece of music continues softly in the background—it's the world outside, resonating faintly in the world within—while a different action plays out in the imagined apartment, proceeding with the same flawlessness that Sir Alfred commands from the orchestra.

The movie has transported you into a dual realm—of art and psychology—where everything is frictionless and yet nothing is ideal. Back and forth: although events in this place of wish fulfillment happen exactly as Sir Alfred intends, with people behaving as his puppets and physical objects yielding smoothly to his will, no scenario gives him what he wants. The first comes closest, effecting a bloody double revenge on Daphne and her lover to the strains of the overture to *Semiramide*; but even though this little thriller leaves Sir Alfred laughing (and the audience in the concert hall cheering him wildly), the victory is hollow. You can tell that from the madness of his cackling in the fantasy, and the brusqueness of his departure from the stage. The other two scenarios—which are much briefer—provide him with even less satisfaction. His dream-play to the *Tannhäuser* overture concludes with him alone and bereft, however noble. The Russian roulette game he imagines while conducting Tchaikovsky (the *Francesca da Rimini* tone poem, with its evocation of a doomed, adulterous love) ends his life in nihilist absurdity.

Even his triumph with the public is bitter. The energy he draws from his fantasies overwhelms the audience. The listeners' enthusiasm is boundless—which as far as he's concerned calls both his work and their taste into question. "I just couldn't wait until the end," Daphne tells him, having rushed backstage after the Wagner. "I had to tell you now how wonderful it is." To which Sir Alfred replies, coldly, "I am relieved to hear it. I thought every emotion was exaggerated." The screenplay, though not the film, continues: "every forte a fortissimo, every piano a pianissimo, every *tutti* a boiler factory."[7]

No doubt he's rebuffing Daphne's praise to show he rejects *her*; but he's also speaking with the authority of someone who knows that the demands of his job go far beyond handling technical details. The ultimate responsibility of a conductor, or film director, is to achieve exactly the right feeling moment by moment, which presupposes the ability to judge what's too much or not enough. Sometimes the forte *ought* to be pushed to fortissimo. That's what Sir Alfred had done earlier in the rehearsal scene, when he instructed his percussionist (a chipper Torben Meyer) to make the biggest cymbal splash he could in the Rossini, and never mind if it seemed a little "wulgar." But sometimes it's better to underplay the moment—and this is where Sir Alfred repeatedly fails, if not in art then in life.

On the excuse of having an artist's temperament—backed up by a baronetcy and the wealth of a manufacturing dynasty—Sir Alfred is a dedicated practitioner of the immoderate in all things. Witness how he converts an airport concourse into his stage for a public spectacle of romantic ardor for Daphne, when at the start of the film he returns to New York from a stay in England. Granted, the prolonged kisses and extravagant endearments serve a narrative function, establishing at the outset that Sir Alfred is mad for his wife and believes his passion is requited. But isn't the show also meant for the other characters in the scene, who wait it out in various degrees of admiration or impatience? Sir Alfred and presumably Daphne have something to prove to all of them about their trans-Atlantic, class-straddling, May-October marriage; and all of them take the proof in their own way.

Daphne's sister (Barbara Lawrence), who is a little wulgar herself, might not believe the demonstration is entirely authentic but spins entertainment from it anyway, using the example of the sexed-up couple to torment her husband, August (Rudy Vallee). Even older and wealthier than Sir Alfred and far stuffier, August endures his wife's barbs (mostly by failing to understand them) while stiffly disapproving of Sir Alfred and Daphne's display. Sir Alfred's manager, Hugo (Lionel Stander), greets the smacking and cooing with a thickly spread Russian indulgence, meanwhile trying to focus the great man momentarily on business. As for Sir Alfred's sleek young secretary (Kurt Kreuger), he merely stands by looking serviceable, though it's not clear for what.

With that, all major characters and their attitudes have been accounted for in just one scene, and Sturges has gotten away with one of the most blatant double entendres of his career:

> SIR ALFRED (*locked in an embrace with Daphne, while absently responding to Hugo's praise of his conducting*): All I have to do is wave a little wand, and out comes the music.
> DAPHNE (*murmuring to him face-to-face*): A little *magic* wand, darling, dipped in a little stardust."

Daphne is very beautiful, and Sir Alfred is very lucky (or so it seems), so the viewer might adopt Hugo's attitude and excuse this early bit of acting-out. The next episode, though, raises questions.

The brother-in-law, August, has come by to say that he hired a detective to follow Daphne during Sir Alfred's absence—as he understands it, he was simply looking out for her, as he'd been asked to do—and now he has a report in hand, which he wants to deliver. Sir Alfred might laugh derisively at this misunderstanding, or wearily deplore the crudeness of August's mind and methods. He might tell August frankly but in even tones that he is shocked that Daphne has been subjected to such treatment. He might even fan through the pages, remarking idly that he's glad it wasn't *his* money that paid for this rubbish, and then tear the report to shreds. But Sir Alfred does none of this. He explodes, backs August through the room while roaring into his face, and rips up not only the report but his brother-in-law's jacket.

Some husbands do respond with violence to disheartening information, the better to avoid thinking about it. It's also true that a man in a demeaning position might make himself feel stronger by attacking the nearest patsy. But as Sir Alfred kicks August out of the suite, to be followed immediately by a wastebasket stuffed with the report's tatters, the possible excuses for his behavior shrink to insignificance beside the magnitude of the eruption. Sir Alfred is not just a husband shaking off a suspicion. He's a man with no sense of proportion.

That much has already been evident from his use of words. Despite being the most relentlessly hyperarticulate of all Sturges's characters, Sir Alfred is also one of the most rhetorically unvaried, relying mostly on hyperbole to win people over, or just as often bully them. He's forever shouting polysyllabic insults, or else cooing to Daphne that "A thousand poets dreamed a thousand years, and then you were born." Perhaps he believes every overblown sentence as it issues from his lips; but when a character carries on so immoderately, and with such either-or passions, you begin to wonder how honest he might be about anything.

Take Sir Alfred's man-of-the-people pronouncements. When told, early in the film, about someone who is proposing to establish a Foundation for the Diffusion of Serious Music, Sir Alfred declares with characteristic élan, "There's nothing serious about music. It should be enjoyed flat on the back, with a sandwich in one hand, a bucket of beer in the other, and as many pretty girls about as possible." He says something similar to the percussionist during the orchestra rehearsal: "There is nothing refined about music." But a few scenes later, when confronting the detective (played by Edgar Kennedy) who had snooped on Daphne, Sir Alfred reverses himself. He's outraged to learn that this rough-spoken man, Sweeney, who practices an inherently shady trade out of a cheap, walk-up office, is devoted to music—especially when *he's* conducting. "I had always believed," Sir

Sir Alfred descends to the film noir milieu of Sweeney's Detective Agency and finds it disconcertingly cordial

Alfred declaims, "that music had certain moral and antiseptic powers quite apart from its obvious engorgement of the senses, which elevated and purified its disciples." So much for buckets of beer.

Given Sir Alfred's situation, you might think he's lashing out reflexively and should not be held to what he says. (That's what the detective thinks, too. "You're just hurt," he says sympathetically. "I can see it. You read that report and naturally it upset you.") But you've already seen enough of Sir Alfred to know how highly he values himself—how he loves to mention, with superb modesty, that he is, after all, a baronet, and though not as wealthy as August does happen to have a *few* million of his own. So maybe Sweeney has unknowingly scratched the ostentatiously unpretentious surface and revealed the snob beneath.

As evidence, look at how Sir Alfred behaves after the scene with Sweeney, with his confidence shaken. He returns to the hotel very late, saying darkly that he'd spent the afternoon at the movies, and delivers a sneering account of the pictures he'd seen. (He makes it sound as if *all* films must be idiotic.) Then, after some beastliness directed at the now-suspect Daphne, he orders her to get dressed for the concert. "Maybe I'll go to the movies instead," she shoots back—to which he replies, "Culturally they might suit you better." The mask of charm drops away, exposing a sneer.

Such theatricalized disdain might appeal to an audience when it's directed at August. (Rudy Vallee can take it. He was *born* to take it.) But after hearing this latest barb, a viewer might think that Sir Alfred routinely disguises his contempt for Daphne, and for other commoners as well. This is no longer the excess of a professional performer who is always on, even when alone with his wife. It's a habit of deception, which demands scrutiny in the context of Sturges's obsession with liars, from Dan McGinty to Woodrow Truesmith.

Even Sturges's seemingly honest characters resort to putting on acts, as Charles Pike does when he mouths his secondhand marriage proposal to Eve. Occasionally, a Jimmy MacDonald or W. T. G. Morton won't know any better than to be guileless; then he's tripped up by the fakers, frauds, and con artists who crowd Sturges's world. The intemperate, inconstant Sir Alfred is apparently another of these shams, despite his need to be true to the music he conducts.

So I might ask: What about himself does he most want to conceal?

I've already noted his snobbism and sexual insecurity (phrased, in more genteel terms, as a worry that his young wife does not truly love him). But something worse comes into sight, very briefly, toward the end of that late-afternoon argument with Daphne. After he's torn her dress—the second item of clothing he's ripped that day—and has provoked her into snapping at him, he shouts menacingly, "I forbid you to speak to your husband in that tone!"

"That's right!" she cries. "Strike me, you brute!" And then, staring him down: "So you don't dare."

He certainly does dare, in his imagination. That will be the main substance of the movie, once the concert and its fantasies begin. But for now, facing Daphne in the parlor of the hotel suite, Sir Alfred backs down. Though she easily sees through the imposture, he pretends he isn't the sort of man who would hit a woman.

Sturges, though, *was* that sort of man. It's painful to say about a great artist, especially one who created some of the strongest female characters in film history, but Sturges was violent toward women.

He chased his second wife, Eleanor, down the stairs while threatening her with a carving knife. With Bianca Gilchrist, he got into rows that once left her with a broken nose and on another occasion sent him to the hospital with a gash in his arm, after he crashed through a pane of glass while running her down. His third wife, Louise, had to welcome guests to a dinner party while wearing sunglasses to hide the black eye he'd given her. By his own account, he often came to blows with Frances Ramsden (though it seems that she gave as well as she got).[8]

Unfaithfully Yours might be described as the movie in which Sturges confessed to a multitude of his faults but denied the worst of them. His on-screen double is arrogant, thin-skinned, two-faced, and far too fond of the sound of his own voice (though, as embodied by Rex Harrison, he's also slimmer and more dashing than Sturges and about a decade younger), and as punishment for these sins he is made ridiculous. But one transgression that Sir Alfred does not commit, though it's suggested he might, is to strike his wife. As soon as the idea comes up, he stalks away to dress for his concert—after which, the movie becomes a machine for evading the reality of violence. Sir Alfred does not act on his murderous impulses but sublimates them into art—and if he *did* act, he'd be too inept to damage anyone but himself.

I suspect that Sturges's conflicted, sometimes brutal feelings toward women do run through the movie, but almost always as a well-managed undercurrent. On the surface, the film is all wit and playfulness. Sturges expresses his worldliness with a new ease in *Unfaithfully Yours*. He takes greater delight in visual storytelling and parody than ever before. And in a striking contrast from *The Sin of Harold Diddlebock*, he laughs from the heart about the vanity of an aging man's concern for his virility.

No doubt *Unfaithfully Yours* reaches an emotional climax in the image of Sir Alfred, in his fantasy, slashing Daphne to death.

Sir Alfred, in his fantasies, enjoying a little wife-slashing

But Sturges has prepared for this horror, and undermined it, by having Sweeney give voice to humble wisdom.

> We fall for these little dames [Sweeney tells Sir Alfred consolingly] and try to believe they're in love with us, when every morning our shaving mirror *yells* they *can't* be.... If it was me, I'd *never* have 'em tailed. I'd never try to find out nothin'. I'd just be grateful for whatever they was willing to gimme—a year, a week—an hour.

Bear in mind that *Unfaithfully Yours* is constructed to convince not only Sir Alfred but also the audience that Daphne has cheated on him. The written evidence comes before him not once but three times, and on the third occasion (as in fairy tales) he finally must pay attention. As in a fairy tale, he does so while looking into a magic mirror of sorts: the face of his fellow-cuckold Sweeney, in which Sir Alfred can see himself as old, bald, doughy, and defeated. Although the urge to slice up Daphne is shocking, the viewer understands that Sir Alfred has been devastated and will remain so until he can adopt Sweeney's advice and aspire to mature resignation. The viewer also intuits that the preening, self-dramatizing Sir Alfred will do no such thing—his inherent character prevents him, as does his job of whipping up grand emotions—and so he must be headed toward a comeuppance.

One more factor comes into play as well and takes Sir Alfred down a notch, even as it excuses the most dreadful of his fantasies. This great artist's imagination is horribly clichéd. Whether it always tosses up corny notions, we don't know; but Sturges has suggested an explanation for this particular set of howlers by stipulating that Sir Alfred spent the afternoon at the movies. As he steps to the podium, the back of his mind is still crammed with the most threadbare stuff Hollywood offers—and this material, reacting with the intoxicating effects of music, produces the ridiculous scenarios projected inside his head.

These fantasies look unlike anything seen before in a Sturges movie: velvety in their shadows, glistening in their play of light, and focused far into the recesses of the frame, so the figures are weighty and rounded in a way that's uncommon in daydreams. And yet this style, atypical for Sturges, is the work of the same cinematographer, Victor Milner, who had produced the flatter, more graphically defined images that suited *Christmas in July*, *The Lady Eve*, and *The Palm Beach Story*.

Milner was, in himself, a lesson in the talent necessary to the studio system. At Paramount during the 1930s, he had served both Lubitsch and DeMille—which is to say, he helped realize not so much varying styles as different worldviews. In 1946, contracting out to Hal Wallis Productions, he had accommodated himself to yet another confluence of theme, mood, and story—film noir—shooting *The Strange Love of Martha Ivers* for Lewis Milestone. With that job in his immediate background, Milner knew exactly how to achieve the brooding, nocturnal tone of Sturges's fantasy sequences.

But pulling back a little from that extreme, Milner also could give *Unfaithfully Yours* the plush and rich feeling Zanuck had asked for, and that Sturges's script demanded, in what might be called the waking scenes. Even when Sir Alfred ventures into the drabness of the detective's office, Milner lights the set to bring out tactile qualities: the pile of Sir Alfred's hat and overcoat, the texture of the detective's wooden file cabinet. And when Sir Alfred, stunned, walks out of the office, Milner extends the space for Sturges, making Sweeney's neighbor, the tailor, visible through two shop windows and across a stair. The world has just stopped for Sir Alfred, but it goes on for the tailor, who stands in the back of the shot calmly eating his lunch.

In the waking scenes, Sturges amplifies this sense of material presence and physical continuity by adding bits of business and camera movements that help place Sir Alfred in solid reality. He's a little clumsy in it, too. Although Sir Alfred makes his living by moving about expressively on the podium, he has a way of bumping into the unyielding space that Sturges has constructed for him. He misjudges a doorframe when carrying a large box of flowers from one room to another, and then makes the same blunder a bit later with a tray of sandwiches and drinks. These small early collisions foreshadow the far more grandiose excursion into indignity that Sir Alfred will eventually take, leaving broken furniture, shattered glass, a persistently yammering telephone, a few yards of electrical cord, enough gaming equipment for a casino, and himself dumped on the parlor floor. But in a larger sense, the misadventures with the flowers and the tray (and Daphne's zipper, for that matter) suggest a general failure on his part to gauge his relationship toward others.

The scene in the detective's office, for example, begins with Sir Alfred jumping to the conclusion that the humble man sitting alone in this place must be Sweeney. Sir Alfred neither sees that the face before him belongs to Julius Tannen nor hears that the man's accent comes straight from the Pale of Settlement. Without pause, Sir Alfred lets loose a tirade against not-Sweeney; and while the invective spouts, Sturges focuses the camera exclusively on its object, the tailor from next door, who keeps craning his head forward to take a bite of sandwich and then pulling back, as if interrupted by the next clause of abuse, and the next.

When Sweeney himself shows up a few moments later, Sir Alfred again can't position himself comfortably with the man, because the detective does not behave like the anticipated ruffian. Instead, he beams joyfully upon seeing the conductor (his artistic hero, as it turns out), begins to reach for a handshake, and then (proving his innate delicacy) crosses to a sink, washes, and dries himself before touching the great man. Talking ecstatically all the while, Sweeney then bustles behind the counter and pours two glasses of whiskey so he can toast Sir Alfred, who by contrast has been standing inert all this time, in awkwardness and uncertainty.

When he returns to the hotel from Sweeney's office, Sir Alfred gives an even more extraordinary demonstration of being lost in space, and (when discomfited) lost in social space, too. Wanting to find out who might lurk in Room 3406—the room

Daphne had visited in his absence—Sir Alfred slips out of his study and walks along the corridor while the camera travels backward, keeping his dazed expression and listless motions steadily in view. Upon knocking on the door of 3406 and being asked to come in, Sir Alfred enters, stares at the man inside— his puzzled secretary, Tony—and after taking a turn around the room, as if looking for something but not trying very hard to find it, walks out again. He hasn't uttered a word.

This is the same Sir Alfred who earlier in the film had shown himself to be the most charming and graceful of men—but that was in the extended rehearsal scene. The camera then had roamed over the orchestra, sometimes finding quasi-abstract images of a line of bows jabbing in unison over strings, sometimes studying the way the harpists kill time when the score has no use for them; and in this extended view of people working together (a subject seldom shown at such length in Hollywood features, and with so little romanticization), Sir Alfred had stood over the ensemble but not apart from it. In the practice of his art, engaging in a give-and-take with other musicians, he earned the expressive gestures and suave grandiloquence with which he's been showing off since the beginning of the film.

It's instructive to compare Sir Alfred here to his as-yet-unnamed counterpart in *Symphony Story* from 1933, as Henderson reproduces that sketch in his introduction to *Unfaithfully Yours*. At the start of the original story, the proud, overbearing conductor cuts short the rehearsal by telling the orchestra, "That's a little better, but it's still terrible. You must do better tonight," before throwing down his baton and hurrying off the stand.[9] In the film, a far more attractive Sir Alfred sends the musicians off with the words "Splendid, gentlemen, splendid. It is already much too good for them. To make it any better would be a total waste of effort." This is Sir Alfred in his amiable professional guise, which he also likes to wear when he's away from the concert hall and things are going his way. Sturges wisely chooses to introduce Sir Alfred in this persona, to gain the viewers' interest and sympathy.

But when things do not go Sir Alfred's way? In emotions and attitudes, he turns out to be much like the nasty piece of work in *Symphony Story*. In physical bearing, he's so maladroit that he sets fire to his dressing room.

By the time of his confrontation with Daphne in the hotel suite, Sir Alfred has abraded everything grand and glamorous about himself except the sheen of his artistic reputation. And even that's tarnished, when he pokes at a sandwich Daphne has ordered for him and the dubious bread gives off the cartoonish noise of a baby's squeeze toy. Inanimate objects from room service now mock the master of organized sound. Nothing can redeem this insufferable man in the audience's eyes until he returns to where he belongs—the podium—and takes up the baton again.

When he does, and Sturges brings the audience directly into Sir Alfred's mind, something happens that's even more unexpected than the three fantasy scenarios. Daphne—a woman who until now has been decorative at best, alternately cloying and lachrymose at worst—turns into someone interesting.

To be more precise: Linda Darnell becomes interesting. An actress who had never quite gotten past her early, repetitive success as Tyrone Power's love interest, she came to *Unfaithfully Yours* after struggling for most of the 1940s through a few intermittent hits and increasingly frequent casting droughts and bit parts. Out of favor for a time with Zanuck, reduced at her nadir to making a miraculous appearance, uncredited, as the Immaculate Conception in *The Song of Bernadette*, Darnell had seemed poised to leap ahead in 1946 when she was given the lead in *Forever Amber*; but that picture failed to meet expectations (which were unattainable, since it was billed as the next *Gone with the Wind*), leaving Darnell stalled. As 1948 began, she was little more than what she'd been when she first showed up in Hollywood—a beautiful thing—only now almost a decade older.

She wasn't even the first choice to play Daphne de Carter. Zanuck had wanted to give the role to the more popular Gene Tierney; but she refused, on the grounds that the part was too small. Zanuck threw the meager leftover to Darnell, who might have protested, or despaired, but instead was thrilled to be put into Sturges's hands. According to Jacobs, she responded to the news by exclaiming, "At last I have found a director!"[10] In the event, Darnell's faith was well placed. Sturges asked her to play a kind of dual role in each fantasy sequence, and she rose to the challenge with utter self-possession.

On one level, Darnell shows the fantasy Daphne to be a mental puppet of Sir Alfred, acting out whichever stereotype of femininity he imagines at the moment: lying minx, contrite sinner, helpless hysteric. On another level, and at the same time, Darnell stands a little apart from each of these impersonations, playfully contorting the tricks that Hollywood actresses used in films noirs, tearjerkers, and psychological thrillers. Sir Alfred is of course the protagonist of each sequence—these are *his* fantasies—but Daphne/Darnell is generally their focus. In the back-and-forth movement that introduces each fantasy, she consistently comes into view as the center of attention, in effect trapped in the line of sight between her two directors: Sir Alfred looming behind her and Sturges in front, his presence with the camera invisible but implicit. And yet, within the unexpected depth of the imaginary space—so uncharacteristic of daydreams,

The musical imagination: Daphne as a marionette in the puppet theater of Sir Alfred's mind

but common enough in films—she finds the freedom of movement needed to roam into parody.

Darnell's performance in the *Semiramide* fantasy begins in near-immobility; she stands facing the camera for minutes on end with her hands in front of her, clutching a handbag. Her head is high, in a semblance of serenity; her voice seldom varies from a tone of passive composure. But as Sir Alfred paces around her, suggesting and insinuating and dissembling, Darnell's eyes react by executing the equivalent of a gymnastic floor routine. They're in continual motion: glancing sneakily to the side, darting upward in fake delight, fluttering to conceal her familiarity with Tony's room number, rolling dreamily downward while she contemplates committing a fresh betrayal. Every emotion is exaggerated, though just enough.

By contrast, in the *Tannhäuser* fantasy, Daphne/Darnell turns her entire body into a sigh of shame. The sound now echoing in Sir Alfred's mind is the same music that had underscored Charles Pike's momentary attempt at noble resignation, when the Lady Eve had tortured him with one scandalous confession after another in their honeymoon Pullman compartment; but in this fantasy, the fallen woman aches with remorse. Daphne/Darnell enters with eyes downcast and head drooping, inching forward with painful steps. She shakes her head in a vain, passing denial of her sin. She clutches her hand to her lips and gasps, groans, weeps. In the rambunctiousness of this heartbreak, Darnell restrains herself only from extending her arm with the palm turned outward, in the immemorial player's gesture of "Pray, no more!" A viewer might be forgiven for falsely remembering even that pose amid all the other mimed confessions of worthlessness, which culminate in Daphne's convulsive sobs at receiving a check for $100,000, free and clear.

The *Francesca da Rimini* fantasy differs from the other two in bringing Tony into the scene. Daphne/Darnell loses a bit of the focus, given that she's now part of a triangle formation; but even here, she retains a central position, and a capacity to make her emotive tropes a little too broad to be taken seriously. As the two men maneuver around her, she's wide-eyed with horror, breathless with fear, and so instinctively ready to flee that she keeps falling back, to the point that you worry she might knock somebody over.

Droll rather than uproarious, these fantasies may rate only chuckles on the laughter scale that Sturges's assistant Edwin Gillette would use for measuring audience reactions. (The scale's "hearty laughs" and "yells" come later, in the knockabout climax.)

But the chuckles are sustained, lifting these sections of the film to a consistent level of wised-up, giddy fun that's generated not only by Harrison's sly posturing but also by Darnell's interplay with him. More muted than her leading man but equally witty, she punctures the fantasies from within.

Even more important: by virtue of her surprisingly chameleonic performance, Darnell suggests that Daphne exceeds the image she's borne in the first part of the film, and the role to which Sir Alfred is pleased to consign her as the beautiful young trophy wife. This shift enables the success of the final section, when the concert has ended and the true crisis begins. That's when *Unfaithfully Yours* at last thrusts an unprepared Sir Alfred into battle with things as they are—both the intractable materiality of objects and the manifold nature of his wife's character—and watches as he goes down to defeat, disgracefully and hilariously.

With characteristic rigor, Sturges matches the events of the climax to the musical fantasies, with Sir Alfred trying to realize each scenario in turn. This means that as the extraordinarily long, continuous final sequence begins, Sir Alfred actually means to get away with murder. Somewhere in the back of the viewer's mind, Daphne lies in a pool of blood—and it's precisely the repressed horror of this prospect that prompts the audience to release wave upon wave of cleansing laughter.

After a very brief bit of suspense-building, in which Sir Alfred lurks about the hotel suite making sure he's alone, Sturges moves quickly to signal that no one is in real danger except the great man himself. The music from *Semiramide* returns, but now in a nose-thumbing, Looney Tunes–style arrangement by the film's great musical director, Alfred Newman, as Sir Alfred fails again and again to carry out the preliminary part of his scheme by concealing his fingerprints. He can't find gloves that will fit. Each new mismatch yields a rude sound effect, establishing that Sir Alfred has overestimated his ability to behave like a film noir character and instead is embedded, unknowingly, in knockabout comedy. At this point, of course, he can't foresee the extent to which he'll be knocked about, and neither can the audience. He's about to be subjected to a solid fifteen minutes of slapstick indignity, in which almost the only lines of dialogue will come from a displaced telephone handset on which an operator keeps asking, "Number, please?"

The repetition, no less than the knowledge that murder is being averted, builds the sequence to its comic height. In a brilliant essay prompted by (or rather against) the remake of *Unfaithfully Yours* from 1984, Veronica Geng wrote about the nearly identical knickknacks that Sir Alfred keeps turning up in cabinets as he searches for the tools of murder, each mediocre, previously forgotten little sculpture as insignificant as the next and each blandly ignored by Sir Alfred as he sets it aside, hardly noticing that he lives amid an inexhaustible surplus of useless "good taste."[11] Other storage items—for example, a large collection of loose light bulbs—make a bigger pop in the scene; but the knickknacks, in their cumulative effect, contribute to the audience's awareness that Sir Alfred is a man stuck in a loop. His stubbornness and self-involvement prevent him from learning anything, no matter how often he flops. The entire fifteen minutes is structured by his determination to make the same mistakes twice, if not three times: to step onto the seat of a chair he'd already broken, to put a telephone back where he'd previously knocked it over, and to move cam dog A-1-3 again on the home recording machine he's attempting to use, when A-1-3 has proved to do nothing but flip the disc.

EVERY EMOTION WAS EXAGGERATED ⟨❧ 311

Like a film director who contrives perfection when on set and makes a mess of his life when out of the studio, Sir Alfred encounters intractable reality

No Sturges protagonist since Henry Fonda had been so physically humiliated. (Eddie Bracken doesn't count; he humiliates himself.) But unlike Fonda, whose resentment of slapstick gives an edge to his performance, Harrison revels in throwing himself into the demolition derby. He knows that Sir Alfred is too vain to feel embarrassed about anything he does; so with unshakeable aplomb Harrison pauses before a mirror, twice, to check the angle of his hat, as if the main requirement while trashing one's own residence is to remain well dressed. When propping an amputated side table against an armchair, he spares a moment to study his uncertain handiwork, in approval, before moving on. And when sprawled backward on a sofa as the result of wrestling with a heavy, ungainly box, he gamely throws one leg in the air and performs a supine kick dance to extricate himself from the curtains. Until this point, his most formidable asset as an actor (and Sir Alfred's as a man of the world) has been his eloquence; but he now seems to abandon language gladly, as if it were a barrier between himself and the audience (for Harrison) or between himself and bloody revenge (for Sir Alfred).

When words return in due course, in response to Daphne's perplexed entrance into a site of disaster, they are preposterous as never before. "I was making an experiment," Sir Alfred haughtily explains of the mess in which he's sitting. "People do, you know. Without them, there would be very little progress in this world." Rather than cover up his foolishness, as he hopes, the excuse strips it bare; and he remains exposed, when soon after he attempts to talk Daphne into submission by complaining that she doesn't know the meaning of the word *simile*, and for once she just doesn't care. Is this new experience of the powerlessness of his words the reason he continues to plot murder—testing the blade of his straight razor—despite having been caught out? If so, he's undone again by his own clumsiness, and by Daphne's kind patience in dressing the wound for him.

From here through the denouement, Sir Alfred continues to thrash about ridiculously, while Daphne steps forward for the first time as a competent adult. While plainspoken—especially in contrast to her husband—she's capable of humorously disparaging Tony as a dancing partner, telling Sir Alfred calmly that she doesn't like the way he's acting, and relieving her irritation by drily mocking the way he proudly clings to his British ways, despite living in New York with an American wife. All the while, Darnell carries herself with a relaxed self-confidence that puts to shame Sir Alfred's dithering behavior, as well as the movie clichés he's entertained about her.

It's almost a happy ending. But just as *The Great McGinty* finished with "Here we go again," and *Christmas in July* concluded with Jimmy's slogan being chosen (in effect) for the second time, and *The Lady Eve* ended with Jean and Charles coming full circle, and *The Palm Beach Story* returned to the altar where it began (times three), so too does *Unfaithfully Yours* reestablish an equilibrium that an alert audience might view with suspicion. No sooner does Sir Alfred learn that Daphne has not committed adultery—at least with Tony—than he resumes addressing her as a "wonderful child," erasing the mature woman she's just shown herself to be. No sooner does his eloquence return at full flood than Daphne belittles herself, saying she doesn't truly understand his burdens as a great man. He decrees that she must put on her most "vulgar" gown—back to the posture of unpretentiousness—so he can show her off to people. She acquiesces, once more accepting her role as a doll he can dress up. And a viewer might wonder, how long will the adoring-couple routine last this time?

Sir Alfred has just gone through an exhaustive demonstration of his tendency to repeat mistakes. Is it possible that his error of the past twelve hours will be repeated, too, or that this isn't the first time he's driven himself mad? Maybe he needs to work himself into a jealous fury in order to conduct at a high level and will find a new cause for suspicion just before the next concert. In that case, maybe Daphne will go on enduring these bouts of abuse, bandaging his wounds, and waiting for his artistic rage to change once more into infantilizing uxoriousness.

The rapturous two-shot on which *Unfaithfully Yours* ends signals that all has been resolved. The audience is welcomed—no, encouraged—to think it's so and go away satisfied. And all the while—as Sweeney might put it—the mirror that *Unfaithfully Yours* holds up to the audience yells it can't be so.

Sturges brought in this thoroughly exceptional picture on time and on budget. But as the editing proceeded, and Fox prepared for previews, Zanuck began to fret that he'd given Sturges too much time and money to work with, and that this decision had somehow been the director's fault. The picture would have to be a runaway success to make a profit for Fox. And Sturges was dawdling over the editing, which cost more money. According to Jacobs's account, Zanuck did not lose faith in the picture, even when the first preview was troubling. He took the editing into his own hands, though, when Sturges continued to tinker, chopping nine minutes of the running time on his own.

Fortunately, Zanuck was neither a Howard Hughes nor a Buddy DeSylva. He preserved the integrity of Sturges's film. But then a horrible turn of events made the cruelest fantasy in the movie seem unnervingly real. In July 1948, as the Fox marketing department was preparing its campaign for *Unfaithfully Yours*, the actress Carole Landis committed suicide. She had been having an affair with Rex Harrison, who was estranged from his wife, Lilli Palmer, but not divorced. No evidence suggested that Harrison had caused Landis's death, but none was wanted. The press had the tragic death of a beautiful though struggling actress at age twenty-nine—and the last man she'd been involved with was a philandering, fancy-talking foreign star.

Fox could not rush out with a comedy in which Harrison seemed to murder his wife; but neither could it write off a two-million-dollar picture. Choosing to wait until the worst of the scandal had abated, the studio released *Unfaithfully Yours* in November, to lukewarm reviews and a cold box office. When business continued to lag, as Curtis relates, Fox scrambled to recast its marketing campaign, opening the picture in Los Angeles in the guise of a murder mystery, with Harrison portrayed in the ads like "the villain in a Sherlock Homes film." Nobody was fooled, Curtis writes. "*Unfaithfully Yours* died a horrible death."[12]

Today it looks more alive than ever. Not to a mass audience, perhaps—though in nonprofit theaters and on video platforms it arguably reaches more people cumulatively, year after year, than Sturges and Zanuck could have hoped to attract in 1948–49. *Unfaithfully Yours* now seems vital for many of the reasons that *Vertigo* has soared in reputation, and that are, paradoxically, the very same reasons why both films were so often declared in the past to be disappointments. They disdain conventional plot-spinning and flaunt their artificiality; they ask the viewer to bathe in music for long periods while very little seems to be going on; they make a puppet of a beautiful but less-than-respected actress and a pitiful weakling of an older leading man. All this, to lay bare the anxieties and fantasies, the desire for control and rage at lack of control, of an artist behind the camera who needs to confess his feelings about women. One film seemed in its day to be an insubstantial *jeu d'esprit*; the other, a puzzling anecdote spun out to inordinate length. But to audiences that now key into the personalities of Sturges and Hitchcock, both can be enthralling. I wonder if *Unfaithfully Yours* isn't the more inventive of the two films, and the more scathingly honest.

INSTEAD OF A CONCLUSION
A Genealogy of Preston Sturges

Orson Welles directed his next-to-last Hollywood film, *Macbeth*, thanks to the inattention of Herbert Yates, president of the Poverty Row studio Republic Pictures.

Sometime in the late 1940s, as Welles told the story, his pal Charles Feldman, a talent agent and independent producer, contracted to make a slate of films with Yates. Feldman helpfully slipped *Macbeth* onto the list of proposed titles, and Yates didn't notice. So Welles, whom the studios no longer tolerated as a director, was set loose to make the film in a mere twenty-three days on the Republic lot, where "shooting" usually involved six-guns and Roy Rogers. Some critics today advance strong arguments for *Macbeth*, but few were heard when the film opened on October 1, 1948. For eight years afterward, Welles busied himself with film, stage, and television work in Europe.[1]

It would take Sturges a while to follow Welles and America's other movie expatriates into the postwar scramble for production in Europe; but by another coincidence in the string I've been following, his final downfall as a studio director coincided almost precisely with the events leading to Welles's departure.

I won't dwell for long on the disheartening tale of Sturges's final decade or belabor his last minor botches, which I include in this book for the sake of completeness.[2] I'd rather end (though not conclude) by thinking with pleasure of his present-day descendants in film and television. Sturges lives on in his artistic genealogy. Before I trace a few of its lines, though, here is a summary of how his career ended.

In September 1948, as *Macbeth* approached release, Sturges began filming the long-delayed Betty Grable vehicle he owed Zanuck, with Technicolor now in order but everything else in disarray.

In retrospect, a few shards of ideas glint within the gluey morass of *The Beautiful Blonde from Bashful Bend*. Ordered to work with the premise of Grable as a hot-tempered saloon entertainer hiding out in a small town in the old West, where she fakes her way through a job as a schoolmistress, Sturges added a pinch of danger by making the heroine an expert pistol shot. (This was less than a brainstorm. *Annie Get Your Gun* had premiered on Broadway in May 1946 and was still running strong when *Beautiful Blonde* went into production.) Sturges also opened the way toward outlandish humor by treating the story as the occasion for another of his parodies of movie genres, in this case the horse operas that had occupied Republic's lot before and after the advent of Orson Welles. Sturges apparently thought that wised-up audiences would enjoy his mockery of Western conventions: the gun battles that somehow leave combatants intact (even though, in this case, they would get shot over and over), or the Native American sidekick who is the butt of the white settlers' jokes. In *Beautiful Blonde*, the purported Indian is actually a Mexican-born dance hall performer, who responds to being addressed in pidgin by telling people to go suck an egg.

Betty Grable and two surrogate Jerry Lewises, in an understated moment in *The Beautiful Blonde from Bashful Bend*.
Courtesy The Museum of Modern Art

Viewers who were not seeking opportunities to look down on the average Western would presumably roar at the lunacies made possible by untethering the film from reality. In effect, Sturges was making a live-action feature that behaved like a cartoon, as Frank Tashlin would soon do with much greater success. Sturges even anticipated Tashlin and other directors of the 1950s by incorporating the biggest comedy sensation of the period, Jerry Lewis, or his near equivalent. In *Beautiful Blonde*, Sturges cast Sterling Holloway and Dan Jackson as goofball brothers with braying laughs, forward-combed hair, and an infantile way of moving about in their adult bodies. They're Lewis surrogates times two, inserted into film history shortly after Dean Martin and Jerry Lewis became stars and shortly before the real Lewis made his feature debut at Paramount in *My Friend Irma*. Sturges's two grotesques ought to have made his picture up-to-the-minute and hilarious. In fact, he did everything expected of him, including exposing Grable's body as amply and often as possible (this was a front-office directive) and tossing in a musical performance for his star, who got to warble her way around a saloon as Julie Gibson had done in *Hail the Conquering Hero*. And yet *The Beautiful Blonde from Bashful Bend* was an ordeal to watch.

The master of the dizzying opening sequence now could think of no better way to begin than with a pedestrian backstory sequence, showing how Grable (or Freddie, as her character is called) was trained as a little girl to become a crack shot. When Sturges cuts to the present, the tempo picks up during a scene in Freddie's saloon, showing how she impulsively shoots at her two-timing fancy man (Cesar Romero) but instead plugs the town judge in the butt. But then, having stirred briefly to life, *Beautiful Blonde* sinks into repetition, spinning like a wheel in mud. Freddie shoots the judge in the pants a second time, and a third. After she escapes from jail and takes refuge in the new town, she endures multiple flirtations from Rudy Vallee, several fits of dialect comedy with El Brendel (as a lawman born in Sweden), and redundant bouts of growling from Cesar Romero. The picture hits bottom with its endless gunfight, in which Sturges replays mirthless gags with the joy of an itchy neurotic scratching himself raw.

Everyone involved saw that disaster was unfolding, but no one could stop it. Jacobs quotes from Zanuck's increasingly fretful memos of late October 1948, which harped on Sturges's failure to stay profitably on schedule but betrayed deeper worries. Zanuck implicitly acknowledged that the material was flimsy—for "the type of scenes you are doing you are spending more time than they are worth"—and wisely noted that the comic Western gunfight was likely to fall flat for lack of an emotional investment from the audience: "We have no story points at issue, therefore we are certainly out on a limb."[3] After the disastrous opening of *Unfaithfully Yours* in early November, Zanuck went into salvage mode on *Beautiful Blonde*, dictating bits of slapstick he wanted Sturges to work into the shoot-out. The overload only made a bad sequence worse.

In December 1948, with production drawing to a close, Zanuck declined to renew Sturges's contract at Fox. The studio waited several months to disgorge *The Beautiful Blonde from Bashful Bend* into theaters, where it opened in May 1949 to strained reviews and pitiful business. By that point, Sturges had managed to pick up an assignment at MGM, writing a comedy for Clark Gable; but that was a one-off. Besides, it consigned him again, after all these years, to the status of a writer for hire; and by October 1949, it had become obvious that his labor was wasted. MGM never made the picture.

The next years were a chaos of abortive projects, mounting debts, and dwindling prestige. At first Sturges's name was enough to attract job offers, including a proposal from Charles Feldman, the man behind Welles's *Macbeth*, to write a screenplay that might be packaged with a couple of stars and sold to a studio. But nothing came of the script for Feldman, *A Present for Uncle Popo*, or any of Sturges's other dealings, in which he almost systematically alienated everyone who attempted to work with him.[4] The only bright spot—a shining beam, actually—was his marriage in 1951 to Sandy Nagle: beautiful, very young, and perhaps stronger and more sharp-witted than he'd anticipated.

The start of 1954 found Sturges following other American filmmakers to Europe, pulled to it by the availability of independent productions and international coproductions and pushed, in his case, not by the blacklist but by creditors, including the U.S. Treasury. He had no plan. First he went to London, on the prospect of making an independently produced film version of Shaw's *The Millionairess* starring Katharine Hepburn. When that project fell through, he sent for Sandy and their toddler son and wandered on to Paris, where he could profit from his fluent French and a reputation that was still fresh, since people there had seen his films only after the war.

The offer that led to his last film came in July 1954, from Gaumont. The studio had bought the rights to a book by Pierre Daninos, *Les carnets du Major W. Marmaduke Thompson: découverte de la France et des Français*, published just that year and wildly popular. It was a compilation of humor articles written for *Le Figaro*, offering droll observations on the contrasting manners of the French and the English as narrated by a fictitious British army major, now retired to Paris with his French wife and son. The book supplied multiple brief stories but no plot, names but no credible human figures (just national characters). It would be a challenge, Gaumont admitted, to pull a script out of this material; but the bilingual Sturges, with his ingenious comic talent, seemed ideal to write and direct the screen version of *Les carnets du Major Thompson*—or two versions, one in French and the other in English.

Sturges struggled for the rest of 1954 to invent a through line that would turn an anthology of newspaper columns into a screenplay. Maybe he would have come up with something, back in the years when he was burning his way through Paramount. Now, his solution was no better than satisfactory. In the frame story, Major Thompson would reminisce about how he'd become a newspaper columnist. Flashbacks would show him dictating a few of his items, which would be acted out using Sturges's old narratage device. Flashbacks would also show how his relationship with his wife during this period conformed to national stereotypes, and how his increasing absorption in writing led to strains in the marriage, to be resolved happily in the last reel.

Gaumont gave its approval, and in July 1955 production began with the great British musical revue star Jack Buchanan in the title role and the French sex goddess of the moment, Martine Carol, cast as his wife Martine. Buchanan had not made the list of Sturges's five or six choices to play Thompson. He exerted little box-office appeal (his best-known film role was in *The Band Wagon*), spoke an unintelligible French, and was suffering in his

Noël-Noël encounters French bureaucracy and modern design in the best segment of *Les carnets de Major Thompson/The French They Are a Funny Race*. Courtesy The Museum of Modern Art

mid-sixties from the spinal cancer that would soon kill him. Carol spoke an unintelligible English, was known as a self-conscious actress (a characteristic that Max Ophüls put to good use in *Lola Montès*), and in her mid-thirties made a somewhat disturbing consort to Buchanan in the film's frequent moments of leering sex comedy. Another recipe for disaster.

Opportunities to watch *Les carnets du Major Thompson* have eluded me, so I can comment only on *The French They Are a Funny Race*, as the shorter, English-language version is called. Its principal attraction is the comic actor Noël-Noël (another veteran of the music halls) in the role of Major Thompson's friend M. Taupin, or the myth-enshrouded Typical Frenchman. Miming his part to the accompaniment of the soundtrack narration, Noël-Noël seems less a human being than a virtuoso chamber ensemble—the instruments are lifted eyebrows, rolling eyes, puffed lips, waggling fingers, flapping elbows, and jiggling hips—gathered to perform a faultlessly elastic scherzo. The best of the sequences has him attempting to file an official document, an impertinence that exposes him to all the indignities that French bureaucracy can inflict. In a scene anticipating Tati's *Mon Oncle*, he makes his way wordlessly along a row of clerks' windows, whose very modern safety glass barriers are furnished with speaking holes of varied, impractical, and increasingly baffling design.

So much for the high point. Much of the rest is labored (a dispute between the major and Martine over their son's governess), predictable (a flashback to the major's experience with his first wife, illustrating the proverbial coldness of Englishwomen), or labored, predictable, and distasteful all at once (an enactment of a Thompson newspaper column about the Frenchman's carefree, life-affirming habit of stalking any woman who strikes him as appetizing). The direction gives the impression that Sturges had at last followed Zanuck's advice not to waste time on scenes that weren't worth the trouble. Jacobs praises the delicacy and restraint of the direction, compared to *The Beautiful Blonde*. I would say that everything needed in the frame is in it, with nothing out of focus.

Les carnets du Major Thompson premiered in France in December 1955 and did tolerably well at the European box office. But Sturges was not going to revive his career on the strength of having made the ninth most popular film in France for 1956. He anxiously awaited the release in the United States of *The French They Are a Funny Race*, which opened at last in May 1957 and promptly bombed. Two months later, Sturges lost his family.

Sandy could no longer bear the strain and isolation of maintaining a household in Paris virtually single-handed, with two small sons in tow, scant funds, no facility in French, and a husband who rolled home when he felt like it. She returned with the children to Los Angeles at the end of July 1957. According to Smedley's account, she and Sturges invented a decent excuse for her to go: she had to dig up a copy of his *Matrix* screenplay. But her departure, in a sense, was already written into the script for *Major Thompson*.

The only affecting moment in the film—affecting, at any rate, for viewers who know the biography—comes when Thompson learns that the newspaper will publish the columns he's been composing, giving him an exciting new career as a writer. He returns to his apartment in professional triumph to find his wife and son gone. In essence, this was the story of Sturges's life with Louise Sargent. They were deeply in love when they married. Then Sturges got Paramount's approval to direct *The Great McGinty*, his career soared, the marriage sank, and Louise went away with their son, Mon. If this experience lived on in *Major Thompson* as memory, it also figured as premonition. Ten years after the break-up with Louise, and a year and a half after the premiere of *Major Thompson*, Sturges found himself once more bereft of wife and children, this time with his career in tatters.

He never saw Sandy or his sons again. Sturges died alone in a room at the Algonquin Hotel in New York early in the morning of August 6, 1959, while working on the memoir that Sandy would eventually adapt into *Preston Sturges by Preston Sturges*. The book was among his few remaining money-making projects. NBC television had expressed enough interest in his ideas to arouse some hopes, and a theatrical producer was preparing to mount two of his stage projects at the Cincinnati Summer Playhouse. He had no promise of film work.

Welles, for all the trouble he made for himself and other people, and all the trouble they made for him, proved to be the more buoyant by far of Hollywood's original writer-directors. In February 1957, while Sturges was still negotiating for the U.S. release of *The French They Are a Funny Race* and fruitlessly pitching an idea for a comic gangster movie, Welles was beginning production on his last studio picture, *Touch of Evil*. Its star, Charlton Heston, had intervened with Universal so that Welles would be allowed to rewrite the script and direct, for which he received no compensation beyond his fee as a supporting actor; and when he was done with the job, the studio botched the editing. Even so, he'd made another classic, and he would direct a couple more before he was through. In July 1959, a month before his sometime friend Sturges would die, Welles was joyfully at work on a new show he intended to perform that fall with his old friends at the Gate Theatre in Dublin. In the event, he had to take a quick acting job to pay some bills, which forced him to cancel the engagement, but he held onto the idea. In 1965, it became *Chimes at Midnight*.

He was the one who figured out how to stay afloat in the waters of independent production—the one who would last long enough to receive lifetime achievement awards and be hailed as one of world cinema's undisputed geniuses. His films remain monuments of dramatic élan, visual magic, and heartfelt engagement with human affairs, giving the literature of the past a contemporary pulse and translating the concerns of his own moment into ageless forms. Even if given the chance, Sturges never could have done what Welles did: make *Touch of Evil*, *The Trial*, *Chimes at Midnight*, *F for Fake*.

And Welles never could have made *The Lady Eve*.

Is anyone today able to approximate a Sturges film? While I assess what his movies have been giving people for eight decades and counting, I scan the ranks of contemporary filmmakers and wonder which of them might be his progeny.

Ethan and Joel Coen come to mind first, but only because they decided, out of antiquarian interest and perversity, to make a film to go with the worst title ever proposed: *O Brother, Where Art Thou?* (2000). Are we to imagine that this is the movie Sullivan would have made from Sinclair Beckstein's classic novel? Not likely. Although *O Brother* is a road movie set in the Depression, featuring elements that include a chain gang and a church service, the few points the picture has in common with *Sullivan's Travels* are as superficial as the movie's resemblances to its other ostensible source, the *Odyssey*. The Coen brothers can be dauntingly clever, and their talent for pastiche recalls Sturges's. That said, they lack a carnivalesque spirit (does anything ever *really* get out of control in a Coen brothers movie?), and the contempt they habitually splash onto their characters, and the audience too, won't mix with Sturges's sympathetic mockery.

Like Renoir's Octave in *La règle du jeu*, Sturges understood that we fallible souls all have our reasons—though he didn't agree with Octave that this is a "terrible thing." On the contrary. It's why we're so funny.

So I set aside the Coen brothers and also David Mamet, another highly sophisticated writer-director of wised-up comedies, including caper movies, to whom the carnivalesque is foreign. While I'm at it, I'll disallow Armando Iannucci, author of *In the Loop* (2009), *The Death of Stalin* (2017), and the television series *Veep* (2012–19), even though he's a formidable political satirist who does enjoy letting events get out of hand. Iannucci differs from Sturges in not caring *why* his characters have their reasons. True, at long intervals he'll deploy the somewhat mechanical writer's trick of making a character blurt out an unexpected backstory or emotion. (Sturges sets a fine example of this technique in *The Great McGinty* when Dan, flustered by Catherine's call for child labor laws, suddenly veers into a petulant boast that *his* factory was "very neat and clean. We'd fold the boxes and then twist the oil paper around the taffy.") The deeper game of enticing you to guess what might be moving about unvoiced under the characters' surfaces is something Iannucci almost never attempts. Scurrying through the rats' mazes of his plots, his people show no side of themselves other than their rage for cheese.

As for first-person confessional comedies, such as Larry David's *Curb Your Enthusiasm* (2000–21) or Issa Rae's *Insecure* (2016–21), they contrast with Sturges more than they compare with him. In their close observation of settings, they remind you of how little Sturges was interested in creating an authentic sense of place (though he did it occasionally, in the first hobo encampment in *Sullivan's Travels* and the orchestra rehearsal in *Unfaithfully Yours*). They also set a benchmark by which you can judge how little information Sturges actually revealed about himself, whatever the adherents of the biographical-psychological method might think. For better and worse, these comedies are eager to tell you, out loud, everything you might want to know about their characters. Much as I admire *Insecure*, I would describe it as School of Sturges only if it had made room for the insincere.

So is there a Sturges genealogy?

I think he has several present-day descendants, among whom I'd include the director Reginald Hudlin, though he didn't write the screenplay for his most Sturgesque (Sturgid?) film, *The Great White Hype* (1996). It's the story of a boxing promoter, the Reverend Fred Sultan, whose champion so predictably overwhelms all opponents that audiences are bored with the matches and no longer bet on them. In search of a payday, Sultan digs up an over-the-hill amateur who arouses tremendous support from a large segment of the public despite being obviously doomed as a competitor. The champ and promoter, you see, are Black, and the challenger is white. If his fans could admit they're enthused only by his skin tone, they might lower their expectations and save their money. But because almost no one in America admits to being *racist*—why, the very suggestion is offensive!—the suckers who rush forward, cash in hand, tell themselves they've discovered a great boxer. The script for this devious exercise in social psychology is the work of Tony Hendra and Ron Shelton, but it's Hudlin who gets credit for the rogues' gallery cast (headed by Samuel L. Jackson) and the kinetic, modern-*commedia* verve of the direction. Most Sturges-like of all, though, is Jackson's gaiety of invention as Sultan. With a righteous joy that's communicable, he convinces the fools to bilk themselves.

In *The Great White Hype*, we see a theme that's often said to define Sturges—the American scramble for success—as well as evidence of why that characterization, by itself, doesn't tell you much. Many authors and filmmakers, in many countries, have had their fun with the ups and downs of avarice, and even with tales of riches falling out of the sky like a sable coat. (*Fox and His Friends*, anyone?) With Sturges, though, the chase after dollars always has a purpose beyond itself. It provides proof that you don't just *think* you've got ideas; or it enacts revenge on a man who has wounded you with his snobbish moralism; or it ends those cries of suffering that get on your nerves so terribly. The Reverend Fred Sultan claims a windfall but also (perhaps more important to him) a victory over racist hypocrisy. (Here, for once, is a specifically American theme.) Similarly, Sturges's other progeny in contemporary film get laughs out of the drive for wealth and status while achieving something more.

Alexander Payne, who shares writing credit with Jim Taylor for the films he directs, has been making satires in this greed-plus mode since his breakthrough feature, *Citizen Ruth* (1996), the story of a pregnant scuffling lowlife (Laura Dern, in the Dan McGinty role) who staggers into an opportunity to make money as a proxy for both antiabortion and prochoice activists. *Election* (1999, based on a novel by Tom Perrotta) also has a female adventurer at its center: Reese Witherspoon, as a high-school girl whose shameless and secretly desperate campaign for class president collides with the equally powerful desperation of a teacher (Matthew Broderick). More recently, Payne's unjustly neglected *Downsizing* (2017) has mocked acquisitiveness (disguised, in this case, as ecofriendly altruism) through a ridiculous sci-fi premise. Matt Damon plays the film's naïf (a mug in all things), while Hong Chau provides a Sturges-like female dynamo as a one-legged Vietnamese political dissident and cleaning woman.

Working in a pushier visual style, and with a looser and more psycholological approach to narrative, David O. Russell has carried on the Sturges tradition with the rambunctious *American*

Hustle (2013), a near-chaotic, based-on-a-true-story caper movie with strong roles for Amy Adams and Jennifer Lawrence. (Carnivalesque? Saturnalian.) His follow-up film, *Joy* (2015), stars Lawrence in the based-on-a-true-story role of Joy Mangano, an upwardly mobile divorced mother whose knack for inventing and promoting useful gadgets might have appealed to the tinkerer in Sturges, and whose squabbling, cast-of-eccentrics family makes the film play like a Sturges comedy from which the cynicism has magically evanesced.

Chris Rock's presence as a performer dominates the films he's written and directed; but he deserves inclusion in the post-Sturges canon for *Top Five* (2014), which I might describe as his *Sullivan's Travels*. Rock plays a stand-up comedian and franchise-movie star (the riches have already been secured) who has sought respectability, and achieved only embarrassment, by making a deadly earnest film about the Haitian revolution. He bounces from setting to setting in New York trying to recover his poise and figure out what to do with the rest of his life, all the while being trailed by a relentless reporter (Rosario Dawson) who is much more than The Girl, given that she has troubles of her own and a devious purpose. Also, the film has a little sex.

Of the recent post-Sturges comedies of imposture and loot, the most highly cultured in setting and tone is *Can You Ever Forgive Me?* (2018), directed by Marielle Heller from a script by Nicole Holofcener and Jeff Whitty. Another based-on-a-true-story film, it stars Melissa McCarthy as Lee Israel, a serious, semi-reclusive, and gravely uncommercial New York author whose rage against the editors and agents who neglect her finds an outlet, and much-needed profit, in literary forgery. As Sturges would have done, Heller takes the side of the abrasive, sharp-tongued Israel (without excusing her wrongdoing), rejoicing with her as she succeeds in her crimes and savoring her friendship with a grandiloquent trickster (Richard E. Grant) who comes across as a kind of latter-day Oscar Wilde, postdownfall.

The cross talk between McCarthy and Grant in *Can You Ever Forgive Me?* keeps alive the crucial Sturges tradition of verbal wit; but for head-spinning dialogue executed at high speed, you now need to look away from the movies toward television productions, such as Amy Sherman-Palladino's *The Marvelous Mrs. Maisel* (2017–22) or *Hacks* (2021–22), created by Lucia Aniello, Paul W. Downs, and Jen Statsky. Both of those shows are about women whose struggle for material success, and emotional survival, depends on their ability to use words to make people laugh. The dueling wit-slingers in *Hacks* are a wealthy, old-style Las Vegas comedian (Jean Smart) and an impoverished, twentysomething, self-defeating agent of change (Hannah Einbinder) who is unwillingly indentured as the sacred monster's joke writer. *Mrs. Maisel*, of course, is about an abandoned housewife (Rachel Brosnahan) who discovers her personal power, a vocation, the esteem of Lenny Bruce, and a wide new world when she realizes she can stand in front of a crowd and let the words flow.

In *Mrs. Maisel*, the most popular of the Sturges offspring, the talent for memorable utterance, whether willed or inadvertent, spreads among the entire cast, as it would in one of his movies. The show also has a pleasing and effective visual style, imitating the look of the Technicolor film comedies of its period in the late 1950s and early 1960s. *Hacks* belongs to the more contemporary mode of staring deadpan at American settings that are either drearily slapped-together or gaudily fake. (For a predecessor, see *Citizen Ruth*.) In its functionalist image-making, *Hacks* recalls the persistent criticism of Sturges as a director who lacked an invigorating, personal visual style.

Before I get to one more Sturges descendant, the writer-director Charlie Kaufman, let me address this complaint.

Granted, Sturges was no Orson Welles, or any of the other directors whose shot sequences could hang on a museum's walls. But even though his images rarely carry an expressive charge in themselves, they are of a piece with the dialogue and performances and serve the larger purpose. Mostly he pulled off the trick by using an abundance of traveling shots, prolonged two-shots, and the presentational images that I've called his buffet shots, giving himself enough space in which to reveal a continually unfolding fictional world and enough time for his performers to build and deepen their interaction, however quickly the words whizzed by. The frequent objections of Paramount's unit producers to his methods (until he'd proved them) suggest that Sturges was being inventive, even though the results weren't pretty. They didn't have to be. They had to convey the same sense as his dialogue: that every place, and every person in it, might be a source of unexpected delight.

He was a whole-language writer, who found amusement in every level and variety of usage. This willingness to discover wonders coming out of everyone's mouth was fundamentally democratic. His camerawork, though plain, was similarly accommodating to all. Sturges thought up the only visual style in which William Demarest could have been a star.

Which leads me to Charlie Kaufman. Of all today's filmmakers, he comes closest to Sturges's inventiveness with language and his daring in narrative construction. (He is also the only living filmmaker to demonstrate a preoccupation with Alexander Pope's "Eloisa to Abelard.") You could take his scripts for *Being John Malkovich* (1999), *Human Nature* (2001), *Adaptation* (2002), *Confessions of a Dangerous Mind* (2002), and *Eternal Sunshine of the Spotless Mind* (2004) and mine them for quotes that would yield a rhetoric of Charlie Kaufman. (One minor example: Drew Barrymore's instructive malapropism in *Confessions* when she hopes her boyfriend, bound for Mexico, doesn't catch Montessori's revenge.) But it's the films that Kaufman has directed as well as written that reveal his deepest affinity with Sturges.

These two filmmakers share the fear of being trapped. *Synecdoche, New York* (2008), *Anomalisa* (2015), and *I'm Thinking of Ending Things* (2020) are all movies about being enclosed in situations of endless, dreadful repetition, from which the only escape is death. Some comedies. Some tribute to "Eloisa to Abelard." (*Relentless walls! whose darksome round contains / Repentant sighs, and voluntary pains.*) And some tribute to Sturges.

In films that are among the most frenetically paced ever made, and yet also among the most flashback-obsessed, his principal characters have a habit of ending where they started. (To quote the feverish John L. Sullivan, "As you are, so shall you remain.") Sturges's cinematic population mostly comprises a dozen or so character actors, who continually play out variations on the same assigned types. His imagined society is a static hierarchy, resilient enough to allow people to grab for their dreams but rigid enough to contain their flailings. (At best, people can deny the impossibility of bettering themselves, as Mr. Waterbury counsels in *Christmas in July*. They can simply *declare* they've succeeded.) At some point, even a naïve, instinctual character such as Dan McGinty realizes, with dread, that circumstances only appear to have changed, while he's stayed the same.

Which is perhaps why I love *The Lady Eve* best of all. It's the film in which the main characters break the circle. At the end, as Jean and Hopsie sail off into a different kind of nowhere, they no longer know where they're going, or what they'll do. They just know they're on the way together. What makes this nonconclusion so joyful—so different, say, from the final shot of Charlie and the Gamin walking into the distance in *Modern Times*—is that Jean and Hopsie are keenly aware of what they've just escaped. Two minutes before the movie ends, they feel they're trapped in their old lives. Then, wonderfully, they're not.

The same is true of Sturges's films. However much you delve into them to understand what they mean and how they work—as I hope I've shown, you can search as deep as you like—these movies in their wholeness behave as if they were alive and so shrug off the bonds of analysis. Perhaps the same could be asserted about the work of every great artist. The truism is worth saying here because Sturges, throughout most of his career, was reluctant to call himself an artist, though I'm certain he understood himself to have been one.

Look at the elegance of construction in *The Great McGinty*, the exuberance of invention in *Christmas in July* (with its castles in the clouds built of airy words), the thematic subtleties of *The Lady Eve*, the sheer comic virtuosity of *The Palm Beach Story* and *The Miracle of Morgan's Creek*, the deepening note of inexpressible sorrow beneath the perpetual-motion parade of *Hail the Conquering Hero*. He knew how good he was. Toward the end of his Hollywood years, he even allowed himself to say "artist" (jokingly) in *The Sin of Harold Diddlebock*. Then, in *Unfaithfully Yours*, he created his portrait of the artist as an insecure blowhard in middle age.

You might imagine that the Sturges who figured himself as the dark and absurd Sir Alfred had a premonition of being unable to evade the decline of his final decade, and a death that would come too soon. But then, by the time Sturges made *Unfaithfully Yours*, he already had triumphed over the odds. After the years that had culminated, by his early thirties, in his rise and fall on Broadway, there was (contrary to F. Scott Fitzgerald) a second act in Sturges's life. It was his Hollywood career. Looking back, you can see the whole thing as a gift—one that let him break the bonds that biography, the business of movies, and mortality itself tried to clamp on an ingenuity that had no limit.

ACKNOWLEDGMENTS

Many people wrote this book, beginning with the man who was my friend from grammar school on, the late Ronald Klein. He was the first person to urge me to watch Preston Sturges's films—this was when we were in our early twenties—and pressed into my hands, when he saw my ignorance, his own ragged paperback of Andrew Sarris's *The American Cinema*. It's the one that still sits on my shelf.

The people responsible for initiating my serious if informal education about movies were the staff of the Department of Film of the Museum of Modern Art, for whom I lucked into a job as publicist. I thank my boss and protector, the late Luisa Kreisberg, and her associate Sharon Zane for putting me forward for the assignment. Those who accepted and guided me—too many of them are gone now—included Laurence Kardish, Mary Lea Bandy, Stephen Harvey, Jytte Jensen, Robert Beers, Zette Emmons, Charles Silver, Alicia Springer, and Adrienne Mancia. Among those at MoMA who very recently gave me material help in completing this book are Josh Siegel, Ron Magliozzi, and Ashley Swinnerton.

My primary berth as a journalist, for thirty-five years, was the *Nation*. Maria Margaronis and Betsy Pochoda invited me in, to my astonishment, to write about fiction and poetry; and when they saw an article about film I'd written for the *Village Voice*—commissioned by another old MoMA colleague, Howard Feinstein—they were the ones who told me I should write about movies for them, too. After Maria and Betsy, so many editors at the *Nation* encouraged and supported me in my film reviewing, until close to the end of my tenure, that I can't name them all. I will single out Art Winslow for his exceptional friendship and care.

Writing for the *Nation* opened the way toward the more expansive and intensive involvement with movies that came from serving on the selection committee of the New York Film Festival and associating with the Film Society of Lincoln Center, as it was then called. I am unendingly grateful to Richard Peña, Wendy Keys, Joanne Koch, Claudia Bonn, my friends on the selection committee—David Ansen, Joan Juliet Buck, Jonathan Rosenbaum, Bob Sklar, and David Sterritt—and other colleagues from Lincoln Center including Kent Jones, Gavin Smith, and Dennis Lim.

About my predecessor on the selection committee, Phillip Lopate, I can only marvel. He somehow took it into his head to be my *rebbe*, as they would have said in his native Brooklyn, and gave me kindness after kindness, including a personal introduction to a pair of eminent Sturgesites, James Harvey and Diane Jacobs. Lawrence Joseph—poet, attorney, and son of Detroit—took it into his head to be not just my friend but my mouthpiece, in the broadest sense. I can never repay him for all the good ideas I've swiped from his monologues.

In the introduction, I mentioned my debt to Henry Abelove: friend, teacher, and mentor. He not only got me started writing about Sturges but also vouched for me when I applied to the John Simon Guggenheim Memorial Foundation for a grant to assist with this book. I gratefully acknowledge the foundation's support, as well as its patience. I am also grateful to Herb Leibowitz, editor of the late, lamented *Parnassus: Poetry in Review*, and his coeditor Ben Downing for their generous moral, collegial, and financial support. Two chapters in this book, on *The Lady Eve* and *The Great McGinty*, appeared in early versions in *Parnassus*.

Carl Bromley, a friend from the *Nation*, took a direct role in getting this book published when he recommended me to Philip Leventhal at Columbia University Press. My thanks go to Philip and his colleagues Monique Briones, Susan Pensak, Robert Demke, and Zachary Friedman for the remarkable combination of professionalism and encouragement they have shown me at every stage of bringing this book to press.

Like many Sturges fans, Ben Sonnenberg and I used to converse in quotations from the films. For years we spoke almost daily—about movies and much else—and with his wife, Dorothy Gallagher, he offered me a kind of intellectual finishing school. Whether I graduated, I'll never know; but Ben is the editor who still hovers over my shoulder as I write. The many DVDs he bequeathed me, some of which I watched repeatedly while writing this book, are known in my family as The Sonnenberg Collection.

With that, I come full circle to the dedicatees of this book: Bali Miller, Jake Klawans, and Ruby Klawans. They are the people I most want to love, support, and spend my hours with. They are the people I have repeatedly abandoned so I could shut myself away and write. Bali, Jake, and Ruby, I apologize for everything. And I thank you for everything, hoping you will somehow feel the outcome has been worth it. All errors are my own.

NOTES

INSTEAD OF AN INTRODUCTION

1. The most exhaustive account of the youth and early career of Orson Welles is found in Simon Callow, *Orson Welles: The Road to Xanadu* (New York: Viking, 1996); the liveliest, in Orson Welles and Peter Bogdanovich, *This Is Orson Welles*, ed. Jonathan Rosenbaum (New York: HarperCollins, 1992). For the youth and early career of Preston Sturges, see especially Diane Jacobs, *Christmas in July: The Life and Art of Preston Sturges* (Berkeley: University of California Press, 1992).
2. Brian Henderson, "Introduction," in *Five Screenplays by Preston Sturges*, ed. Brian Henderson (Berkeley: University of California Press, 1985), 17.
3. Stuart Klawans, "Habitual Remarriage: The Ends of Happiness in *The Palm Beach Story*," in *Reading Cavell*, ed. Alice Crary and Sanford Shieh (London: Routledge, 2006), 218–30.
4. In general, quotations are from the completed films and are transcribed with standardized punctuation. Passages that appear only in the screenplays are flagged as such and retain Sturges's idiosyncratic punctuation.
5. In "Misspeaking in the Films of Preston Sturges," Jeff Jaeckle argues that malapropism is found everywhere in Sturges; but Jaeckle uses the term to mean any sort of twist on words. See Jaeckle, ed., *Film Dialogue* (London: Wallflower, 2013), 140–53.

1. YA CAN'T GET AWAY FROM ARITHMETIC

1. Preston Sturges, *Preston Sturges by Preston Sturges: His Life in His Words*, ed. Sandy Sturges (New York: Simon and Schuster, 1990), 218.
2. Brian Henderson, ed., *Five Screenplays by Preston Sturges* (Berkeley: University of California Press, 1985), 32.
3. Sturges, *Preston Sturges by Preston Sturges*, 276.
4. Diane Jacobs, *Christmas in July: The Life and Art of Preston Sturges* (Berkeley: University of California Press, 1992), 201.
5. Jacobs, 143.

2. HE THINKS HE HAS IDEAS

1. Brian Henderson, ed., *Five Screenplays by Preston Sturges* (Berkeley: University of California Press, 1985), 186.
2. Diane Jacobs, *Christmas in July: The Life and Art of Preston Sturges* (Berkeley: University of California Press, 1992), 159.
3. Jacobs, 161.
4. Preston Sturges, *A Cup of Coffee* (New York: Samuel French, 1989), 63–64.
5. George Bernard Shaw, *Major Barbara*, in *The Bodley Head Bernard Shaw*, vol. 3 (London: Bodley Head, 1971), 174.
6. Jacobs, *Christmas in July*, 223.

3. I'M NOT A POET, I'M AN OPHIOLOGIST

1. Brian Henderson, ed., *Five Screenplays by Preston Sturges* (Berkeley: University of California Press, 1985), 323.
2. Henderson, 364.
3. James Harvey, *Romantic Comedy in Hollywood, from Lubitsch to Sturges* (New York: Da Capo, 1998), 568.
4. Joseph Anthony, "A Modern Lilith," *Century* (March 1928): 635.
5. Harvey, *Romantic Comedy*, 571.
6. Henderson, *Five Screenplays*, 488.
7. Henderson, 498.

4. AS YOU ARE, SO SHALL YOU REMAIN

1. Diane Jacobs, *Christmas in July: The Life and Art of Preston Sturges* (Berkeley: University of California Press, 1992), 262.
2. Sturges, *Preston Sturges by Preston Sturges: His Life in His Words*, ed. Sandy Sturges (New York: Simon and Schuster, 1990), 295.
3. Jacobs, *Christmas in July*, 256.
4. Elliot Rubinstein made this point in "Hollywood Travels: Sturges and Sullivan," *Sight and Sound* (Winter 1977), 50: "If the likes of Sullivan did make *O Brother, Where Art Thou?*, we'd have only an undistinguished representative of precisely the wrong genre, with 'social significance' thrown in even more gratuitously than that 'little bit of sex' one of the executives keeps trying to work into any scenario."
5. Jacobs, *Christmas in July*, 245.
6. Joseph McBride, *Searching for John Ford: A Life* (New York: St. Martin's, 2001), 314.
7. Brian Henderson, ed., *Five Screenplays by Preston Sturges* (Berkeley: University of California Press, 1985), 641.
8. Henderson, 662.
9. Penelope Houston, "Preston Sturges," in *Cinema: A Critical Dictionary: The Major Filmmakers*, ed. Richard Roud (New York: Viking, 1980), 2:995.
10. Anthony Wood, "Jess Lee Brooks: A Black Western Actor in the Narrative of the American West," in *High Altitude History: Writing History at Montana State University*, May 17, 2017, https://historymsu.wordpress.com/2017/05/17/jess-lee-brooks-a-black-western-actor-in-the-narrative-of-the-black-west/.
11. Brander Matthews, *A Study of the Drama* (Boston: Houston Mifflin, 1910), 171–74.
12. Manny Farber and W. S. Poster, "Preston Sturges: Success in the Movies," in *Farber on Film: The Complete Film Writings of Manny Farber*, ed. Robert Polito (New York: Library of America, 2009), 470–71.
13. James Agee, *James Agee: Film Writing and Selected Journalism*, ed. Michael Sragow (New York: Library of America, 2005), 164.
14. Henderson, *Five Screenplays*, 599.
15. Jacobs, *Christmas in July*, 264.

5. TOPIC A

1. Brian Henderson, ed., *Four More Screenplays by Preston Sturges* (Berkeley: University of California Press, 1995), 26.
2. Diane Jacobs, *Christmas in July: The Life and Art of Preston Sturges* (Berkeley: University of California Press, 1992), 271.
3. Henderson, *Four More Screenplays*, 84.
4. Richard Wilbur, *Responses: Prose Pieces, 1953–1976* (New York: Harcourt Brace Jovanovich), 16–38.
5. Sturges, *Preston Sturges by Preston Sturges: His Life in His Words*, ed. Sandy Sturges (New York: Simon and Schuster, 1990), 259.

6. HOMO SAPIENS, THE WISE GUY

1. James Curtis, *Between Flops: A Biography of Preston Sturges* (New York: Harcourt Brace Jovanovich, 1982), 168.
2. Brian Henderson, ed., *Four More Screenplays by Preston Sturges* (Berkeley: University of California Press, 1995), 366.
3. Robert Stam, "Orson Welles, Brazil, and the Power of Blackness," *Persistence of Vision*, no. 7 (1989): 93–112.
4. Orson Welles and Peter Bogdanovich, *This Is Orson Welles*, ed. Jonathan Rosenbaum (New York: Harper Collins, 1992), 115–20.
5. Thomas Schatz, *The Genius of the System* (New York: Pantheon, 1988), 298–300.
6. Schatz, 298.
7. Henderson, *Four More Screenplays*, 381.
8. Diane Jacobs, *Christmas in July: The Life and Art of Preston Sturges* (Berkeley: University of California Press, 1992), 285.
9. Welles and Bogdanovich, *This Is Orson Welles*, 155.

7. PSYCHOLOLOGY

1. Brian Henderson, ed., *Four More Screenplays by Preston Sturges* (Berkeley: University of California Press, 1995), 561.
2. Henderson, 548.
3. James Harvey, *Romantic Comedy in Hollywood, from Lubitsch to Sturges* (New York: Da Capo, 1998), 682.

4. James Curtis, *Between Flops: A Biography of Preston Sturges* (New York: Harcourt Brace Jovanovich, 1982), 183.
5. Diane Jacobs, *Christmas in July: The Life and Art of Preston Sturges* (Berkeley: University of California Press, 1992), 302.
6. Henderson, *Four More Screenplays*, 540.
7. Sturges, *Preston Sturges by Preston Sturges: His Life in His Words*, ed. Sandy Sturges (New York: Simon and Schuster, 1990), 256.
8. David Thomson, *Showman: The Life of David O. Selznick* (New York: Knopf, 1992), 422–28.
9. James Agee, *Film Writing and Selected Journalism*, ed. Michael Sragow (New York: Library of America, 2005), 392.
10. Jacobs, *Christmas in July*, 298.

8. THAT'S ALL YOU KNOW HOW TO HURT

1. Diane Jacobs, *Christmas in July: The Life and Art of Preston Sturges* (Berkeley: University of California Press, 1992), 310.
2. Sturges, *Preston Sturges by Preston Sturges: His Life in His Words*, ed. Sandy Sturges (New York: Simon and Schuster, 1990), 301.
3. Andrew Sarris, *Hollywood Voices: Interviews with Film Directors* (Indianapolis: Bobbs-Merrill, 1971), 93.
4. Brian Henderson, ed., *Five Screenplays by Preston Sturges* (Berkeley: University of California Press, 1985), 687.
5. Henderson, *Five Screenplays*, 731.
6. Sturges, *Preston Sturges by Preston Sturges*, 297.
7. Manny Farber, *Farber on Film: The Complete Film Writings of Manny Farber*, ed. Robert Polito (New York: Library of America, 2009), 187.

9. YOU AROUSE THE ARTIST IN ME

1. Diane Jacobs, *Christmas in July: The Life and Art of Preston Sturges* (Berkeley: University of California Press, 1992), 323–24.
2. See, for example, the two-part profile by Alva Johnston, "How to Become a Playwright," *Saturday Evening Post*, March 8 and March 15, 1941.
3. Jacobs, *Christmas in July*, 336–38.

4. James Curtis, *Between Flops: A Biography of Preston Sturges* (New York: Harcourt Brace Jovanovich, 1982), 207.
5. Donald Spoto, *Madcap: The Life of Preston Sturges* (Boston: Little, Brown, 1990), 209.

10. EVERY EMOTION WAS EXAGGERATED

1. Thomas Schatz, *The Genius of the System* (New York: Pantheon, 1988), 435.
2. "60 Top Grossers of 1946," *Variety*, January 8, 1947, 8; "Top Grossers of 1947," *Variety*, January 7, 1948, 63; and "Top Grossers of 1948," *Variety*, January 5, 1949, 46.
3. Diane Jacobs, *Christmas in July: The Life and Art of Preston Sturges* (Berkeley: University of California Press, 1992), 359–61.
4. Jacobs, 366.
5. Jacobs, 373.
6. Sturges, *Preston Sturges by Preston Sturges*, 235.
7. Brian Henderson, ed., *Four More Screenplays by Preston Sturges* (Berkeley: University of California Press, 1995), 937.
8. Jacobs, *Christmas in July*, 99, 134, 325, and 394; Sturges, *Preston Sturges by Preston Sturges: His Life in His Words*, ed. Sandy Sturges (New York: Simon and Schuster, 1990), 312.
9. Henderson, *Four More Screenplays*, 763.
10. Jacobs, *Christmas in July*, 373.
11. Veronica Geng, "Compare the New Movie with the 1948 Preston Sturges Classic and You'll Find a Case of Champagne Comedy Gone Flat," *Film Comment*, March 1, 1984, 57–58, 77.
12. James Curtis, *Between Flops: A Biography of Preston Sturges* (New York: Harcourt Brace Jovanovich, 1982), 232.

INSTEAD OF A CONCLUSION

1. Orson Welles and Peter Bogdanovich, *This Is Orson Welles*, ed. Jonathan Rosenbaum (New York: HarperCollins, 1992), 203–7.
2. For the full, painful account, see Nick Smedley and Tom Sturges, *Preston Sturges: The Last Years of Hollywood's First Writer-Director* (Bristol: Intellect; Chicago: University of Chicago Press, 2019).

3. Diane Jacobs, *Christmas in July: The Life and Art of Preston Sturges* (Berkeley: University of California Press, 1992), 384.
4. It seems just as well that nothing came of *A Present for Uncle Popo*, the description of which sounds like the cacklings of an old lecher interspersed with vatic wheezing. See Smedley and Sturges, *Preston Sturges*, 58–63.

BIBLIOGRAPHY

Agee, James. *Film Writing and Selected Journalism*. Edited by Michael Sragow. New York: Library of America, 2005.

Bazin, André. *The Cinema of Cruelty: From Buñuel to Hitchcock*. Edited by François Truffaut. Translated by Sabine d'Estée with Tiffany Fliss. New York: Seaver, 1982.

Callow, Simon. *Orson Welles: Hello Americans*. New York: Viking, 2006.

———. *Orson Welles: One-Man Band*. New York: Viking, 2015.

Cavell, Stanley. *Pursuits of Happiness: The Hollywood Comedy of Remarriage*. Cambridge, MA: Harvard University Press, 1981.

Corliss, Richard. *Talking Pictures: Screenwriters in the American Cinema*. New York: Penguin, 1975.

Curtis, James. *Between Flops: A Biography of Preston Sturges*. New York: Harcourt Brace Jovanovich, 1982.

Erskine, John. *Adam and Eve: Though He Knew Better*. Indianapolis: Bobbs-Merrill, 1927.

Farber, Manny. *Farber on Film: The Complete Film Writings of Manny Farber*. Edited by Robert Polito. New York: Library of America, 2009.

Geng, Veronica. "Compare the New Movie with the 1948 Preston Sturges Classic and You'll Find a Case of Champagne Comedy Gone Flat." *Film Comment*, March 1, 1984.

Harvey, James. *Romantic Comedy in Hollywood: From Lubitsch to Sturges*. New York: Knopf, 1987.

Haskell, Molly. *From Reverence to Rape: The Treatment of Women in the Movies.* 2nd ed. Chicago: University of Chicago Press, 1987.

Houston, Penelope. "Preston Sturges." In *Cinema: A Critical Dictionary,* edited by Richard Roud. New York: Viking, 1980.

Jacobs, Diane. *Christmas in July: The Life and Art of Preston Sturges.* Berkeley: University of California Press, 1992.

Jaeckle, Jeff, ed. *Film Dialogue.* New York: Wallflower, 2013.

Jaeckle, Jeff, and Sarah Kozloff, eds. *ReFocus: The Films of Preston Sturges.* Edinburgh: Edinburgh University Press, 2015.

Matthews, Brander. *A Study of the Drama.* Boston: Houston Mifflin, 1910.

Pirolini, Alessandro. *The Cinema of Preston Sturges: A Critical Study.* Jefferson, NC: McFarland, 2010.

Rozgonyi, Jay. *Preston Sturges's Vision of America: Critical Analyses of Fourteen Films.* Jefferson, NC: McFarland, 1995.

Rubinstein, Elliot. "Hollywood Travels: Sturges and Sullivan." *Sight and Sound,* Winter 1977.

Sarris, Andrew. *The American Cinema: Directors and Directions, 1929–1968.* New York: Dutton, 1968.

———. *"You Ain't Heard Nothin' Yet": The American Talking Film—History and Memory, 1927–1949.* New York: Oxford University Press, 1998.

Schatz, Thomas. *The Genius of the System: Hollywood Filmmaking in the Studio Era.* New York: Pantheon, 1988.

Smedley, Nick, and Tom Sturges. *Preston Sturges: The Last Years of Hollywood's First Writer-Director.* Bristol: Intellect, 2019.

Spoto, Donald. *Madcap: The Life of Preston Sturges.* Boston: Little, Brown, 1990.

Stam, Robert, Susan Ryan, and Catherine Benamou. "Dossier on *It's All True.*" *Persistence of Vision,* no. 7 (1989).

Sturges, Preston. *A Cup of Coffee: A Comedy About Business.* New York: Samuel French, 1989.

———. *Five Screenplays by Preston Sturges.* Edited by Brian Henderson. Berkeley: University of California Press, 1985.

———. *Four More Screenplays by Preston Sturges.* Edited by Brian Henderson. Berkeley: University of California Press, 1995.

———. *Preston Sturges by Preston Sturges: His Life in His Words.* Edited by Sandy Sturges. New York: Simon and Schuster, 1990.

———. *Three More Screenplays by Preston Sturges*. Edited by Andrew Horton. Berkeley: University of California Press, 1998.

Ursini, James. *The Fabulous Life and Times of Preston Sturges: An American Dreamer*. New York: Curtis, 1973.

Welles, Orson, and Peter Bogdanovich. *This Is Orson Welles*. Edited by Jonathan Rosenbaum. New York: HarperCollins, 1992.

INDEX

Academy Award, 166
Adam (biblical), 65, 70, 80–83, 89, 93
Adams, Amy, 331
Adventures of Huckleberry Finn, 27
African Americans: audiences, 119; characters, 63, 107, 120–21, 133; church life, depictions of, 96, 117, 120–21, 131; hyperarticulation in Black speech, 7; performers, 119, 125
Agee, James, 2–3, 124, 225
Alger, Horatio, 267
Algonquin Hotel, 326
American Hustle, 330–31
Angelus, Muriel, 22–23
Aniello, Lucia, 332
Annie Get Your Gun, 318
anonymity, in *The Great McGinty*, 14
Anthony, Joseph, 83
Argosy Pictures, 262
Arno, Sig, 152
Arnold, Edward, 36, 41–42, 44, 46
Arthur, Jean, 42, 45
aspirations, Sturges's, 20
Astor, Mary, 154, 158

"Ave Maria," 189–90
Awful Truth, The, 195

Ball, J. B. (*Christmas in July* character), 36, 43–49, 54, 58, 60
Banque Nemo, La, 264
Barnes, Binnie, 42
Barrymore, Drew, 333
Bartlett, Jeanne, 69
Baxter, Ephraim (*Christmas in July* character), 38–40, 42–43, 49–50, 53–54, 56, 58–60
Bazin, André, 124
Beau Geste, 173
Beautiful Blonde from Bashful Bend, The, 318–21, 325
Beckstein, Sinclair (*Sullivan's Travels* fictional author), 101, 327
Beery, Wallace, 24
Beggar's Opera, The, 23
Being John Malkovich, 333
Benny, Jack, 130
Betty (*Christmas in July* character), 34, 54–58, 60–61, 63–64, 199

Bible, 66–68, 70, 80, 94, 193, 273
Biden, Sturges's birth name, 162
Bildocker (*Christmas in July* character), 52, 62, 64
Bissell, Doc (*Hail the Conquering Hero* character), 253, 257
Blake, William, 93
Blitzstein, Marc, 125
Bloom, Molly, 161
Blore, Eric, 104
Borden, Lizzie, 263
Boss, The (*The Great McGinty* character), 12–14, 16, 21–24, 26, 28–29, 31–32; *The Miracle of Morgan's Creek* and, 194, 197, 199, 212, 226; *The Palm Beach Story* and, 148, 160; *Sullivan's Travels* and, 96, 122
Bracken, Eddie, 195, 218, 227, 229, 231–33, 248, 252, 311
Brady, "Diamond Jim," 41–43. *See also Diamond Jim*
Brazil, Welles and, 126, 130, 170–71
Bridge, Al, 117, 121, 212, 214, 243, 278
Broderick, Matthew, 330
Brooks, Jess Lee, 117–19, 121
Brosnahan, Rachel, 332
Bruce, Lenny, 332
Buchanan, Jack, 323–24
Bugsy (*Hail the Conquering Hero* character), 234–37, 243–45, 247–48, 251, 259–60
Burrows (*Sullivan's Travels* character), 103–4

Caine, Georgia, 198, 243, 245
California Pictures, 262–64, 284

Calloway, Cab, 158
candor, 60, 97, 142, 235
Cantor, Eddie, 239
Can You Ever Forgive Me?, 331
Capra, Frank, comparisons to, 61–63, 98, 101, 107, 109–10, 126, 130, 136, 161, 258
Carey, Harry, 185
carnets de Major Thompson, Les. *See The French They Are a Funny Race*
Carol, Martine, 323–24
Carter, Daphne de (*Unfaithfully Yours* character), 290–1, 303–9, 312–13
Carter, Sir Alfred de (*Unfaithfully Yours* character), 8–9, 90, 290–313, 335
Caspary, Vera, 43–45
Catherine (*The Great McGinty* character), 21–25, 27–29, 32, 328
Catholic League of Decency, 193
Cavell, Stanley, 3–5, 66, 161
censors, 193–94, 200, 214, 218, 252
Chaplin, Charlie, 20, 96, 98
Child of Manhattan, 39
Christmas in July, 33–64; *The Great McGinty* and, 17; *The Great Moment* and, 166, 182; *Hail the Conquering Hero* and, 238; influences and comparisons, 334–35; *The Lady Eve* and, 71; *The Miracle of Morgan's Creek* and, 199; *The Palm Beach Story* and, 148–49; *The Sin of Harold Diddlebock* and, 271, 278; *Sullivan's Travels* and, 96; *Unfaithfully Yours* and, 301, 313

INDEX ❧ 355

Citizen Kane, 125–26, 167
Citizen Ruth, 330, 332
Clair, René, 264
Coburn, Charles, 67
Coen, Joel and Ethan, 327–28
Colbert, Claudette, x, 109, 135–39, 147, 149, 153–54, 160–61, 281
College Swing, 130
Columbia University, 81, 291
Confessions of a Dangerous Mind, 333
Conlin, Jimmy, 121, 243, 272
Consider the Lily, 39
contract screenwriting, 20–21, 27, 35, 40, 73
Coolidge, Calvin, 34
Cooper, Gary, 166
Coughlin, "Bathhouse John," 19
Cranach, Lucas, 76
Crosby, Bing, 154, 289
Crowther, Bosley, 124
Cup of Coffee, A (play), 38–39, 41, 43, 49–50, 55, 59, 115, 134. See also Christmas in July
Curious George, 278–79
Curtis, James, 2, 166, 195, 262, 264, 269–70, 314–15

Damon, Matt, 330
Daninos, Pierre, 322
Daphne. See de Carter, Daphne (*Unfaithfully Yours* character)
The Dark Horse, 24
Darnell, Linda, 290, 305–9, 312
David, Larry, 328
Davis, Bette, 24
Dawson, Rosario, 331
death, Sturges's, 163, 326

Demarest, William, 333; *Christmas in July*, 52, 62; *The Great McGinty*, 26, 32; *The Great Moment*, 176, 183–84; *Hail the Conquering Hero*, 231, 233–36, 238, 243, 251; *The Lady Eve*, 69; *The Miracle of Morgan's Creek*, 199, 206, 221; *Sullivan's Travels*, 121
DeMille, Cecil B., 130, 302
Dempsey, Mary (Sturges's mother), 1, 162, 264. See also Desti, Marie
Dern, Laura, 330
Desti, Marie (d'Este), 36, 162–63, 264. See also Dempsey, Mary (Sturges's mother)
DeSylva, Buddy, 133, 169–71, 175–77, 193–94, 231, 255–56, 314
dialect, 55, 64, 320
dialogue: Black speech, 7; candor, 60, 97, 142, 235; dialect, 55, 64, 320; double entendres, 294; doubletalk, 6, 35, 55; hyperarticulation, 7–8, 270, 295; hypoarticulation, 6–7, 129, 216; malapropisms, 7–8, 275, 333; metaphor, 86; poetic, 79–80; retorts, 11–12, 62, 101; Sturges's talent for writing, 5–9, 79–80, 106
Diamond Jim, 41–43
"Diamond Jim." See Brady, "Diamond Jim"
diatribes, 190–191
Dickens, Charles, imagery, 53, 102
Diddlebock, Harold (*The Sin of Harold Diddlebock* character), 261, 266–84, 289, 291, 299, 335
Disney, Walt, 117

domestic violence, 298–99
Donlevy, Brian, 15, 194
double entendres, 294
doubletalk, 6, 35, 55
Downs, Paul W., 332
Downsizing, 330
"Down Went McGinty" (song), 14
Dr. Ehrlich's Magic Bullet, 165
Drew, Ellen, 34, 54–55
Dudley, Robert, 37, 138, 280–81
Dumont, Margaret, 37
Duna, Steffi, 21
Duncan, Isadora, 36, 82–83, 162, 291
Dunne, Irene, 195

Easy Living, 33–34, 36, 41, 43–46, 61, 71, 148, 290
Eden, Garden of, 69–71, 84
Edwards, Bill, 254–55
Eggerth, Marta, 96
Einbinder, Hannah, 332
Emma (*The Lady Eve* snake), 65, 80
Emmy (*The Miracle of Morgan's Creek* character), 195, 198, 205, 211–13, 215, 219–21, 223, 228–29
Erskine, John, 81–83
Eternal Sunshine of the Spotless Mind, 333
Eugenia (character). *See* Harrington, Jean (*The Lady Eve* character)
Evans, Walker, 110
Eve, 90, 134, 298. *See also* Harrington, Jean (*The Lady Eve* character); *The Lady Eve*

Fanny, 227
Farber, Manny, 123, 257, 280
Federal Theatre Project, 125–26
Feldman, Charles, 317, 321
Field, Betty, 176
Fitzgerald, F. Scott, 335
Flagler, Henry, 137
flashbacks, 16, 40, 177, 323–24, 334
flops, 24, 39, 130, 264, 284, 287, 310
Flynn, Joseph, 14–15
Fonda, Henry, 66, 85, 87, 89–90, 101, 311
Ford, John, 27, 101, 110, 126, 130, 262–63
Forrest (*Hail the Conquering Hero* character), 254–55
Fox, 19–20, 110, 239, 284–88, 314, 321, 330. *See also* Twentieth Century-Fox
Francesca da Rimini, 292, 308
Freeman, Frank, 170
French They Are a Funny Race, The, 322–26
Freud, Sigmund, 201–2, 208
Frost, Eben (*The Great Moment* character), 176, 184, 186–88
Fülöp-Miller, René, 165

Gable, Clark, 109, 136, 138–39, 146, 160, 321
Garner, Tom (*The Power and the Glory* character), 40, 42–43, 46, 49
gender and gender roles, 146, 156
Geng, Veronica, 310

INDEX 357

George (*The Great McGinty* character), 24
Gerry (character). *See* Jeffers, Gerry (Geraldine) (*The Palm Beach Story* character)
Gibson, Julie, 246, 249, 320
Gilchrist, Bianca, 198, 298
Gillette, Edwin, 308
GIs, 194, 199–200, 202, 209–10, 213, 237. *See also* Marine Corps; U.S. Army
Gish, Lillian, 263
Goethe, 84, 102
Goldwyn, Samuel, 174, 201–2
The Good Fairy, 33, 41
Grable, Betty, 286–87, 318–20
Grant, Richard E., 332
The Grapes of Wrath, 101, 110–11
Great Depression, 17, 37, 109, 173, 267, 272, 280, 327
Great McGinty, The, 11–32; *Christmas in July* and, 33, 35; *The Great Moment* and, 166, 183; *Hail the Conquering Hero* and, 238, 245, 257; influences and comparisons, 325, 328, 330, 334–35; *The Lady Eve* and, 70–71; *The Miracle of Morgan's Creek* and, 197, 199, 212, 226; *The Palm Beach Story* and, 148, 160; *The Sin of Harold Diddlebock* and, 262, 267; *Sullivan's Travels* and, 96, 122–23; *Unfaithfully Yours* and, 290, 297, 313. *See also The Miracle of Morgan's Creek*

Great Moment, The, 165–91; *Christmas in July* and, 40; *Hail the Conquering Hero* and, 233–34, 238, 249; *The Lady Eve* and, 70; *The Sin of Harold Diddlebock* and, 262
The Great White Hype, 329–30
The Green Pastures, 120
Greig, Robert, 103
Griffith, D. W., 263
Guadalcanal, 239–41, 247, 252, 254
Guinea Pig, The, 115

Hackensacker, John D., III (*The Palm Beach Story* character), 37, 60, 151–52, 154–59, 199
Hadrian (*Sullivan's Travels* character), 37, 100–3
Hail the Conquering Hero, 231–60; *Christmas in July* and, 33; dialogue in, 8; *The Great Moment* and, 169–70; influences and comparisons, 320, 335; *The Lady Eve* and, 71; *The Palm Beach Story* and, 148; *The Sin of Harold Diddlebock* and, 262, 272, 282
Hall, Porter, 37, 100, 183
Hal Wallis Productions, 302
Harrington, Colonel (*The Lady Eve* character), 67, 74, 78, 80, 88
Harrington, Jean (*The Lady Eve* character), 66–67, 69, 71–94; comparisons, 23, 134, 148, 212, 221, 255, 313, 334–35
Harrison, Rex, 290, 299, 309, 311–12, 314–15

Hartman, Don (*Christmas in July* character), 51
Harvey, James, 74, 85, 195, 246
Hathaway, Henry, 166
Hayden, Harry, 52, 253
Hayes, Margaret, 106
Hays Office, 134–35, 153, 193–95
Hearst, William Randolph, 126
Heller, Marielle, 331
Henderson, Brian, 2; on *The Great McGinty*, 19, 21; on *The Great Moment*, 166, 169; on *Hail the Conquering Hero*, 242; on *The Lady Eve*, 68; on *The Miracle of Morgan's Creek*, 195–96; on *The Palm Beach Story*, 134; on *The Sin of Harold Diddlebock*, 282; on *Unfaithfully Yours*, 304
Hendra, Tony, 329
Hepburn, Katharine, 322
Hergesheimer, Joseph, 263
Heston, Charlton, 326
Heydt, Louis Jean, 21, 183
Hinky Dinky. *See* Truesmith, Hinky Dinky (*Hail the Conquering Hero* character nickname)
Hitchcock, Alfred, 22, 286, 289, 315
Hoffe, Monckton, 68–69
Hoffenstein, Samuel, 165–66
Hollander, Frederick, 14
Holloway, Sterling, 319
Holofcener, Nicole, 331
"Home to the Arms of Mother" (song), 246
Hope, Bob, 154

Hopsie (character). *See* Pike, Charles "Hopsie" (*The Lady Eve* character)
horses: interfering, 65, 87; talking, 284
Hotel Haywire, 130
Houston, Penelope, 119
Howard, Esther, 107, 138, 183
Hudlin, Reginald, 329
Hughes, Howard, 262–65, 270–71, 280, 283–84, 314
Hugo (*Unfaithfully Yours* character), 294
Human Nature, 333
Human Strong Box, 264
Huston, John, 126, 237
Hutton, Betty, 195, 209, 237, 287
Hutton, Edward F., 38
Hutton, Eleanor Close, 18, 38–39, 137, 298
hyperarticulation, 7–8, 270, 295
hypoarticulation, 6–7, 129, 216

Iannucci, Armando, 328
If I Were King, 173
independent production, 174, 327
Insecure, 328
Is Marriage Necessary? (screenplay), 134

Jackie (*The Sin of Harold Diddlebock* lion), 269, 277–81
Jackson, Charles Dr. (*The Great Moment* character), 182–85, 187
Jackson, Dan, 319
Jackson, Samuel L., 329

Jacobs, Diane, 2, 320, 325; on *Christmas in July*, 43, 55; on *The Great McGinty*, 20, 30; on *The Great Moment*, 183; on *Hail the Conquering Hero*, 237; on *The Miracle of Morgan's Creek*, 195, 225; on *The Palm Beach Story*, 135; on *The Sin of Harold Diddlebock*, 262–63, 284; on *Sullivan's Travels*, 128; on *Unfaithfully Yours*, 289, 306, 314
Jean (character). *See* Harrington, Jean (*The Lady Eve* character)
Jeffers, Gerry (Geraldine) (*The Palm Beach Story* character), 136–59, 163, 199, 255, 281
Jeffers, Tom (*The Palm Beach Story* character), 137, 143–45, 154–56, 158–59, 162, 180
Jewell, Richard, 173
Jimmy. *See* MacDonald, Jimmy (*Christmas in July* character)
Johnson, Mr. (*The Miracle of Morgan's Creek* character), 212, 214, 221–22
Johnson, Samuel, 102
Jones, Norval (*The Miracle of Morgan's Creek* character), 195, 197, 199, 202–9, 211–13, 215–19, 221–29, 245
Joslyn, Allyn, 24
Joy, 330–31
Judge Dennis (*Hail the Conquering Hero* character), 243, 253

Kaufman, Charlie, 332–34
Kenna, Michael "Hinky Dink," 19
Kennedy, Edgar, 270, 283, 296
King, Henry, 263
Kockenlocker, Constable (*The Miracle of Morgan's Creek* character), 199, 205, 221, 224
Kockenlocker, Trudy (*The Miracle of Morgan's Creek* character), 195, 197–200, 202–28, 277
Koerner, Charles, 171
Kreuger, Kurt, 294

Lady Eve, The, 65–94; *Christmas in July* and, 36, 47; *The Great McGinty* and, 16, 23; *The Great Moment* and, 166, 182; *Hail the Conquering Hero* and, 238, 249; influences and comparisons, 327, 334–35; malapropism in, 8; *The Miracle of Morgan's Creek* and, 201, 212, 221; *The Palm Beach Story* and, 134, 148; *The Sin of Harold Diddlebock* and, 262; *Sullivan's Travels* and, 96; *Unfaithfully Yours* and, 290, 301, 308, 313
Lake, Veronica, 105, 108–9, 122, 255
Lamour, Dorothy, 154
Landis, Carole, 314
Lange, Dorothea, 110
language: use for character building, 8–9. *See also* dialogue
La Vell, Jeannie, 256, 268
Lawrence, Barbara, 294
Lawrence, Jennifer, 331
LeBaron, William, 172–73
LeBrand (*Sullivan's Travels* character), 100–3

Leisen, Mitchell, 46
Lewin, Albert, 68–69
Lewis, Jerry, 319–20
Libby (*Hail the Conquering Hero* character), 235–36, 243–44, 254–59
Lilith (Erskine), 83
Lilith theme/myth, 80–84, 87, 92–93
Lizzie (*The Great Moment* character), 176–78, 180–81, 185, 187, 189, 263
Lloyd, Harold, 265–66, 269, 271, 273, 275, 279, 281–82
Lola Montès, 324
Lombard, Carole, 37
Love Before Breakfast, 130
Lubitsch, Ernst, 129, 302
Lynn, Diana, 195, 229

Macbeth (film), 317
MacDonald, Jimmy (*Christmas in July* character), 34–35, 49, 52–64; comparisons, 122, 148, 199, 278, 298, 313
Mad Wednesday, 284
Magi, 197
The Magnificent Ambersons, 126, 171
Major Barbara, 49, 115
malapropisms, 7–8, 275, 333
Mamet, David, 328
Mangano, Joy, 331
Mankiewicz, Herman, 166
Mar-a-Lago, 137
Marie Antoinette, 166
Marine Corps, 71, 232–36, 239–41, 243–44, 247–50, 253–54, 257–59. See also *Hail the Conquering Hero*

marriage and marital issues, 321, 323, 325; *Christmas in July*, 39, 42, 54–55; *The Great McGinty*, 18, 21–24, 26, 29; *The Great Moment*, 177–78, 186; *Hail the Conquering Hero*, 254–56, 258; *The Lady Eve*, 85, 87, 93; *The Miracle of Morgan's Creek*, 193, 207, 211–12, 214–15, 217, 219–20, 222; *The Palm Beach Story*, 134, 136–38, 144, 146, 153, 159–60, 162; *The Sin of Harold Diddlebock*, 262, 268; *Sullivan's Travels*, 113, 122; *Unfaithfully Yours*, 294, 298
Marshall, Tully, 24
Martin, Dean, 319
Marvelous Mrs. Maisel, The, 332
Mary (*Easy Living* character), 45–49
Massachusetts General Hospital, 178–79, 185, 187
Matthews, James Brander, 121, 291
Mauzens, Frédéric, 264
Maxford, Dr. (*Christmas in July* character), 51–54, 59, 62
McCarey, Leo, 195
McCarthy, Melissa, 331–32
McCrea, Joel: *The Great Moment*, 178, 180–82; *The Palm Beach Story*, 136–38, 145, 147, 151–52, 160–61; Sturges on set with, x; *Sullivan's Travels*, 100, 109, 120–21
McCreery, Andrew J., 18–19
McGinty, Dan (character). See *The Great McGinty*
McGlennan-Keith, Sir Alfred (*The Lady Eve* character), 90

INDEX ❦ 361

McGlue, Captain (*The Palm Beach Story* pseudonym), 152
Meet John Doe, 98, 101
Mercury Productions, 262
Mérimée, Prosper, 264
Meyer, Torben, 58, 121, 249, 293
Milestone, Lewis, 302
military. *See* Marine Corps; U.S. Army
Millionairess, The, 322
Milner, Victor, 301
miming, 229, 324
Minnelli, Vincente, 105
Miracle of Morgan's Creek, The, 193–229; *Christmas in July* and, 33, 49; *The Great Moment* and, 167, 169–70, 182; *Hail the Conquering Hero* and, 231, 233, 237, 239–40, 252; influences and comparisons, 335; *The Lady Eve* and, 70; *The Palm Beach Story* and, 148; *The Sin of Harold Diddlebock* and, 262, 276–77
"Modern Lilith, A" (article on Isadora Duncan), 82–83
Modern Times, 334
Mohan, Alice (*The Great Moment* character), 189–90
Molnar, Ferenc, 41
Montez, Maria, 239
Moore, Charles R., 121, 157
Moran, Frank, 121, 200
Morton, W. T. G., 166–70, 175–90, 298. *See also The Great Moment*
mothers and motherly love, *Hail the Conquering Hero*, 234–35, 244, 246, 248–50, 257

Mudge, Estelle de Wolfe, 17, 201
Muggsy (*The Lady Eve* character), 8, 69, 71, 81, 88

NAACP, 96
Nagle, Anne Margaret. *See* Sturges, Anne Margaret
"Sandy" Nagle
Never Say Die, 130
Newman, Alfred, 309
Next Time We Love, 130
Noble, Mr. (*Hail the Conquering Hero* character), 8, 235, 243
Noël-Noël, 323–24
Norval. *See* Jones, Norval (*The Miracle of Morgan's Creek* character)

Office of War Information, 193
Ophüls, Max, 264, 324
Otis, Miss (*The Sin of Harold Diddlebock* characters), 261, 266, 268–70, 282–83

Pagnol, Marcel, 227
Pallette, Eugene, 36, 47
The Palm Beach Story, 133–63; *Christmas in July* and, 33, 37, 47; *The Great Moment* and, 166–67, 169, 182; *Hail the Conquering Hero* and, 238; influences and comparisons, 335; *The Lady Eve* and, 70–71; *The Miracle of Morgan's Creek* and, 194; *The Sin of Harold Diddlebock* and, 281; Sturges on set, x; *Sullivan's Travels* and, 109; *Unfaithfully Yours* and, 290, 301, 313

Palmer, Lilli, 314
Pangborn, Franklin, 51, 138
Paradise Lost, 261
Paramount, 320, 322, 325, 333; *Christmas in July*, 43, 57; *The Great McGinty*, 14–15, 20; *The Great Moment*, 165–67, 169–70, 172–73, 175, 177–79, 191; *Hail the Conquering Hero*, 231, 237, 239–40, 253, 256; *The Lady Eve*, 68; *The Miracle of Morgan's Creek*, 194, 218; *The Palm Beach Story*, 133, 135, 154; screenwriting on contract, 20; *The Sin of Harold Diddlebock*, 262, 267, 269, 271; *Sullivan's Travels*, 101, 121, 127–29; *Unfaithfully Yours*, 301; *The Vagrant* screenplay and, 20
parody, 13, 150, 299, 307
Pascal, Gabriel, 174
Payne, Alexander, 330
people of color. *See* African Americans
Perrotta, Tom, 330
Peters, Jean, 44
Pierce, Franklin, 183
Pike, Charles "Hopsie" (*The Lady Eve* character), 66–72, 74–80, 84–94; comparisons, 16, 36, 47, 96, 134, 148, 201, 298, 308, 313, 334
Players, The (restaurant), 237–38, 269
playwriting, Sturges and, 18. *See also specific plays by title*
politics. *See The Great McGinty*
Pope, Alexander, 333

Poster, W. S., 123
Potel, Victor, 194
Powell, Dick, 34, 54–55, 60–61
Power and the Glory, The, 18–20, 39–40, 70, 73, 167, 176
Present for Uncle Popo, A, 321
Private Life of Helen of Troy, The (Erskine), 82
public works projects, 19

Rae, Issa, 328
Rafferty, Mr. (*The Miracle of Morgan's Creek* character), 182–83, 210, 224, 226
Raines, Ella, 239, 243, 255–56
Ramsden, Frances, 269–70, 282, 299
Rand, Ayn, 34
reading a film, 3–5
Reinhardt, Max, 285, 288, 291
reinvention of character, 15–16
Remember the Night, 107
Renoir, Jean, 264
Republic Pictures, 317
RKO, 170–171, 173–74, 284
Rock, Chris, 331
Rockefeller, John D., 49
Rockefeller, Nelson, 170–71
Rogers, Roy, 317
Romero, Cesar, 320
Romm, May (Dr.), 202
Roosevelt administration, 19, 63, 115, 125–27
Ross, Barney, 241–42
Rossini, 91, 293
Russell, David O., 330–31

Safeguarding Military Information, 127
Sam, janitor (*Christmas in July* character), 63–64
Sargent, Louise. *See* Tevis, Louise Sargent
Sarris, Andrew, 240
Schaefer, George, 171, 173–74
Schultz the grocer (*Hail the Conquering Hero* character), 249–50
screwball comedy: *The Lady Eve*, 74, 92; *The Palm Beach Story*, 138, 159; *Sullivan's Travels*, 96, 108–9, 128
script. *See* dialogue
Seeger, Pete, 238
Segal, Lore, 249
Seitz, George, 107
Selznick, David O., 202
sex and sexual love, 331; *Christmas in July*, 46, 49, 54, 59–60; *The Great McGinty*, 23; *The Great Moment*, 183; *The Lady Eve*, 69–70, 75, 77, 87, 89; *The Miracle of Morgan's Creek*, 204, 207, 215; *The Palm Beach Story*, 137, 144, 146–48, 150, 153–54, 159–61; *The Sin of Harold Diddlebock*, 268, 271; *Sullivan's Travels*, 96, 101, 106–9; *Unfaithfully Yours*, 292, 294, 298
Shaw, George Bernard, 5, 39, 49–50, 114–15, 174, 322
Shelton, Ron, 329
Singer, Paris, 36–38, 137

Sin of Harold Diddlebock, The, 261–84; *Christmas in July* and, 33; influences and comparisons, 335; *The Lady Eve* and, 71; *The Palm Beach Story* and, 148; *Unfaithfully Yours* and, 289, 291, 299
slapstick comedy, 5, 29, 321; *Christmas in July*, 55, 61; *The Great Moment*, 167, 180, 186; *The Lady Eve*, 66, 84, 91–92; *The Sin of Harold Diddlebock*, 264; *Sullivan's Travels*, 96, 98, 106, 127–28; *Unfaithfully Yours*, 288, 310–11
Smart, Jean, 332
Smedley, Nick, 325
snakes, 65, 67–70, 76–78, 80, 87, 134
Songs for John Doe (album), 238
Southern belles, 42, 177, 185
Spoto, Donald, 270
Stander, Lionel, 294
Stanwyck, Barbara, 47, 66, 74–75, 77, 84, 86, 89
Statsky, Jen, 332
Steele, Freddie, 234, 237–38, 242–44, 259–60
Steinbeck, John, 101
Story of Louis Pasteur, The, 165
Strictly Dishonorable (Broadway play), 18–19
Study of the Drama, A (Matthews), 121, 291
Sturges, Anne Margaret "Sandy" Nagle, 2, 321–22, 325–26
Sturges, Mary (mother of Preston Sturges). *See* Dempsey, Mary; Desti, Marie

Sturges, Preston: Chicago roots, 18–19; defiance of Production Code Authority, 5, 23, 134–35, 153, 193–94, 196; disguise of own artistry, 16–17, 27–28, 129–30, 264, 270–71, 289, 335; horror of recurrence, 5, 29, 31–32, 70–71, 93, 105, 131, 161, 258–59, 261, 313–14, 334; mother, 1, 36, 162–63, 264; portrayals of adventurous women, 23, 148, 162, 209–11, 255, 330–31, 332; sense of social hierarchy, 37, 61–63, 104–5, 122–24, 184, 258, 334; use of stock characters, 5–6, 53–54, 121–24, 184. *See also* wives, Sturges's; *specific topics*

Sturges, Solomon (stepfather), 18–19, 37–38, 53, 162

success, American scramble for, 329–30

Sullivan, John L. (*Sullivan's Travels* character), 95–132, 148, 180, 199, 269, 289, 327, 334. *See also Sullivan's Travels*

Sullivan's Travels, 95–132; *Christmas in July* and, 37, 53, 62; *The Great McGinty* and, 16–17; *The Great Moment* and, 166–67, 180, 182–83, 189; *Hail the Conquering Hero* and, 237–38, 253; influences and comparisons, 327–28, 331, 334; *The Lady Eve* and, 70; *The Miracle of Morgan's Creek* and, 194, 199; *The Palm Beach Story* and, 133, 135, 141, 148, 150, 157;

The Sin of Harold Diddlebock and, 263, 269; *Unfaithfully Yours* and, 289–90

Sweeney (*Unfaithfully Yours* character), 296–97, 300–3, 314

Tamiroff, Akim, 29, 194
Tammany Hall, 18–19, 29
Tannen, Julius, 182–83, 194, 303
Tannhäuser overture, 290, 292, 308
Tashlin, Frank, 319
Taylor, Jim, 330
Tevis, Louise Sargent, 256, 262, 299, 325–26
Thalberg, Irving, 172
Three Black Pennies, The, 263
Three Stooges, 246, 249
Tierney, Gene, 306
"Tol'able David," 263
Toland, Gregg, 110
Tony (*Unfaithfully Yours* character), 304, 307–8, 312–13
Toones, Fred "Snowflake," 63, 121, 150
Top Five, 331
Toto (*The Palm Beach Story* character), 7, 152, 157–58
Tracy, Spencer, 40, 264
Triumph Over Pain. *See Great Moment, The*
Trudy (character). *See* Kockenlocker, Trudy (*The Miracle of Morgan's Creek* character)
Truesmith, Hinky Dinky (*Hail the Conquering Hero* character nickname), 248, 250–51

Truesmith, Woodrow (*Hail the Conquering Hero* character), 233–37, 243–55, 257–59, 297
Truex, Ernest, 53
Twain, Mark, 27
Twentieth Century-Fox, 284–85
tycoons, 36–44, 47, 49–50, 52, 59–61, 64, 279

Undershaft, Andrew, 49, 115
Unfaithfully Yours, 285–315; influences and comparisons, 321, 328, 335; *The Palm Beach Story* and, 148, 159
Universal Studios, 40–41, 43, 96, 239, 256, 326; screenwriting on contract, 20–21
Upperman, Dr. (*Hail the Conquering Hero* character), 240
U.S. Army, 203, 215, 239

Vagrant, The (screenplay), 19–20. See also *The Great McGinty*
Vallee, Rudy, 37, 151–52, 154, 294, 297, 320
Vendetta, 264
Verneuil, Louis, 264
Vidor, King, 120
Viel, Marguerite, 264

Waggleberry, Mr. (*The Sin of Harold Diddlebock* character), 265, 267, 271–72, 276, 280, 282
Wagner's music, 91, 211, 214, 293
Walburn, Raymond, 53, 243, 271
Warner Bros., 20, 24, 115, 166, 172, 239
War of the Worlds, The, 125
Warren, Dr. John Collins (*The Great Moment* character), 185, 187–90
Warwick, Robert, 37, 100
Waterbury, Mr. (*Christmas in July* character), 52, 58, 60–64, 334
weddings, 23–24, 42, 137–38, 207, 211, 219, 258. See also marriage and marital issues
Welles, Orson, 317–18, 321, 326–27; Brazil sojourn, 126, 130, 170–71; comparison to Sturges, 1–2, 118, 125–26, 130–31, 174–75, 189–90, 262, 333; influences on, 40; Oscar, 166; *Sullivan's Travels*, mention in, 124
Wells, H. G., 125
West, Mae, 173
Whippet (tank), 106, 238
Whitty, Jeff, 331
Wienie King (*The Palm Beach Story* character), 37, 47, 59–60, 138–42, 147, 199, 280
Wilbur, Richard, 154
Wilde, Oscar, 332
William, Warren, 24
Witherspoon, Reese, 330
wives, Sturges's: divorces, 17–18; domestic violence, 298–299; Hutton, Eleanor Close, 18, 38–39, 137, 298; Mudge, Estelle de Wolfe, 17, 201; Sturges, Anne Margaret "Sandy" Nagle, 2, 321–22, 325–26; Tevis, Louise Sargent, 256, 262, 299, 325–26

World War I, 106, 127, 234
World War II, 124, 174, 237
Wormy (*The Sin of Harold Diddlebock* character), 8, 272–73, 275, 277–78, 280–81
Wyler, William, 41, 126, 242–43, 291

Yates, Herbert, 317

Zanuck, Darryl F., 284–91, 302, 305–6, 314–15, 318, 320–21, 325
Zimmerman, Mr. (*Christmas in July* character), 182–83